W9-AQE-714

TECHNOLOGY AND MEDIA

INSTRUCTIONAL APPLICATIONS

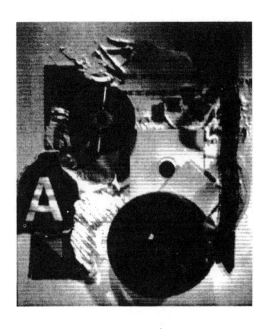

FRED A. TEAGUE
DOUGLAS W. ROGERS
ROGER N. TIPLING

KENDALL/HUNT PUBLISHING COMPANY
4050 Westmark Drive   Dubuque, Iowa 52002

TABLE OF CONTENTS

PREFACE

The purpose of this book is to help teachers develop proficiency in the application of instructional media and computer technology in the classroom. The book is written specifically to teachers and to those preparing to be teachers. This book may be appropriately used for inservice professional development workshops or used independently by people desiring to improve their proficiency in using media and technology, as well as a text in media and technology courses for teachers.

Part I includes foundational information teachers must have in order to become maximally proficient in the use of media and technology in the classroom. Information describes the contributions media and technology make to learning, general principles that are foundational to the use of media and technology in education, and basic procedures educators may follow in using media and technology effectively in teaching.

Part II focuses on techniques that may be used in the appropriate selection and use of media and technology in the classroom. The emphases here are basic projection, and audio and video materials. Resources are included to help readers acquire proficiency in the operation and maintenance of equipment.

Part III includes an overview and specific guides for developing proficiency in the use of computer technology in teaching. Included are the components of classroom computer systems, computer terminology, and computer equipment operation. Also discussed are microcomputer uses in teaching, use of word processors, spreadsheets, databases, graphic applications, telecommunications, and multimedia and other emerging computer technologies.

Part IV includes information and tools designed to help the teacher develop proficiency in production of certain types of media. Areas covered include visual design principles; graphics for use in teaching; and mounting, laminating, and enlarging classroom resource materials.

The authors have been purposefully selective in the specific content and in the proficiency areas included. Therefore, readers will not gain exposure through this publication to all information needed to select, prepare, and use media and technology in every teaching/learning setting. However, the more basic content is included in such a way as to start a person on the path to becoming proficient in the use of a wide variety of instructional media and technology.

ACKNOWLEDGMENTS

This is the fifth textbook to be published in a sequence that has extended over a period of almost two decades. Many individuals have influenced the design and development of this publication. Special appreciation is expressed to Barbara S. Newhouse of Manhattan, Kansas, and Les D. Striet of Topeka, Kansas, who were coauthors of previously published textbooks with some of the writers of this publication. Their previous research and writing activities have inspired the current team of authors to maintain the excellence and utility essential in helping teachers make effective use of media and technology in the classroom.

Several reviewers have made significant suggestions and some have experimented with the materials in their classes. Judith Lechner of Auburn University made many helpful suggestions and contributed materials that were used in this publication. The late Dave Cropp, who taught at Emporia State University, provided extensive suggestions that were highly valuable. Nancy Vick of Longwood College, Farmersville, Virginia, and Gerald Rabbit of Jamestown College in North Dakota were both very helpful with their reviews and suggestions for revision. Ralph Hawkins of Southwest Missouri State University, Ernie Ferguson of Southwest Baptist University, Bob Price of Texas Tech University, and Eric Moore of Southwest Baptist University have been especially helpful in reviewing the text and recommending improvements.

The authors also wish to acknowledge the support and encouragement of family, colleagues, students, and friends during the writing of this book.

Part I

Foundations of Instructional Media and Technology

Major Characteristics of Instructional Media

Using Media and Technology in the Classroom

Media Selection and Evaluation

Development of Instruction

Introduction

Nowhere in the field of education is change more rapid or more noticeable than in the area of instructional media and technology. In recent years microcomputers have moved into instructional settings at a pace unparalleled to any other form of instructional technology. This illustrates the dynamic nature of instructional media and technology and the extent to which educators must stay alert to innovations and changes in this area.

Persons just entering the education field often are overwhelmed by the technological systems that they must master. They face the double challenge of familiarizing themselves with all major forms of technology, as well as keeping up with new developments in technology as they occur. Instructors must understand the fundamental concepts that undergrid the selection and use of media and technology in education to be able to take advantage of this everchanging resource. The focus of Part I is on basic concepts that provide a solid base for developing instructional competencies related to media and technology.

Chapter 1

MAJOR CHARACTERISTICS OF INSTRUCTIONAL MEDIA

PURPOSES

▶ To be able to identify the major characteristics of each type of commonly used instructional media.

▶ To describe the unique features of each media type and the features some media have in common.

Developments in modern technology have made available to teachers an array of media and technologies that can be of real value in improving the quality of instruction, the outcomes of learning, and the vibrance of the learning environment. These materials and devices are the essential tools that teachers use in the practice of their profession. They are powerful and flexible tools in the hands of those who are skilled in their use.

For several decades educators have recognized that well-produced materials such as films, videotapes, and sound-slide sets can bring the world into the classroom in very exciting, informative and authentic ways. Such media enable the teacher to create within the classroom a genuinely exciting learning environment. In such a setting more learning occurs, it becomes a more enjoyable endeavor, and teaching becomes a joy rather than a chore.

Media and technology can bring excitement to the classroom.

Educational media and technology of many types are available today and make unique contributions to the quality of the learning environment. One form of media or technology used in harmony with another can often have an even more dynamic impact on learning. For example, learning experiences usually yield significant results when microcomputers are appropriately coupled with videodisc technology in well-developed interactive programs. Likewise, the learning experience is filled with excitement when distant places are brought into the classroom in multi-images, projected in vibrant color and accompanied with realistic and authentic sound. Well-produced and appropriately used media are powerful and flexible tools in the hands of teachers who are skilled in their use.

The use of instructional media must begin with a thorough understanding of the characteristics of each major type of such media. Although there are many types of instructional materials and equipment available for use today, the purpose here is to develop acquaintance with a few of the more common ones.

Media and technology vary widely in form and use.

The teacher should know what benefits each type of media can provide.

Building on acquaintance with a wide range of print, nonprint, motion, still, passive and interactive media, the classroom teacher must then perfect a wide range of methodologies employing whatever technologies are needed. The teacher who has become highly competent in using modern technologies in the classroom will be able to integrate such systems into a variety of group and individualized learning approaches that yield the desired learning outcomes.

Instructional media and technology must, however, be viewed not just in terms of their physical characteristics but also in terms of the ways in which they are applied to the learning process. These applications may be viewed primarily as presentation (one-way exchanges) or as interaction (two-way exchanges). Consequently, instructional technologies are often referred to as presentation technology and interactive technology.

PRESENTATION MEDIA AND TECHNOLOGY

Presentation technologies are ones that lend themselves well to use by teachers, students, and others in making formal presentations to groups. Such technologies range from a simple picture or graphic projected on a screen to a sophisticated, computerized presentation in which several forms of visual images are combined with sound to produce highly dramatic and compelling learning experiences. Presentation technologies are usually aimed at group instruction but are effective in presenting information to individual learners as well.

INTERACTIVE MEDIA AND TECHNOLOGY

Interactive technologies are designed and applied in the learning environment in ways that enable the learner to interact with the technology. These technologies are programmed to elicit responses from the learner and usually evaluate student responses, give feedback to the learner, and enable the learner to ask questions or seek assistance in other ways. Interactive technologies have the major advantages of facilitating active learning and enabling the learner to know at all times how well he or she is accomplishing the learning objectives. Many instructional materials produced for interactive technologies are designed for individual use, but many are suitable for use in group learning settings as well.

Various types of media and technology may be used in either presentation or interactive applications. However, to introduce the major types of media and technology, the types are discussed briefly in this chapter as either primarily presentation technologies or as primarily interactive technologies.

Filmstrips

Many types of materials may be enlarged by projection for use by groups of students or may be used by one student on an individual basis. One of the more common of these is the 35mm filmstrip. Most schools have a collection of filmstrips available either in the classroom or in a centrally located media center or school library. Many types of equipment are available for both group use and individual viewing of filmstrips. Some filmstrips have captions at the bottom of each frame or picture so that a brief printed message or story can accompany the picture series.

If more verbal information is needed, the filmstrip may be accompanied by either a record or tape, referred to as a sound filmstrip. Special equipment is available that will both show these filmstrips and play the records or tapes that accompany them. If a sound filmstrip projector is not available, one may make use of sound filmstrips by using a record player or tape recorder along with a filmstrip projector.

Slides

Photographic slides are similar to filmstrips in terms of their use in instruction. They are usually used in a series but may be shown one at a time. However, using an automatic slide projector makes it convenient to show slides. Changing from one picture to the next is accomplished by simply pushing a remote button or lever. Because slides are mounted in separate 2 × 2 inch frames, they are very flexible and can be rearranged. Slide trays provide convenient storage and usage.

As with filmstrips, sound recordings may be used with slides when an accompanying verbal message is needed. Special recorders are designed to play the sound and also advance the slides at the proper time.

Motion Picture Films

Motion picture films are valuable in communication because they include both moving pictures and sound. Sound films provide a natural means for one to acquire information and to participate in exceptionally valuable vicarious learning experiences. In addition to images in motion, instructional films are enhanced in the power of their communicating effectiveness by their potential for effective use of natural sound, natural color, and narration synchronized with visuals that show motion at a fixed pace.

Video Recordings

Videotape recordings are similar to sound motion picture films, because both picture and sound can be easily reproduced. Small portable video recording systems are becoming increasingly available. In addition to enabling one to make and show instructional videotapes, these systems are being used extensively for taping and review of student performance. This makes it possible for students in areas such as physical education, speech, and drama to evaluate and consequently improve overt, observable behaviors. In areas such as civics, ecology, and current events, students may use video recording for in-depth "live reporting" of events as they occur.

Audio Recordings

The same capabilities are available in sound only with the use of audio recorders now available to virtually all learners. In addition, a very wide range of prepared audio materials is available in both tape and disc record formats. Most of the tape-recorded materials are especially well-suited for use by individual students. All audio recordings lend themselves well to both group and individual listening activities. Imaginative instructors record many audio materials specifically prepared for use by their particular students.

Overhead Transparencies

Overhead transparencies are valuable tools in many situations. Because the transparency is out in the open, rather than inside the machine as the visual is shown, one may easily point to, draw on, or block out part of the transparency as it is being shown. This enables a person to direct the attention to a specific part of the visual that is being emphasized. The overhead transparency may also be constructed in several parts so that the information can be presented in whatever sequential order is necessary for the development of an idea. Another of their major advantages is the ease with which one can prepare transparency materials. These features, plus the fact that the projector operates in a fully lighted room, make the overhead projector a valuable instructional tool.

Microcomputers

A newer instructional resource available to teachers today is the microcomputer. Recent advances in the development of microprocessors or "chips" have revolutionized the hardware equipment costs of computers. Microcomputers operate with the same functional components as larger computer systems: input, memory, output, and central processing unit, but now an entire system can fit on a desktop. Applications for instruction include such usage as drill and practice, tutoring, gaming/simulations, and problem solving. Computers may also be used to manage instruction in support functions such as testing, scheduling, recordkeeping, and information retrieval. In classrooms, microcomputers are used most often to develop computer literacy and as personal productivity tools. Unlike most other forms of educational technology, microcomputers are interactive in nature and have the unique capability of being used to control other instructional equipment.

Disc Technologies

Disc technologies make vast amounts of information in various forms available to students for their interactive use. Laser technology stores digital information in large quantities on a disc, and students or teachers can call up specific parts or segments of the information on demand. Information may be still

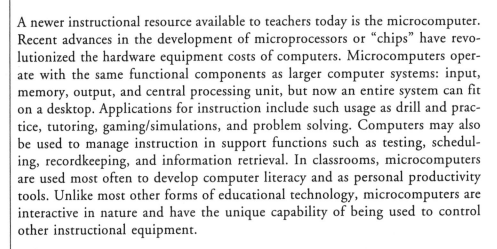

graphics, animated, video, audio, print, or any combination of such forms. The visual materials may be motion pictures or still media similar in appearance to projected slides or filmstrips. The current and potential disc technologies are so extensive that disc technologies may in the immediate future be used for virtually all of the instructional and learning applications of media and technology.

Liquid Crystal Displays (LCDs)

Liquid crystal displays take several forms, from the small display windows on calculators to laptop computer screens to devices used to enlarge and present computer and video images on large projection screens. Therefore, LCDs enable instructors to display computer and video-based media to students in various sizes of groups. Many LCDs make use of an overhead projector to enlarge computer or video images on the screen. These devices enable a group of students to corporately interact with materials programmed and stored in computer and video-based systems.

Multimedia

Media and technology appear to have major impacts on learning when multiple media are used together in a well-orchestrated system. Frequently included in multimedia instruction are print text, still graphics, moving visual images, and sound. Today, most multimedia delivery of instruction is computer based and controlled. User friendly "authoring" programs have been developed so that teachers and other educational personnel may develop their own multimedia instructional programs. The most sophisticated uses of multimedia involve experimentation with "virtual reality" in learning. Virtual reality involves an individual entering a simulated environment of three-dimensional images and realistic directional sound, so that the characteristics of the real environment are virtually re-created by the media and technology.

Display Media

Some of the most valuable instructional materials are simple-to-make and simple-to-use materials that do not require special equipment for their uses in education.

The oldest and most frequently used teaching device is the ever-present chalkboard. It can communicate many types of information to students. Colored chalks and special devices such as templates and patterns make the chalkboard an effective communication device, usable in virtually all classrooms and laboratories.

The capability to add materials, move them around, and take them away from a display contributes to the flexibility and instructional effectiveness of clingboards such as flannel boards and felt boards. Other types of clingboards include peg boards, hook-and-loop boards, and magnetic boards. Clingboards enable instructors and students to build a story visually or represent a situation as it is communicated with others in the learning environment.

Posters are available for many instructional uses and can be easily made by teachers and students. They offer an attractive and interesting means of communicating a single idea, and when kept on display, are a continuing reminder of information being used within an instructional segment.

Bulletin boards are available in most classrooms and can be used as a valuable learning display in many instructional settings. A well-developed bulletin board may provide an interesting general impression of a topic of study or may include materials in considerable detail that are available for individual study over an extended time period. Students often do their most productive work when researching information and translating it into bulletin board exhibits of their own creation and design.

Object Media

Three-dimensional instructional materials such as objects, models, and mockups have the advantage of providing realism and opportunities for detailed study in many areas. They contribute to many types of learning outcomes and often make learning interesting and meaningful to many students.

Maps and globes are extensively used in some subject areas and are readily available for most of the special applications that teachers and students need to make of them.

Certain critical criteria are related to the media and technology used in today's classrooms. Important among such criteria are

▶ *Appropriate group size:* Some types of media, such as overhead transparencies, motion picture films, and video tapes and discs, work well for presentations to large student groups (groups of 30 or more). Some, especially microcomputers and some disc technologies, may best be used in individualized applications. Others, such as chalkboards, slides, filmstrips, and some audio media, are best used with medium or small groups.

▶ *Pacing:* Some types of media, such as filmstrips, motion picture films, and videotapes, appear in a fixed order and usually are presented sequentially. Others, including slides, chalkboard materials, overhead transparencies, disc technologies, and microcomputer materials, are flexible in sequence or nonsequential, so they can be presented in various ways.

▶ *Software production:* Teachers and students may produce some types of materials themselves, such as overhead transparencies, slides, and chalkboard illustrations. Other formats are more difficult to produce and require specialized production services that school media specialists or commercial production firms must provide.

▶ *Software cost:* Teachers continuously decide what instructional materials to use. The teacher is wise to have information at hand concerning potential costs of the materials. Although the costs of media vary greatly, some types generally cost more than others. Among the least costly are chalkboards, overhead transparencies, filmstrips, and audio recordings. Materials that usually are more expensive are motion picture films, some videotapes, and some microcomputer software.

▶ *Communication channels:* Communication criteria such as color, motion, sound, and randomness are often critical to the quality of classroom instruction. Most materials afford appropriate communications, but the teacher must check carefully to ensure that media being considered are designed to communicate clearly and appropriately.

▶ *Physical facilities:* Some media and technologies must be used in certain kinds of physical settings. For example, some materials require a darkened room; some technologies require the proximity of several electrical outlets. When special facilities must be used, such requirements should be planned for well beforehand. An unfortunate circumstance may arise if prior arrangements for media requirements are not thorough and carried through.

SUMMARY

This brief review of various types of instructional media should develop an awareness of the wide range of instructional materials currently available to teachers. The list given here is not exhaustive, but rather includes only the most common and most traditional of the teaching and learning media. All teachers should become increasingly skilled in using a wide variety of instructional materials and equipment. The learning success of students, as well as the professional growth of the instructor depend extensively on the effectiveness with which the tools and resources of the teaching profession are employed.

SUGGESTED ACTIVITIES

1. Read Chapter 1 and analyze the check sheet titled "Instructional Media Characteristics." Mark an "X" in each square in which the type of media and technology listed at the top of the sheet generally meets the criteria given along the left side of the sheet.

2. Be prepared to discuss your results of activity 1 in a group setting.

3. Select a school that is familiar to you or visit a school and observe uses to which media and instructional technologies are put.

INSTRUCTIONAL MEDIA CHARACTERISTICS

This chart shows certain characteristics of instructional media in relationship to circumstances in which they may be used. Study the chart carefully and insert an X in each square where you believe the media listed at the top of the sheet meet the citeria listed on the left.

		Media Type	Chalkboard	Overhead Transparencies	35mm Slides	35mm Filmstrips	Disc Technology	Audio Recordings	Video Recordings	Sound Filmstrips	Sound-Slide Series	16mm Motion Picture Film	Microcomputers
	Criteria												
Group Size	Large (30+)												
	Medium												
	Small (Under 12)												
	Individual												
Pacing	Fixing												
	Flexible												
Software Production	Commercial												
	Media Specialist												
	Teacher Produced												
	Student Produced												
Software Cost	High ($300+)												
	Medium												
	Low (less than $50)												
Communication Channels	Color												
	Motion												
	Sound												
	Visual												
Room Facilities	Darkening												
	Acoustics												
	Electricity												

Chapter 2

USING MEDIA AND TECHNOLOGY IN THE CLASSROOM

PURPOSES

- ▶ To become acquainted with the major reasons for using media and technology in the classroom.
- ▶ To become familiar with basic procedures for media usage.
- ▶ To become acquainted with research and theory that undergird the use of media and technology in the classroom.

INTRODUCTION

Dramatic changes are occurring in today's classrooms.

Today's students have grown up in a technological society. Applications of technology are extensive in business, industry, and society at large. Today's students know technology more intimately than older generations and have come to accept and depend on it. The typical American student is literally in touch with the world through personally owned communications technology such as multiband radios, television sets, CD players, push-button telephones, C.B. transceivers, camcorders and recorders, electronic calculators, and an unlimited assortment of electronic games. It is evident that a person nurtured in such a technological environment is indeed a stranger if the learning environment lacks similar technologies.

Some of the most exciting and innovative occurrences in education and training during recent years have been the development and use of new instructional technology. New approaches have breathed fresh air into many classrooms. Penmanship has been revolutionized by the felt tip marker, science teaching has come alive with new laboratory equipment. Videotapes and films have brought the world itself into the heart of the social science classroom. However, we are only in the initial stage of a technological revolution in teaching and learning. Microcomputers gave instructors the capacity to greatly change the learning environment. The speed at which newer instructional technologies will become a meaningful part of education and training remains to be seen. Progress is underway. The purpose of this chapter is to introduce you to the major ways that instructional media and technology can help in teaching and to present some of the more important research and theoretical bases for using media and technology in teaching.

Technology is changing the learning environment.

Integration of media into classroom activities is essential.

MULTIPLE INTELLIGENCES

Learning is multi-dimensional.

Just as instructional technology is being developed at an accelerating rate, so is knowledge about intelligence and learning. Recent research and its interpretation have emphasized that intelligence is not fixed at birth and static throughout life but rather a multidimensional phenomenon that occurs at multiple levels of a person's brain/mind/body system. Today educators know that intelligence can be learned and taught.

Gardner was one of the first to emphasize the multidimensional, changing nature of intelligence when he gave the following definitions of learning:

> An intelligence entails the ability to solve problems or fashion products that are of consequence in a particular cultural setting. The problem-solving skill allows one to approach a situation in which a goal is to be obtained and to locate the appropriate route to that goal. The creation of a cultural product is crucial to capturing and transmitting knowledge or expressing one's views or feelings. The problems to be solved range from creating an end to a story to anticipating a mating move in chess to repairing a quilt. Products range from scientific theories to musical composition to successful political campaigns.

GARDNER'S SEVEN INTELLIGENCES

Media can strengthen intelligence.

Based on the dynamic view of intelligence, Gardner and others have identified seven intelligences and have studied ways in which individuals may increase their intellectual capacities. Media and technology have major roles in expansion of several of these intelligences. Each of the intelligences is examined here, and examples show how the use of media and technology can strengthen intellectual capacities.

Verbal/Linguistic Intelligence

Verbal/linguistic intelligence is used any time a person deals with written or spoken words and language. Activities involving this intelligence include conversation, formal speaking; any kind of writing; creating and telling stories; or any other uses of speaking, listening, or reading. Media and technology can enhance students' verbal/linguistic intelligence by involving them in playing word games, solving verbal puzzles, using language-oriented games, watching a TV show's sequel or successive episodes, making a presentation using media, or producing a video or computer-generated report.

Logical/Mathematical Intelligence

Logical/mathematical intelligence deals with deductive thinking, reasoning, numbers, and recognition of abstractions. It is often associated with scientific thinking. Students use logical/mathematical intelligence in activities such as counting by twos; counting change received during a transaction; seeing relationships among multiple pieces of information; and in making lists, setting priorities, or planning for the future. Students and teachers may use media and technology to strengthen logical/mathematical intelligence by comparing and classifying groups of real objects by shape, color, size, use, and so on; by creating and following cooking recipes; by watching a video and then reconstructing its main points, subpoints, and so on; and by creating and displaying a sequence of numbers that have a hidden pattern and asking learners to discover the pattern.

Visual/Spatial Intelligence

Visual/spatial intelligence deals with the sense of sight and involves visualizing objects and creating internal mental images. This intelligence enables people to build structures based on blueprints, win at chess, or visualize concrete objects from design specs. It is involved in the imaginations of children when they daydream, pretend to be someone else, or pretend to be in another time or place.

There is extensive potential for the use of media and technology in developing visual/spatial intelligence. Visual images used in many media can spark the imaging processes in students. Students can use their imaginations to find animals, faces, and objects as they view clouds. Students can view films or videotapes of life in other times or at other places and then pretend they are there. Visual/spatial intelligence may be strengthened as students pretend they are interacting with the people they meet via media. Learners may express ideas or feelings by working with clay, paint, markers, crayons, and other art supplies to create personally meaningful visual images. A group activity such as creating a montage with cutout pictures may employ media in developing visual/spatial intelligence.

Visual media can kindle students' imaging processes.

Body/Kinesthetic Intelligence

Body/kinesthetic intelligence deals with physical movement and involves knowing and making proper use of the body. This intelligence comes into play when a person uses the typewriter or computer keyboard without looking at the key labels; or when a person rides a bicycle, drives a car, catches a ball, or walks on a balance beam. Media and technology are frequently used to develop body/kinesthetic intelligence. Uses may involve video to enable the learner to evaluate and find ways of improving body movement. Video or drawings may also be used to demonstrate proper, effective use of the body in activities such as using a snowblower or lifting heavy items. Media are valuable tools in developing proper skills involved in sprinting, dancing, and jogging, all of which make use of body/kinesthetic intelligence.

Musical/Rhythmic Intelligence

Musical/rhythmic intelligence deals with the recognition of tonal patterns, and sensitivity to rhythm and beat. This intelligence is applied when a person hears a jingle on television and automatically hums it over and over throughout the day. This type is active when people use tones and rhythmic patterns to communicate how they are feeling. Musical/rhythmic intelligence enables people to associate certain sounds with intense joy, fear, and excitement, or with expressions of religious devotion and patriotism.

Media and technology, especially those involving the production or reproduction of sound, are used extensively to involve learners in using and enhancing musical/rhythmic intelligence. Recorded sound may be used to prompt feelings, evoke images, or spark memories. Rhythm patterns recorded from nature, such as traffic flowing, coffee brewing, wind blowing, bells ringing, or rain beating on the window, may enhance the capability of learners to express feeling or engage in a variety of creative expression. Students may also use sound effects, music, and rhythm beats to embellish stories they have written and are reading aloud to others.

Learners can express feelings and personal creativity by hearing rhythm patterns from nature.

Interpersonal Intelligence

Interpersonal intelligence operates primarily through person-to-person relationships and communication. Students experience interpersonal intelligence when they participate in joint efforts such as committees, team sports, or task forces. This intelligence uses all of the other intelligences, especially the abilities to engage in verbal and nonverbal communication. It enables individuals to develop empathy and caring for each other. Media and technology may be used to promote interpersonal intelligence. Students may learn to express encouragement and support for others by observing occurrences of such support in videotapes or other media. They may observe this in facial expression, body posture, gestures, sounds, words, and phrases in the media. Media may be used to expose students to models of supportive behavior and to encourage students to avoid prejudice and bias. Media and technology may also be used to teach the mechanics of working productively in groups and to show the geometrical rewards of a unified group effort.

Intrapersonal Intelligence

Intrapersonal intelligence deals with inner states of being, self-reflection, metacognition, and awareness of spiritual realities. It involves the capability to step back and watch oneself, almost as a outsider. It involves inner feelings, thinking processes, intuition, and spirituality. Self-identity and the ability to transcend self are parts of intrapersonal intelligence.

Students can track the high and low points of their day with mood graphs.

Media and technology may be used to encourage and enhance the use of intrapersonal intelligence. Students may graphically depict a "mood graph" to show high and low points of the day, and to note external events that affected them internally. Drama and role-playing may be used to create a situation or problem to which learners will react. Individuals can then be encouraged to personally and privately analyze their thoughts, feelings, emotions, and inner states of being. Students may also be assigned to keep a reflective log in which they record their thoughts, feelings, ideas, insights, and events that are important to them. A variety of media, such as writing, drawing, singing, acting, painting, photography, or sculpting may be used to depict these thoughts, feelings, and insights.

Instructional media and technology help students learn, because students learn very effectively in well-planned lessons that include a combination of instructional media and learning activities. Media must be an important part of teaching if maximum learning occurs. Research and practice indicate that instructional media contribute to learning in several ways.

Vicarious Learning Experiences

One of the most challenging and difficult tasks faced by teachers is organizing relevant experiences for students. Because students are typically confined to the four walls of the school building, learning activities must give accurate and meaningful information about the real world. This challenge may be faced confidently by teachers who use instructional media to bring the world into the classroom. Furthermore, many teachers are discovering the wealth of visual materials available in filmstrips, films, slides, videotapes, computer programs, and study prints that enable students to vicariously see the world. Likewise, audio records and tapes enable natural, dramatized, or narrated sounds to be transported directly into the learning environment.

Students appear to learn when they are involved in one or more of the four major types of learning experiences shown in the left column of the following table. The right column indicates the instructional methods that are often used to implement each type of learning experience.

Learning Experiences	Instructional Methods
Learning in the real situation	Field study Internships On-the-job training
Learning through interpreting the real situation	Demonstrating Collecting Computer simulation Role-playing Dramatizations
Learning through vicarious representations of the real situation	Viewing filmstrips Interacting with computer programs Watching videotapes Listening to audio recordings
Learning through verbal descriptions of the real recorded situation	Listening to live lectures Discussions Reading

CONTRIBUTIONS OF MEDIA TO LEARNING

Bring the world into your classroom through media and technology.

15

Media and technology are used to implement a variety of learning experiences.

Media and technology enhance clarity in classroom communications.

A careful examination of the instructional methods column reveals that instructional media may be used in conjunction with several other methods to achieve learning. However, instructional media are used in almost all vicarious learning experiences. Therefore, instructional media make a major contribution to teaching by providing these experiences within the classroom.

Precise Communication

Instructors today direct a learning environment in which communication occurs in a variety of forms. Instructors and students alike are confronted with many complex communication problems.

Instructional media can serve as the primary tools for communicating information. Instructors must present information that is essential in the development of complex concepts. In schools it is important communicated information that enables students to construct behavior patterns representative of the attitudes and values being encouraged in class.

To build complex concepts and value systems, accurate information must be communicated. Instructional media often provide the means for the precise communications required.

Alert educators recognize that visual media are often best suited to communicate information of a visual nature. Instructors have often been in the difficult position of explaining verbally what something looks like. For example, imagine an instructor describing a marsupial verbally to a group of primary students who have never heard of a marsupial. The correct picture can accomplish the communication job quickly, easily, and effectively. A motion picture or videotape can show a marsupial in action. Visual materials such as these are absolutely essential to the effective communication of the vast amount of information necessary to implement a modern curriculum.

Audio materials may also be used to achieve a great deal of accuracy in educational communication. For example, how could teachers tell students what the croak of a bullfrog sounds like? Tape recordings can store natural sounds and bring them to life at the precise moment needed.

These are oversimplified examples of instructional media used to communicate information with the accuracy demanded in learning environments. Successful teachers turn with ease and confidence to many types of instructional media when such media are appropriate. More repetitive tasks can be managed by instructional media, enabling instructors to devote more time to personalized work with students. Instructional media are vehicles by which teachers can establish effective channels of communication.

Interest in Learning

Responsive instructors are continuously searching for refreshing ways of generating and expanding interest in learning. Instructional media can contribute to interest in learning because they present information, represent situations, and pose questions in exciting ways.

Some types of instructional media can generate interest by virtue of the physical conditions under which the student's media are used. Materials that are shown by projection are usually shown under partially darkened room conditions. A contrast is created between the darkened room environment and the brilliantly lighted screen. This contrast in light naturally directs the students' attention to the lighted area, ensuring an opportunity for interest to develop in the materials being shown. When motion is added, a contrast is created between the relative stillness of the classroom and the simulated movement on the screen. This contrast in motion further expands the likelihood that students will become interested in the materials being projected on the screen. Interest may be further heightened by adding color to the projected materials.

In addition, accompanying the pictures with "true to life" sounds contributes to interest in the materials. These visual and audio stimuli alter the normal physical environment and as such may be expected to influence interest in the information being presented via film, videotape, or similar media.

Instructors in various subject areas find that instructional media help to create interest in the academic subject. In some situations, this is true simply because instructional media such as films, filmstrips, and tapes provide an interesting means for students to receive learning stimuli. For example, students studying about the period of the American Revolution might become increasingly interested in the subject as they view films depicting the midnight ride of Paul Revere or the drama of the Boston Tea Party. In an entirely different learning situation, home economics students in a sewing class might be motivated to improve their skills as they see an expert at work via film or videotape. Also, teachers may show students a series of film loops demonstrating the various skills they must learn.

Instructional media such as films, filmstrips, tapes, film loops, displays, exhibits, and models have tremendous potential for increasing student interest in learning. Teachers who are effective in creating lively, interesting learning environments will be found using a wide range of instructional media.

Increased Options for Learning

If there were only one way to teach, teaching would be a boring task for creative and imaginative individuals. There are many ways to direct students toward attainment of learning goals. Teachers who are alert to the needs of students welcome opportunities to choose between many possible means of

Interest in learning is enhanced when media and technology are properly used in the classroom.

Some types of media are especially effective in capturing the attention of learners.

There are many ways to teach and many ways to learn.

accomplishing a teaching task. There are so many ways to teach that instructors may select activities to match the needs, interests, and capabilities of students.

Instructional media increase the options available to teachers. Without instructional media, teachers might make reading assignments, lead discussions, lecture, and involve students in various projects. However, teachers who employ a large assortment of instructional materials have many choices.

Students may experience the world and never leave the classroom.

When students study another culture, instructors may choose to take them there via videotape. If students need to study a specific historical event, they may go back in time via film. When they need to see the world from a perspective in space, they may do so with slides taken from a spaceship. Likewise shortwave radio can enable students to engage in up-to-date study in areas such as foreign language, music, world events, geography, and economics.

Instructors who teach students specific skills will discover an increasing number of choices because of the instructional media available. They may develop audio tapes, photos, or a combination of both so that students can move through a skill development process step-by-step on an individual basis. Teachers and trainers may wish to assign students to view materials that provide a model of expert performance that the student can imitate.

Professional educators make choices of the most crucial nature as instruction is planned and implemented. They welcome a great number of alternative methods for leading students toward learning goals. Teachers who are dedicated to providing the most meaningful experiences possible for their students welcome the increased options that media afford and the many potential ways of employing the media to enhance learning.

FIVE STEP UTILIZATION PROCEDURES

When teachers present information by using instructional media, utilization techniques should always be employed. There is no "one" specific procedure for using slide sets, tape recordings, films, or any other type of instructional media. However, general procedures should govern the use of all instructional media. These utilization procedures can be analyzed in five steps.

1. Prepare Yourself

1

Educators prepare themselves by carefully reviewing instructional materials to be used and by making decisions pertaining to specific teaching acts involving the use of the materials. Teachers must have a thorough knowledge of instructional media content and must know in advance how to ensure that maximum learning results from the use of the materials.

Usually this familiarization is done through previewing the media format prior to presenting it. Often a study or utilization guide is provided with the media and is a valuable tool in assessing summary content, identifying vocabulary usage, assessing visual information, and exploring possible related and extended follow-up activities. Previewing instructional materials allows teachers to decide whether the entire media selection should be used or just a portion of it relates to the particular situation or needs of the audience. It is perfectly acceptable to use just a portion of a media item, and previewing allows teachers to make this decision. Preparing themselves also enables teachers to check the datedness of the media. Media pertaining to historical events or media employing animation techniques do not become dated as quickly as most others.

Although clothing styles, models of automobiles, and hair styles tend to date media quite rapidly, the media *content* is what should be considered in deciding if the media is current enough to use. Content that is still accurate and realistic is acceptable. Teachers may decide to allow a student to preview the media with them. This is acceptable and will provide other reactions, questions, and concerns. Research has shown that every time people view a cognitive media format, they learn one-third more information from it.

2. Prepare the Environment

This step involves making physical environmental arrangements for using instructional media. Such tasks include obtaining and setting up necessary equipment, obtaining extension cords, controlling room lighting and ventilation, arranging seating for optimum viewing and listening, and being aware of safety and fire hazards and exit possibilities.

3. Prepare the Audience

This is the most crucial step in the entire process of using instructional media. Educators must bring students to the point where they are ready to learn from the materials that are to be used. When unfamiliar vocabulary is used, the new terms should be explained to students in advance so that they will understand the terms when they occur in the presentation. When unfamiliar or unusual visual information is included, students must be prepared in advance to deal with it.

In many situations, instructional materials include some information that does not specifically relate to the desired learning outcomes. Instructors may deal with such situations by directing the students' attention to the desired information, with the intent that students will "tune out" information that is not a part of the concept being developed. This may be accomplished by telling students what to "look for" in the materials.

Students may also be assigned to seek answers to specific questions, or to construct summaries or other responses on the basis of having used the instructional media.

Regardless of the specific activities educators employ to prepare students to use specific media items, students should always know what they are expected to learn from the materials or what they should be able to do as a result of having

2

3

used the materials. When instructors carefully prepare students for the use of instructional materials, rather than simply showing films or playing records, students become more active participants in the media event, and instructional media are more likely to make the intended contributions to students' growth and development.

4. Use the Media

Instructors who have adequately prepared themselves, the learning environment and their students can implement the use of materials with confidence that the planned outcomes will occur. They have reason to be enthusiastic about teaching with the use of instructional media. Their use of instructional media such as films will occur with technical ease, because they know when to turn on each switch, how loud to play the sound, and how to fade the picture in and out on the screen at exactly the right time.

They also know how to "troubleshoot" if there is a technical breakdown in the equipment. Today's students are accustomed to experiencing effective media presentations by watching television at home, attending movies, and playing video games that feature sophisticated graphics techniques. They expect the same effective media utilization practices in schools, and educators who are capable of being "good media showpeople" can match the outside media influences as they use media in teaching.

5. Follow Media with Other Learning Activities

Instructional media are not used in a vacuum but rather are vital parts of planned sequences of learning activities. The impact of a film or tape does not stop when the machine is turned off. Some of the most important media utilization tasks involve connecting and integrating media with other learning activities. Students should be given opportunities to relate information gained from instructional media and that acquired from sources such as teachers, other students, and reading materials.

Integrating activities may include rather elaborate procedures such as constructing displays, building models, or writing plays using information acquired from use of instructional media. In other circumstances integrating activities may be limited to rather short discussions of media-related information or short answers to questions posed prior to the use of the materials. Regardless of the specific activities teachers use, they should understand that instructional media cannot stand alone. It must *integrate* with the total ongoing instructional design in order to make maximum contributions to learning.

RESEARCH AND THEORY

The contributions media and technology make to learning should be viewed in reference to the body of research and experiential knowledge from which they are drawn. A systematic theory undergirding the use of instructional media and technology is only now maturing, despite the accumulation of fairly extensive research data throughout the twentieth century.

Research during the first half of the century focused on proving the validity and worth of such resources. These early studies tended to address questions such as "are audiovisual materials of value in teaching?" "can students learn from them?" and "what benefits derive from their use?"

Early studies by Meierhenry, Knowlton and Tilton, Wittich and Fowlkes, Roulton, Anspiger, and Wise all indicated that instructional media made significant contributions to the improvement of teaching and to the enhancement of learning when used appropriately. These and other studies answered whether people can learn effectively when media and technology are significant components of the learning process.

Early research demonstrated that media could improve instruction.

Having alleviated remaining doubts about the learning worth of media and technology by midcentury, researchers and theorists turned their attention to questions of how media and technology could best be used in teaching and learning. Research tended to be highly localized and often focused on narrow applications. However, some generalizations were discernible, and theorists began to point out how media and technology could make significant improvements in the classroom and other learning environments.

Dale's Cone of Learning Experiences

One of the first theorists to be heard widely was Edgar Dale, who first published his ideas in 1946 in a book, *Audiovisual Methods in Teaching,* and later clarified them in *Theory of Audiovisual Instruction,* published in 1954. Dale indicated that teachers are severely limited in what they can transmit to students out of their experiences alone. He pointed out, however, that media and technology provide students with effective means of learning from vicarious experiences. Dale argued that a greater extent of contact with reality was desirable in the classroom which audiovisual resources could facilitate by bringing the world into the classroom through pictures and sound.

How can media and technology be most effectively employed in the classroom?

The teacher who must rely only on personal experience is severely limited.

Dale desired to show a clear relationship between experience and knowledge. To demonstrate this relationship he constructed a cone of learning experiences in which he depicted experiences ranging from the most direct to the most abstract. His cone contained the following experiences (p. 46):

Experience and knowledge belong together.

- ▶ Verbal symbols
- ▶ Visual symbols
- ▶ Recordings, radio, still pictures
- ▶ Motion pictures
- ▶ Television
- ▶ Exhibits
- ▶ Field trips
- ▶ Demonstrations
- ▶ Dramatized experiences
- ▶ Direct, purposeful experiences

Learning experiences vary—some are highly abstract, and some are very concrete.

Based on previous research and on thinking that was current at midcentury, Dale cited the following as the contributions audiovisual materials made to learning (p. 65):

Media and technology make definite contributions to learning.

1. "They supply a concrete basis for conceptual thinking and hence reduce meaningless word-responses of students."

2. "They have a high degree of interest for students."

3. "They make learning more permanent."

4. "They offer a reality of experience which stimulates self-activity on the part of pupils."

5. "They develop a continuity of thought; this is especially true of motion pictures."

6. "They contribute to growth of meaning and hence to vocabulary development."

7. "They provide experiences not easily obtained through other materials and contribute to the efficiency, depth, and variety of learning."

The results obtained from media and technology vary from one circumstance to another.

Dale made major contributions toward constructing a theoretical basis for using audiovisual materials in teaching, but his works drew considerable criticism from his contemporaries. Some questioned whether it was necessary or possible to sequence learning experiences on a scale of concrete to abstract. Others found it difficult to defend the premise that verbal symbols are more abstract than visual symbols or that visual symbols are more abstract than single-sensory materials such as recordings, radio, and still pictures. Nevertheless, Dale's influence on the growing field of knowledge about media and technology was extensive and his contributions, spanning more than three decades, were of major importance.

Studies of Instructional Technology

Skinner focused attention on a technology of instruction.

Dale's initial work was followed shortly by several studies and publications that made significant contributions to the emerging field of instructional media and technology. B.F. Skinner's early publications, *Verbal Behavior* and *The Science of Learning and the Art of Teaching,* stimulated a flurry of activity in programmed instruction. This led to a greater understanding of the objectives and events of instruction and provided much of the basis for the development of computerized instruction. The basis and means of employing computers in instruction were further advanced significantly by Gagne's book, *The Conditions of Learning,* which was published in 1967 amid growing interest in computerized instruction.

Other researchers and theorists focused on the processes of communication in the classroom with specific interest in the communications functions of media

Figure 2.1

Model of Technology as an Instructional Communication Element

Media and technology can improve communication in the classroom.

and technology. Communications models such as that shown in Figure 2.1 illustrate the manner in which media and technology were viewed as major communication elements in the classroom.

Media and technology can improve classroom learning.

What is known about learning is probably an even more important consideration than what is known about communications. Benjamin S. Bloom focuses attention on three major elements in learning, as shown in Figure 2.2.

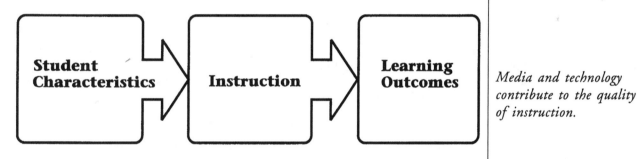

Figure 2.2

Bloom's Elements of Learning

Media and technology contribute to the quality of instruction.

Of prime concern in Bloom's theory as presented in *Human Characteristics and School Learning* is the quality of instruction (pp. 115–127). Four elements of instruction are cited as critical to quality:

Media and technology remove barriers to learning.

1. "Cues or directions provided to the learner." The cues are often presented or provided by media employed in the instructional process.

2. "Participation of the learner in learning activity." Participation in meaningful learning activity often involves the learner with media and technology. This is especially the case in regard to interactive technologies such as microcomputers.

3. "Reinforcement which the learner secures in some relation to the learning." Media have been found to be highly effective as reinforcers of learning in a wide variety of classroom settings.

Improved communications and learning result from use of appropriate media and technology.

4. "A feedback and corrective system must be included . . . because much of school instruction is fraught with error and difficulty." Because of the consistency with which media and technology present information and regulate learning activity, their use can play an important role in correcting learning.

Media and technology should be chosen with the learners in mind.

Other writers and classroom practitioners believed that media and technology were important elements in the classroom because they helped the teacher remove barriers to communication and learning. Among them were Wittich and Schuller who identified five such barriers (pp. 10–12):

1. Verbalization—Too much verbalization becomes an annoying stimulus and causes students to tune teachers out. Some forms of media, on the other hand, communicate by visual means, removing this barrier.

2. Referent confusion—This barrier develops when two people use the same words to mean completely different things. It was believed that this is most likely to occur in verbal communication and that the use of various media as illustrations of meaning remove the barriers.

3. Daydreaming—Daydreaming was believed to be lessened or eliminated by making lessons more interesting or easier to understand. A suggested means of doing this focused on the use of media with multisensory appeal.

Media and technology extend students' experiences.

4. Perceptual difficulties—These difficulties are overcome by presenting concrete and clear sensory messages to learners so that students obtain accurate interpretations and perceptions.

5. Physical discomfort—It was held that a favorable environment would enhance learning and that instructional media would help create a more favorable physical setting than might otherwise exist.

Physical difficulties are overcome through use of media and technology.

From a broad research review, the same authors pointed out that teachers should select and use media on the basis of six learning tenants (pp. 12–20):

▶ Each learner is unique.
▶ Perception is the foundation of learning.
▶ Learning requires involvement.
▶ Both content and media must be suitable to the learner.
▶ Teaching strategies must be appropriate.
▶ Creativity is the goal of learning.

Media and technology are the teacher's kit of modern tools.

The roles of media and technology in teaching and learning was also the subject of a review by Erickson. On the basis of comprehensive reviews of research pertaining to the use of media and technology, he asserted that they play one or more of the following roles in the classroom:

▶ "provides the teacher with the means for extending the horizons of experience." (pp. 11–13)

► "helps the teacher provide meaningful sources of information." (pp. 14–18)
► "provides the teacher with interest-compelling springboards into a wide variety of learning activities." (pp. 18–19)
► "assists the teacher in overcoming physical difficulties of presenting subject matter." (pp. 19–23)
► "provides the teacher with rich sources of pupil purpose when communicative materials are produced jointly by pupils and teachers." (pp. 23–26)
► "provides the teacher with a kit of tools to carry out diagnostic, research, and remedial work demanded by up-to-date instructional purposes." (pp. 27–28)

Such research findings and conclusions demonstrate clearly that media and technology are of proven value in the classroom. However, teachers must continuously consider which strategy is best for achieving a given learning outcome, and must select and make effective use of media and technology.

Students today have been raised in a technological environment that evolves constantly. Educators must provide a variety of approaches to the learning environment if they want to meet the needs and challenges of present day learners. Instructional media provide four observable contributions to learning. (1) Instructional media provide for vicarious learning experiences by substituting for the real situation through the use of a media format, such as a film, filmstrip, videotape, audio recordings, or study pictures. (2) Instructional media make communications more precise by serving as primary tools for communicating information precisely and accurately. (3) Instructional media contribute to interest in learning through physical conditions, motivation, color, realism, and creativity. (4) Instructional media increase options for establishing learning experiences for educators by providing choices and alternative methods in guiding students toward learning goals.

1. Explain what is meant by "vicarious learning experiences" and cite an example of how you might provide a vicarious learning experience for learners under your direction.

_____

_____

_____

_____

_____

_____

_____

_____

_____

_____

SUMMARY

The classroom is a changing environment.

SUGGESTED ACTIVITIES

2. Explain some specific ways in which accuracy of communication is important in your teaching field or professional area.

_____

_____

_____

_____

_____

_____

_____

_____

_____

3. Identify a contribution media can make to teaching as concluded from research. Relate the research conclusion to your work as a teacher and explain how using media in the manner suggested might impact learning in your classroom.

_____

_____

_____

_____

_____

_____

_____

_____

_____

4. Identify an instructional task within your teaching area in which you feel various types of instructional media could effectively be used. Example: To teach the rotation system in volleyball.

Teaching Task (not a unit) _____

_____

_____

_____

_____

5. Describe the various types of media that might be used to teach your particular concept. Think of as many as you can, although you may actually use only one or two items of instructional media to teach the concept. Example: A film or videotape would probably be effective in teaching the rotation system in volleyball because it would show sequence from one position to the next.

_____

_____

_____

_____

_____

_____

_____

_____

_____

_____

6. Choose one of your media formats described in activity 5 and locate through media catalog resources a current title and information on your subject. Example: *Volleyball in Action,* a 16mm sound film available from many film rental libraries. Take the item you choose through the five utilization steps suggested in this chapter, describing what you would do in each step.

Media format _____

Title and description

_____

Five step utilization procedure for this particular media format

_____

_____

_____

_____

_____

_____

_____

_____

_____

Chapter 3

MEDIA SELECTION AND EVALUATION

PURPOSE

▸ To become acquainted with the principles, procedures, and sources employed in the selection and evaluation of instructional materials.

Sound media selection decisions are most apt to result when media are selected by carefully making use of appropriate source materials and procedural guidelines. This chapter describes such guidelines and then explores evaluation criteria and sources of educational media.

INTRODUCTION

Instructors should use instructional media in ways which appear to best fit immediate learning situations. Instructional media should be selected on the basis of the needs of students and the characteristics which instructional materials must possess in order to meet these needs. Certain general principles, described here, should be used as the basis for selecting and using all types of instructional materials.

MEDIA SELECTION GUIDELINES

Instructional Media Should Follow, Not Dictate, Learning Objectives

Instructors are often accused of building their instruction around a textbook, thereby letting the text dictate the learning outcomes. Educators should begin planning instruction by carefully formulating the goals and objectives to be achieved. All instructional media, both books and audiovisual materials, should be selected on the basis of the contributions they will make to the attainment of the learning objectives being sought.

Consider the objectives of instruction prior to choosing media.

Instructors Must Be Thoroughly Familiar with the Content of All Media Used in Instruction

Selection of instructional media should follow complete review of the materials rather than simply the reading of a catalog description. Adequate instructional planning demands a thorough knowledge of instructional media content. Only

The teacher must have a thorough knowledge of media content.

Media and technology must fit the instructional plan.

when this knowledge is present will the teacher be able to construct meaningful sequences of learning activities.

The Instructional Media Must Be Appropriate to the Teaching Formats

Some instructional materials are designed specifically for use by individual students and are not appropriate for group use. Also, some materials designed for group use are difficult to use on an individual basis. Instructors should be aware of general limits of various types of instructional media. For example, materials in 8mm film loop format should not be selected for use with a large student group. Likewise, persons planning individualized instruction should not select materials in overhead transparency format, because this medium may be appropriate only in group presentations.

Instructional Media Should Be Consistent with Student Capabilities and Learning Styles

A thorough study of the intended learners should precede decisions regarding media selection.

Instructors should continually be aware of the conceptual level of their students in order to select materials that are consistent with students' levels of comprehension. Materials available from commercial publishing companies are usually designed for a general student population. Instructors can adapt many materials so that they can be used successfully with particular students. However, if the materials are too "far above" or "below" the developmental level of the students, they should not be used.

Strive for objectivity in choosing media.

Instructors should also select materials that are suited to the individual learning styles of students. Some students are uniquely capable of learning from visual materials. The same students may have difficulty in learning from highly verbal reading materials prepared at the same conceptual level. Visual materials are a natural path to learning for "visually oriented" learners. Materials should be selected to suit the learner's unique learning characteristics and styles.

Instructional Media Should Be Chosen Objectively, Not on the Basis of One's Personal Preference

Teachers may tend to select instructional media solely on the basis of an attractive appearance. However, a colorful, exciting filmstrip, film, or display is valueless if it fails to establish the desired student response.

Look for variety in media.

Instructors should avoid predetermining the type of instructional media to use and should be open to using whatever format of media is most suitable. For example, one should not look for a "filmstrip" that shows the physical characteristics of the Grand Canyon. Rather, one should seek to devise the "best way" of showing the physical characteristics of the Grand Canyon to the particular student group, whether that way constitutes use of a filmstrip or some other means.

Educators should experiment with many types of materials rather than limiting themselves to the few with which they are most comfortable. Often a teacher will discover that a medium such as slides is a particularly effective means of teaching. Instructors should continue to use slides as long as they are effective but guard against becoming limited to them. Good instructors constantly search for "better" procedures for using all types of media in instruction.

Choose media that can impact learning in a significant way.

Media Should Be Chosen on the Basis of Their Contribution to Learning Outcomes

Some instructional materials are much more readily available than others. Some are located in the classroom or elsewhere in the local school. Others must be ordered from a central location in the school system or from outside the district. Teachers should not limit instructional media usage to items easily available, but should engage in detailed advance planning, so that orders can be made for materials that must be obtained from outside the local setting.

Physical Conditions Surrounding the Use of Instructional Media Affect Their Results

When projected materials are shown, seating arrangements should ensure that each student has an adequate view of the screen. Likewise, when group listening activities are used, sound must be evenly distributed throughout the room.

Use media under the best conditions possible.

Control of room light is necessary for effective use of many projected materials. Teachers must be alert to the amount of light needed in the room and see that the light is adequately controlled at that level.

When instructional media are used for individual viewing and listening, learning is usually enhanced by isolating students in private study areas or listening carrels. Physical arrangements should ensure an undisturbed learning environment when a class uses individualized viewing and listening. Students should listen using headsets that fit comfortably and provide for quality sound reproduction.

Instructional Materials Produced Locally by Instructors Usually Make Significant Contributions to Learning

Media that teachers create for their own students are tailored specifically to the students' needs, interests, and capabilities. Research indicates that teachers make better instructional uses of the materials they have produced than of materials obtained from commercial sources.

Try new media and new ways of using them.

For these and other reasons, it is desirable for instructors to produce many of the instructional materials needed in their teaching. To do so, teachers must obtain certain skills necessary in the production of instructional media and must be acquainted with the total process of planning and developing various types of instructional materials.

No Single Medium Is Best for All Purposes

Just as there is no one "best" way to teach under all situations, there is no "best" medium of instruction to use at all times. Instructors should experiment with the use of a variety of instructional media and select the medium most appropriate to the learning task.

CRITERIA FOR MEDIA EVALUATION

Beyond these general underlying principles, several important specific criteria should be employed as instructional materials are chosen and their uses assessed. Educators can best apply such criteria by thinking of the criteria in terms of observable characteristics of the materials.

Curriculum Concerns

Choose media that fit the curriculum.

Among these characteristics are consistency with the local curriculum and with the specific objectives of the instruction in which the materials are to be used. The first of these relates to the extent to which the materials fit into the over-all educational program of the school, firm, or agency. Materials should be selected only if they are consistent with the overall purposes of the program and only if they enable learners, through their use, to achieve specific objectives or planned outcomes of the learning activities in which they are engaged. The person selecting materials must look for a positive fit with both the overall program purposes and the specific learning outcomes to be achieved by each student.

Content Criteria

Choose media that have the correct content.

As teachers evaluate materials, they should give careful attention to several characteristics relating to the content of the materials. One characteristic relates to the amount of content included in the materials. If too much is included the learner may become confused and turn away from learning processes. If too little is included, the learner may be left lacking the knowledge base necessary to make meaningful application of the acquired facts. Therefore, teachers should seek to select materials which have appropriate amounts of content in regard to the entry knowledge base of the learner and the terminal learning outcome to be achieved.

The content of the materials must be sequenced to lead the learner logically from simple to complex ideas or from start to finish in a process. One should also examine the content carefully to determine that it is both current and accurate.

Materials will make their maximum contribution to learning when they capture and hold the interest of learners. Only the actual use of the materials will demonstrate the extent to which students maintain interest in the materials, but instructors must pre-assess the extent to which they believe a media selection provides potential for stimulating student interest.

Learner Characteristics

One must also examine materials to ensure that they match the ability level of the learners. Materials that are too complicated for the students will result in frustration and failure to learn, whereas those that are too simplistic will result in boredom and possibly antisocial behavior.

Materials should be selected that can be adapted to various learning situations and styles. Such materials afford the instructor freedom to adapt the materials both to the unique characteristics of a group and to the specific needs of individuals.

Match the media to the learners.

Only materials that make positive contributions to the self-image of learners should be selected. Therefore, the person selecting the materials should ensure that they are free from bias and prejudiced attitudes and concepts.

Technical Concerns

Certain technical characteristics of materials should also be considered. The amount of time necessary to see, hear, or read the materials should be appropriate to the content presented and the conceptual level of the learners. Materials presented too rapidly for given learners will create confusion and materials presented over too long a time period may result in boredom and an absence of attention to what is being presented.

Choose media that are of acceptable technical quality.

Consideration should also be given to the durability of the materials. Teachers should select materials that will hold up under anticipated uses. For example, printed materials or pictures that are to be handled by learners should be printed or mounted on heavy paper or cardboard and the surfaces should be laminated.

If the materials have an audio or sound-reproducing capacity, educators should determine whether the sound quality is sufficient for the planned uses of the materials. Consideration should be given to such aspects as the composition of the narration, speed at which the materials are presented, tone quality, and the quality and appropriateness of music if such is a part of the audio presentation.

Likewise, the technical quality of visual materials must be examined carefully in relation to planned uses for the materials. Characteristics such as color, photography, lettering style, graphics, and size of visual symbols should receive special attention.

Choose media that have the required support materials.

Supporting Materials

Finally, teachers should consider whether adequate supporting materials are available. Materials such as teacher's guides, suggestions for using the materials, information to supplement the materials, and reports on the development and testing of the materials should be carefully examined.

These principles and criteria, properly applied, provide a solid base for selecting and evaluating instructional materials. Instructors who select and use media on these bases will discover that a wealth of instructional media is available and can be used to develop the learning outcomes being sought.

MEDIA SOURCES

Look within your school to get the necessary media for your classroom.

Local Sources

One of the major concerns of educators relates to where instructional materials may be obtained. The best source is usually the most localized one. The school's media center (usually the learning resource center or LRC) is a most crucial element in the supply of both locally produced and purchased instructional materials. LRC staff use various means to acquaint users with available materials. Catalogs may be available in the forms of printed booklets, card catalogs, or computer databases. It is the teacher's responsibility to become thoroughly familiar with materials available locally.

Additional Media Center Sources

Other materials are available from various offsite sources. Such sources include school districts and regional and state media centers that serve elementary and secondary schools. These media centers distribute catalog information to persons who are eligible to obtain materials from their collections. The following section includes addresses for many of these centers.

INFORMATION SOURCES

Selection Tools

Several types of tools are helpful as teachers select instructional materials. Directories, indexes and guides list materials for use in most educational settings. The National Information Center for Educational Media (NICEM) publishes extensive indexes covering the major types of media. Particularly helpful are *Film and Video Finder, Audiocassette Finder,* and *Filmstrip and Slide-Tape Finder.* These are available from NICEM, Access Information, Inc., Box 40130, Albuquerque, NM 87196.

The R.R. Bowker Company, 205 East 42nd Street, New York, NY 10017, publishes indexes to several types of materials. The *Educational Film/Video Locator* is an excellent general index covering these types of media. Another valuable tool is the *Video Source Book,* published by the National Video Clearinghouse,

Inc., 100 Lafayette Drive, Syosset, NY 11791. These and other indexes are kept up-to-date through regular supplements.

Look outside the district.

Available free of charge is the *Multimedia Source Guide*, a supplement to *T.H.E. Journal*. This guide gives descriptions and sources for computer-generated multimedia software. It is available from: *T.H.E. Journal*, 150 El Camino Real, Suite 112, Tustin, CA 92680.

The correct tool is essential to accurate selection of media.

Examples of valuable guides for use in selecting free and inexpensive materials are those published by Educators Progress Service, Randolph, Wisconsin 53956. This firm publishes several guides listing hundreds of items that may be obtained free of charge for use in teaching. Some guides cover materials of one media type (such as videotapes) in all subject areas, while others include materials in one subject area (such as Science) listing media of all types.

Some selection tools relate specifically to one type of media.

Several types of media directories are also available covering certain types of items. The most comprehensive guide for use in selecting equipment is *The Directory of Video, Computer, and Audio-Visual Products,* published annually by the International Communications Industries Association, 3150 Spring Street, Fairfax, VA 22031.

Some selection tools guide you to "free" materials.

Two excellent sources of information about microcomputers and instructional software are *The Source,* published by The Source Library Services, McClean, VA 22101, and *School Microware Directory,* published by Dresden Associates, Inc., Dresden, ME 04342.

The National Audiovisual Center, The National Archives and Records Service, Information Branch, Washington, D.C. 20401, can provide a wealth of information about instructional materials produced by federal agencies. Information about general equipment and technology manufacturers and distributors may be found in *The Thomas Register of American Manufacturers,* published by Thomas Publishing Company, Inc., 461 Eighth Avenue, New York, NY 10001.

Some selection tools indicate where you may obtain equipment.

The American Library Association, 50 East Huron Street, Chicago, IL 60611, publishes *Library Technology Reports,* which includes evaluations of materials and equipment. The *Educational Media Yearbook,* published annually by Libraries Unlimited, P.O. Box 263, Littleton, CO 80106, is a rich source of information pertaining to media and technology-oriented publications and organizations.

Some selection tools give information about microcomputer software.

The *A.M.I. Directory* has over 8,000 listings of products and services related to the production of audio, video, music, software, film, lighting, and related services. The directory is available from A.M.I. Publishing, P.O. Box 35, 20 Wellington Street, East Aurora, Ontario, Canada L4G 3H1.

Some selection tools give evaluations of materials.

Many periodicals furnish valuable up-to-date information pertaining to new materials and technologies. Among such periodicals:

Educational Technology. Educational Technology Publications, Inc., 140 Sylvan Ave., Englewood Cliffs, NJ 07632.

Some journals and magazines tell about new materials.

Electronic Learning. 902 Sylvan Ave., P.O. Box 2001, Englewood Cliffs, NJ 07632.

ERIC/IR Update. ERIC Clearinghouse of Information Resources, School of Education, Syracuse University, Syracuse, NY 13210.

Tech Trends. Association for Educational Communications and Technology, 1126 16th St. N.W., Washington, D.C. 20036.

Library Journal and *School Library Journal.* R.R. Bowker Company, 1180 Avenue of the Americas, New York, NY 10036.

Media and Methods. American Society of Educators, 1511 Walnut Street, Philadelphia, PA 19108.

Materials are available from a very extensive number and range of sources.

Media Review. Media Review, 343 Manville Road, Pleasantville, NY 10570.

School Library Media Quarterly. American Association of School Librarians, 50 Huron Street, Chicago, IL 60611.

T.H.E. Journal, 150 El Camino Real, Suite 112, Tustin, CA 92680.

Training and Development Journal. American Society for Training and Development, 600 Maryland Avenue S.W., Washington, D.C. 10023.

Many other sources may be used to become aware of available materials and to keep up-to-date on new materials being produced in any subject area. Most professional journals provide listings of new audiovisual materials as they are made available in the subject area covered by the journal. Producers of instructional materials also issue catalogs on a regular basis covering all materials currently in print. Likewise, many local distributors issue catalogs of materials sold by their firms.

Instructors will also find a wealth of instructional materials available in their own communities. Local firms such as the telephone company, banks, offices of professional or trade associations, local government offices, museums, special interests groups, and clubs often have useful materials that are available to educators.

Look for selection tools that are unbiased and that are up-to-date.

Governmental agencies are a valuable source of materials of many types. For example, the U.S. Department of Agriculture has vast resources related to agriculture, energy, engineering, and nutrition. These materials are available from many USDA offices, including Washington, D.C., in regions, states, and counties. Often local governmental offices have valuable instructional materials that are freely distributed to teachers and trainers.

CLASSIFIED SOURCES

Space does not permit an exhaustive listing here of sources useful in the selection of all types of materials in all subject areas. However, a limited number of sources is given as examples so that teachers may become acquainted with the general sources that they may use to obtain information about various types of media.

Audio Recordings

Audio Cardalog. Jeffrey Norton Publishers, 145 East 49th Street, New York, NY 10017.

Caedmon Records. 110 Treemont Street, Boston MA 02107.

Folkways Records. 701 5th Avenue, New York, NY 10036.

The National Center for Audio Tapes. 384 Stadium Building, University of Colorado, Boulder, CO 80302.

W. Schwann, Inc. 137 Newbury Street, Boston MA 02116.

Spoken Arts. Inc. 310 North Avenue, New Rochelle, NY 10801.

Display Materials

American Museum of Natural History. Central Park West at 79th Street, New York, NY 10024.

Artex Prints. Inc. Westport, CT 06680.

Bulletin Boards and Directory Products. 724 Broadway, New York, NY 10003.

Denoyer-Geppert. 5235 Ravenswood Avenue, Chicago IL 60640.

Documentary Photo Aids. Inc. P.O. Box 2237, Phoenix, AZ 85002.

Instructo Corp. 1635 North 55th Street, Paoli, PA 19301.

Museum of Modern Art. 11 West 53rd Street, New York, NY 10019.

National Audubon Society. 11305 5th Street, New York, NY 10028.

National Geographic Society. School Service Division, 16th and M Streets, N.W., Washington, D.C. 20036.

Oravision Company. Inc. 321 15th Avenue, South, St. Petersburg, FL 33701.

Filmstrips and Slides

Denoyer-Geppert Co. 5235 Ravenswood Avenue, Chicago, IL 60640.

General Aniline and Film Corp. 140 West 51st Street, New York, NY 10020.

Guidance Associates. 23 Washington Avenue, Pleasantville, NY 10570.

C.S. Hammond and Co., Inc. Maplewood, NJ 07040.

Popular Science Publishing Co. Audio-Visual Division, 355 Lexington Avenue, New York, NY 10017.

Society for Visual Education. 1345 Diversey Parkway, Chicago, IL 60614.

Free and Inexpensive Materials

Ruth H. Aubrey Selected Free Materials for Classroom Teachers. Fearon Press, Belmont, CA 90738.

Educators Guide to Free Materials. Educators Progress Service, Randolph, WI 53596.

The Elementary Teachers Guide to Free Curriculum Materials. Educators Progress Service, Randolph, WI 53596. (Several other guides to free materials are available from this source)

Free and Inexpensive Learning Materials. Division of Surveys and Field Services, Peabody College, Nashville, TN 37028.

Microcomputer Software

Chisholm. 910 Campisi Way, Campbell, CA 95008.

Educational Software Directory. Sterling-Swift Publishing Co., 7901 So. I.H. 35, Austin, TX 78744.

Hartley Courseware, Inc. 133 Bridge Street, Dimondale, MI 48821.

Interactive Communication Systems, Inc. 8050 North Port Washington Road, Milwaukee, WI 53217.

International Microcomputer Software Directory. Imprint Software, 1520 So. College Ave., Ft. Collins, CO 80521.

Kirkwood Community College. 6301 Kirkwood Blvd., SW, P.O. Box 2068, Cedar Rapids, IA 52406.

Microcomputer Index. Microcomputer Information Services, 2464 El Camino Real, Suite 247, Santa Clara, CA 95051.

Satellite Educational Resources Consortium. 939 South Stadium Road, Columbia, SC 29201.

Tandberg Educational, Inc. Orchard Ridge Corporate Park, Building No. 2, Fields Lane, Brewster, NY 10509.

Telecourse People, Miami-Dade Community College, 11011 SW 104th Street, Miami, FL 33176.

Overhead Transparencies

Lansford Publishing Co. P.O. Box 8711, San Jose, CA 95155.

Scott Graphics, Inc. 28 Gaylord Street, South Hadley, MA 01075.

3M Company. Visual Products Division, 3M Center, St. Paul, MN 55101.

Print Materials

The Booklist. 50 East Huron St., Chicago, IL 60611.

Center for Humanities. 2 Holland Avenue, White Plains, NY 10603.

Scholastic Book Services. 904 Skyulvan Avenue, Englewood Cliffe, NJ 06632.

Walt Disney Educational Media Co. 5005 Buena Vista Street, Burbank, CA 91521.

Video Recordings and Motion Picture Films

Agency for Instructional Television. Box A, Bloomington, IN 47401.

Ambrose Video Publishing. 1290 Avenue of the Americas, Suite 2245, New York, NY 10104.

Annenberg/CPB Project. 901 East Street, N.W., Washington, D.C. 20004.

Association Sterling Educational Films. 866 3rd Avenue, New York, NY 10022.

Chip Taylor Communications. 15 Spollett Drive, Derry, NH 03038.

Cornet International Films and Video. 65 East South Water Street, Chicago, IL 60601.

Encyclopedia Britannica Educational Corp. 425 North Michigan Avenue, Chicago, IL 60611.

Eye-Gate House, Inc. 146-01 Archer Avenue, Jamaica, NY 10570.

Great Plains National TV Library. P.O. Box 80669, Lincoln, NE 68501.

McGraw-Hill/Contemporary Films. 1221 Avenue of the Americas, New York, NY 10020.

The National Film Board of Canada. 680 5th Avenue, New York, NY 10019.

Pheonix/BFA Films and Video. 468 Park Avenue, South, New York, NY 10016.

The Public Television Library. 475 L'Enfont Plaza, S.W., Washington, D.C. 20024.

Pyramid Films. Box 1048, Santa Monica, CA 90906.

Rainbow Educational Video, Inc., 170 Keyland Ct., Bohemia, NY 11716.

Silver Burdette Division of General Learning Corporation. 460 Northwest Highway, Park Ridge, IL 60068.

Time-Life Films. 43 West 16th Street, New York, NY 10011.

U.S. Government Films. National Audiovisual Center, Information Branch, Washington D.C. 20409.

Videoplay Program Source. C.S. Tepfer Company, Ridgeford, CT 06877.

EVALUATION PROCEDURES AND TOOLS

Evaluation of instructional materials involves the formulation of value judgments about the materials. Teachers always make such a judgment, even if the evaluation consists of casually looking back on the experience and commenting that the students really learned from the materials or that their use was a waste of time.

The process of evaluating instructional materials can be enhanced if teachers employ carefully developed and proven evaluation tools. One such tool is the Evaluation Guide for Instructional Materials, which appears at the end of this chapter. This guide was developed and tested over a period of several years at Kansas State University and is used extensively by teachers and media specialists across the United States to guide them through the process of evaluating instructional materials.

SUGGESTED ACTIVITIES

1. Pages 43, 45 and 47 consist of three copies of the Evaluation Guide for Instructional Materials. Examine carefully an item of instructional materials using this guide as a tool to guide your evaluation of the materials. Make two copies of your evaluation, leaving one copy in your book. Turn in one copy to your instructor if asked to do so. This will leave one copy for your future reference and use in evaluating instructional materials.

2. Read and review carefully the guidelines for instructional media selection given at the beginning of the chapter. Select the three principles you regard as most important to your teaching area and tell why you selected each.

(a) _____

_____

_____

_____

_____

_____

_____

_____

(b) _____

_____

_____

_____

_____

_____

(c) _____

_____

_____

_____

_____

_____

3. Review the sources listed in this chapter from which instructional materials may be obtained. Identify five or more organizations that appear to have materials that could be used in your teaching area(s). Write to the organizations, requesting detailed information about these materials.

EVALUATION GUIDE FOR INSTRUCTIONAL MATERIALS

1. Type of Media _____ 2. Subject Area _____
3. Title _____ 4. Producer _____
5. Technical Characteristics: Size _____ Speed _____ Length _____
   Color _____ Sound _____ Date _____
6. Cost: Purchase $ _____ Rental $ _____

Review the Materials in Detail Before Proceeding
7. Suggested Use Levels: Early Childhood _____ Primary _____ Intermediate _____
   Jr. High _____ Sr. High _____ College _____ Adult _____
8. Brief Description _____
   _____
   _____

Evaluate the materials on the basis of each of the following characteristics. If one of the characteristics does not apply, leave all spaces for that item blank.

	Excellent	Good	Fair	Poor
1. Consistency with the local curriculum	___	___	___	___
2. Consistency with the objectives of the instruction in which their use is anticipated	___	___	___	___
3. Inclusion of appropriate amount of content	___	___	___	___
4. Development of a logical sequence	___	___	___	___
5. Currentness of content	___	___	___	___
6. Accuracy of content	___	___	___	___
7. Potential for stimulating student interest	___	___	___	___
8. Consistency with the intended learners' ability levels	___	___	___	___
9. Adaptability to various learning situations	___	___	___	___
10. Freedom from bias, prejudiced attitudes, and concepts	___	___	___	___
11. Appropriateness of time or length to content	___	___	___	___
12. Durability of materials	___	___	___	___
13. Sound quality (narration, speed, tone, music, etc.)	___	___	___	___
14. Visual quality (photography, color, size, graphics, etc.)	___	___	___	___

	Yes	No
15. Are teachers' guides and supplemental information available with the materials?	___	___
16. Do the materials make distinct and important contributions not currently available in the collection?	___	___
17. Is the cost of the materials justified by the instructional values they exhibit?	___	___
18. Do you recommend purchase of the materials?	___	___

Evaluated by _____ Date _____

EVALUATION GUIDE FOR INSTRUCTIONAL MATERIALS

1. Type of Media _____ 2. Subject Area _____
3. Title _____ 4. Producer _____
5. Technical Characteristics: Size _____ Speed _____ Length _____
                                Color _____ Sound _____ Date _____
6. Cost: Purchase $ _____ Rental $ _____

Review the Materials in Detail Before Proceeding
7. Suggested Use Levels: Early Childhood _____ Primary _____ Intermediate _____
   Jr. High _____ Sr. High _____ College _____ Adult _____
8. Brief Description _____
_____
_____

Evaluate the materials on the basis of each of the following characteristics. If one of the characteristics does not apply, leave all spaces for that item blank.

	Excellent	Good	Fair	Poor
1. Consistency with the local curriculum	___	___	___	___
2. Consistency with the objectives of the instruction in which their use is anticipated	___	___	___	___
3. Inclusion of appropriate amount of content	___	___	___	___
4. Development of a logical sequence	___	___	___	___
5. Currentness of content	___	___	___	___
6. Accuracy of content	___	___	___	___
7. Potential for stimulating student interest	___	___	___	___
8. Consistency with the intended learners' ability levels	___	___	___	___
9. Adaptability to various learning situations	___	___	___	___
10. Freedom from bias, prejudiced attitudes, and concepts	___	___	___	___
11. Appropriateness of time or length to content	___	___	___	___
12. Durability of materials	___	___	___	___
13. Sound quality (narration, speed, tone, music, etc.)	___	___	___	___
14. Visual quality (photography, color, size, graphics, etc.)	___	___	___	___

	Yes	No
15. Are teachers' guides and supplemental information available with the materials?	___	___
16. Do the materials make distinct and important contributions not currently available in the collection?	___	___
17. Is the cost of the materials justified by the instructional values they exhibit?	___	___
18. Do you recommend purchase of the materials?	___	___

Evaluated by _____ Date _____

EVALUATION GUIDE FOR INSTRUCTIONAL MATERIALS

1. Type of Media _____ 2. Subject Area _____
3. Title _____ 4. Producer _____
5. Technical Characteristics: Size _____ Speed _____ Length _____
     Color _____ Sound _____ Date _____
6. Cost: Purchase $ _____ Rental $ _____

Review the Materials in Detail Before Proceeding

7. Suggested Use Levels: Early Childhood _____ Primary _____ Intermediate _____
   Jr. High _____ Sr. High _____ College _____ Adult _____
8. Brief Description _____
   _____
   _____

Evaluate the materials on the basis of each of the following characteristics. If one of the characteristics does not apply, leave all spaces for that item blank.

	Excellent	Good	Fair	Poor
1. Consistency with the local curriculum	___	___	___	___
2. Consistency with the objectives of the instruction in which their use is anticipated	___	___	___	___
3. Inclusion of appropriate amount of content	___	___	___	___
4. Development of a logical sequence	___	___	___	___
5. Currentness of content	___	___	___	___
6. Accuracy of content	___	___	___	___
7. Potential for stimulating student interest	___	___	___	___
8. Consistency with the intended learners' ability levels	___	___	___	___
9. Adaptability to various learning situations	___	___	___	___
10. Freedom from bias, prejudiced attitudes, and concepts	___	___	___	___
11. Appropriateness of time or length to content	___	___	___	___
12. Durability of materials	___	___	___	___
13. Sound quality (narration, speed, tone, music, etc.)	___	___	___	___
14. Visual quality (photography, color, size, graphics, etc.)	___	___	___	___

	Yes	No
15. Are teachers' guides and supplemental information available with the materials?	___	___
16. Do the materials make distinct and important contributions not currently available in the collection?	___	___
17. Is the cost of the materials justified by the instructional values they exhibit?	___	___
18. Do you recommend purchase of the materials?	___	___

Evaluated by _____ Date _____

Chapter 4

DEVELOPMENT OF INSTRUCTION

PURPOSES

▶ To become acquainted with seven procedures involved in the systematic planning of instruction.
▶ To become acquainted with the place of media and technology in the systematic development of instruction.

Teachers are more likely to arrive at sound decisions regarding the use of media and technology as part of a systematic instructional planning and development process. Many models have been designed to depict how instruction might be systematically developed. The instructional development model presented here should not be regarded as "the" plan for use in all instructional planning. Rather, it is presented as one means of demonstrating a type of systematic process that should enable media and technology to be selected and used in appropriate ways.

Figure 4.1 indicates seven elements involved in systematic development of instruction. These elements form the basis of effective planning and depict clearly the place of media and technology in an overall instructional scheme.

Conduct Student Assessment

Systematic instructional development must be built on an accurate assessment of students' needs. Instruction must be planned in relation to an assessment that includes the best data available regarding students needs, capabilities, interests, learning styles, and overall readiness for involvement in the planned learning activities.

It is essential to make an accurate assessment of the entry mastery level of the student. Learning activities can then be planned to take the students from their entry level toward the desired learning outcomes. A thorough student needs assessment will also enable teachers to make appropriate media selection decisions. For example, students with limited entry mastery will require concrete learning activities such as role playing and field study. On the other hand, students with advanced entry competencies can make use of abstract media such as graphic and print materials.

INTRODUCTION

Effective planning is an integral part of effective instruction.

SYSTEMATIC INSTRUCTIONAL DEVELOPMENT

A thorough knowledge of students is essential to effective instruction.

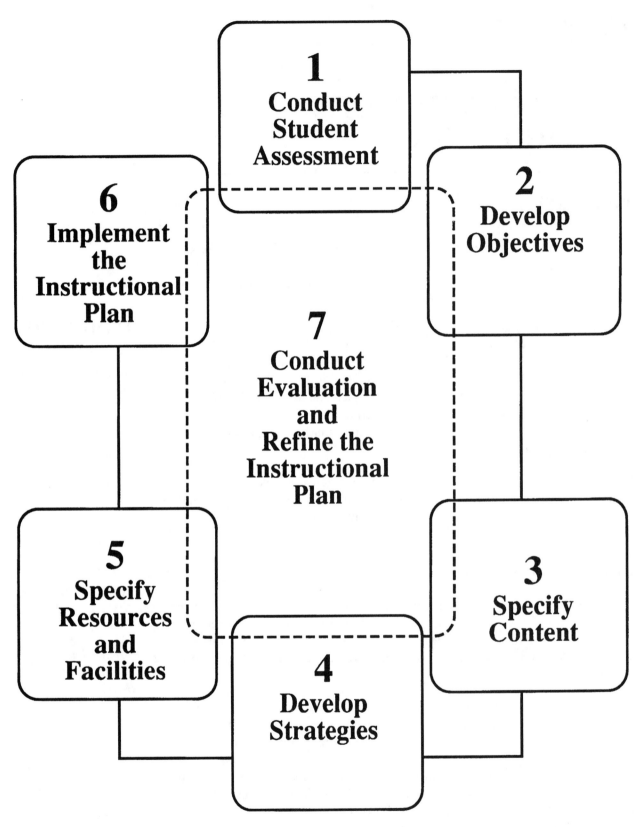

Figure 4.1

Elements of Systematic Instructional Development

Develop Objectives

Sound instruction is based on established goals and objectives. *Goals* are broad statements that describe student learning outcomes. Goals are stated in general terms and may be interpreted in various ways. Some examples of instructional goals are these:

Objectives point clearly to what students are to learn.

- ► Students will know the alphabet by the end of kindergarten.
- ► Students will understand basic mathematic operations.
- ► Students will be culturally literate.
- ► Students will have a basic knowledge of the major cities of the world.

These broad statements of expectations about student performance are usually expressed in the curriculum plans of the school district. Instructional *objectives*, on the other hand, are more specific and describe the means by which these educational goals may be attained.

Appropriate content is essential in directing students to the attainment of specified objectives.

Instructional objectives are clearly stated, specific descriptions of what students are expected to learn through instruction. Instructional objectives are usually stated in behavioral terms, such as the following:

- ► The student will be able to recite the alphabet in sequence.
- ► The student will recognize and name a given letter no matter where it appears in a word.

Objectives are crucial elements in the instructional development process because they describe the performance or competency that will result in the learner as a product of the instruction. When teachers prepare to teach, it seems logical to ask, "what will I do to cause students to learn?" However, appropriately developed instructional objectives are always stated in terms of what *students* will do as a result of learning, not in terms of what instructors will do as they teach.

An effective instructional plan must deal with how instruction will be implemented.

An instructional objective stated in behavioral terms must focus on the student, what the student will do as the outcome of learning, and what the teacher will do to ensure that learning occurs. An instructional objective should consist of four parts:

- ► an identification of the learner (usually stated as "The student will . . . ")
- ► the performance or behavior
- ► the condition under which the performance is to occur
- ► the standards or criteria by which the performance will be evaluated

Certain terms are help to pinpoint objectives in statements of learning performances. Some useful performance verbs are these:

A behavioral objective has three focuses: the learner, the planned outcome, and the path to learning.

add	design	outline
alphabetize	distinguish	prepare
analyze	estimate	produce

apply	evaluate	read
build	explain	reconstruct
categorize	identify	remove
choose	illustrate	revise
classify	indicate	select
compare	label	sort
compute	locate	specify
construct	manipulate	suggest
contrast	measure	translate
deduce	modify	verbalize
defend	order	verify
define	organize	write
describe		

Other terms are useful in stating the conditions under which performance occurs. Among them are these:

given
when
while
without

Standards or criteria by which the performance will be evaluated may be stated as follows:

degree of accuracy
amount of time
a number of occurrences.

An example of an instructional objective consisting of the four parts follows:

1. Learner: The student

2. Performance: will be able to mark statements with an "F" for fact and an "O" for opinion

3. Condition: given an article from a newspaper,

4. Standard: with 75 percent of the statements marked correctly.

Well-developed instructional objectives should result in three major advantages in instruction. First, student achievement should be enhanced, because students know clearly what they are to learn and how they are to show that they have learned. Second, communications and interaction in the classroom should be improved by the common knowledge of what is to be learned and how learning is to occur. Third, planning and evaluation should be enhanced by the development and use of specific objectives and assessment procedures.

Student achievement, classroom communications, and planning and evaluation all are improved by the use of instructional objectives.

Specify Content

As objectives are developed, statements of content or reference to printed sources of content should be made. Thus, content statements compose the next layer of building blocks in a systematic instructional development process. In the past, content necessary to reach stated objectives has been selected from textbooks or drawn together from other print sources. Much content now used is taken from either print or nonprint media sources.

However, as computers assume larger roles in instruction, content is being written to facilitate computer entry by programmers. Extreme care must be taken in selecting, sequencing, and pacing. Only factual information to attaining the objectives should be included. Main points should stand out and all supporting information should relate to and clarify the major ideas.

Develop Strategies

Once the student characteristics are known, the objectives set, and the content stated, teachers are prepared to develop the major instructional strategies necessary to guide students toward the objectives. Teachers have traditionally presented substantial amounts of information to students using methods such as lectures and teacher-directed discussions. Research has long shown that media may be selected and used to effectively disseminate information to students.

However, with advanced technology now available media may be employed for a broad range of instructional purposes and within a variety of strategies. Also, it should be remembered that instructional media are crucial elements when discovery strategies are used. A wide range of relevant media are essential when learners are motivated and set free to find their own answers and solutions.

The strategy teachers select will determine the most appropriate organizational scheme to be employed. Systematic developmental activities often reveal the necessity of organizing in ways different from the classroom groups used traditionally in teaching. Research has indicated that in many instances individualization or small groups are the best organizational approaches to use to attain the desired learning outcomes.

Media and technology enhance and expand the range of strategies that teachers can use.

Technologies now available make possible a wide range of choices pertaining to instructional organizational patterns. Microcomputer and videodisc technologies have potential for directing a large part of the learning activities needed in instruction today. Thus, decisions as to instructional organization are crucial ones and are no longer limited to schemes for merely moving learners from one size of group to another within a self-contained classroom.

Specify Resources and Facilities

Resources and facilities, including media and technology, are keys to effective instruction.

The effectiveness of the instructional design rests heavily on the human and material resources available and on the manner in which each is employed in the learning activities. Designs in teaching and training rest increasingly on an instructional team, rather than on a single teacher or trainer. The instructional plan should specify each teacher, trainer, aide, intern, and so on, who is to be involved in the instructional process and should indicate the role each is to play.

Instructors should identify and use facilities that help the learner to meet the learning objectives. Instructional designs that make use of high-state technologies such as computers and video must include specifications relating to these facilities. Even the more traditional media such as films and slides require facility considerations such as light control and ample electrical outlets. Facility considerations must also be related to instructional modes so that adequately sized spaces are available for the student grouping patterns to be used.

Implement the Instructional Plan

Performance is the ultimate test of the quality of an instructional plan.

Actual instruction must be conducted with the same diligence that has been advocated here for planning and development. No instructional medium or device can compensate for instructional personnel who do not function with a high level of professional competence. All planned learning activities *must* be directed and monitored expertly and all instructional activities carried forward with professionalism.

Special care should be taken to ensure that effective use is made of all media integrated in the learning activities. Instructional personnel should progress with ease to the use of a variety of media and should apply technological approaches with confidence.

Evaluation must answer questions pertaining to the quality of the instructional plan.

Even with the most precise planning, instructional activities often fail to result in the desired student learning outcomes. It is essential, therefore, for teachers to be flexible enough to change plans and approaches and that their planning process be flexible enough to accommodate changes necessitated by class responses. Often students with varying learning styles and with various intelligences, as indicated previously in Chapter 2, do not perform precisely as planned. It is wise for teachers to take into consideration the need to devote additional time to those students who do not master the objectives originally intended.

Teachers should gear instruction so that most students may reasonably be expected to master a majority of the stated objectives but should also plan to provide alternative instruction or reteaching for students who encounter difficulty or fail to attain the learning outcomes in the planned timeframe.

Conduct Evaluation and Refine the Plan

Assessment data in a variety of forms may be used as bases for evaluative decisions regarding the progress of learners toward attainment of the instructional objectives. Such data usually take the forms of test results, formalized observations recorded on observation guides, performance checklists, and informal observations that may or may not be recorded.

Although evaluation of student achievement is essential, it is important to look beyond immediate learner assessment to the evaluation of the overall instructional approach. Evaluations must be made on the basis of the best available information throughout the entire process of designing, developing, and implementing the instruction.

Criterion-referenced tests are usually effective in measuring how well students achieve specific learning objectives. Well-developed criterion referenced tests should enable the teacher to measure what the students can do, what they cannot do, and the major difficulties they are encountering. In teaching the skills emphasized in most curricula today, teachers find it more appropriate to compare each student's performance to a prestated standard or criterion than to the performance of other students. Evaluation must relate specifically to the student attainment of the objectives regardless of the kinds of evaluation tools, techniques, or activities used. The evaluation process must enable the teacher to address two basic questions:

▶ Has the student attained the stated objectives?
▶ To what extent was the instruction effective?

Evaluation of instructional materials warrants special consideration in the context of this publication. For this reason, Chapter 3 included a discussion of evaluative criteria for such materials. The chapter concluded with copies of a guide that is being used extensively in the evaluation of all forms of instructional materials.

Evaluation of an instructional plan leads quite naturally to its revision and ultimate improvement. The margin that always exists for improvement; changes in content, methods, and technologies point continuously to the need for revision. The alert instructor is constantly searching for means of improving instruction. The final element in this instructional development process appropriately makes provision for the continuing instructional improvement that must occur in a dynamic instructional process.

No instructional plan is perfect. Revision is always in order.

**SUGGESTED
ACTIVITIES**

1. Distinguish between "goals" and "objectives" by writing "G" or "O" in front of each statement:

   __Students in this course will know how learning theory applies to using educational technology in the classroom.

   __Students in first-year English will be able to write a term paper in correct format.

   __Students in European History class will be able to write a two-page essay explaining the relationship between nationalism and World War I.

   __Students will select a balanced lunch in the school cafeteria, demonstrating that they know what constitutes a nutritious meal.

   __The second grade class will be acquainted with all the major holidays of the United States.

2. Identify the expected performance or behavior, conditions, and standards or criteria in the following by writing these in the spaces provided:

   Students will be able to operate all equipment, using the materials provided in the laboratory, with a high level of proficiency (no hesitation or mistakes).

   Performance/behavior

   Conditions

   Standards/criteria

   Using the information in the textbook and based on experience, students will be able to list a minimum of eight advantages and three disadvantages of using filmstrips.

   Performance/behavior

   Conditions

   Standards/criteria

Given a photocopier and photocopy acetate the student will be able to create a well-designed, clean and clear overhead transparency.

Performance/behavior

Conditions

Standards/criteria

Students will create or use appropriate media when giving a presentation in any college course.

Performance/behavior

Conditions

Standards/criteria

Third grade students will be able to use guide words in a beginning dictionary with 80 percent accuracy.

Performance/behavior

Conditions

Standards/criteria

Second grade students will be able to subtract two digit numbers requiring borrowing, in columnar form. They will be able to do this for 10 problems with 80 percent accuracy within 5 minutes.

Performance/behavior

Conditions

Standards/criteria

3. List three broad goals of a school district where you attended:

4. Construct three objectives stated in behavioral terms in your interest area of teaching, being certain to include:

   (a) identification of the learner

   (b) performance or behavior

   (c) conditions

   (d) standards or criteria

Recommended Readings

Anspiger, Varney C. *Measuring the Effectiveness of Sound Motion Pictures as Teaching Aids.* New York: Teachers College, Columbia University, 1933.

Armsey, J.W. and N.C. Dahl. *An Inquiry into the Uses of Instructional Technology.* New York: Ford Foundation, 1953.

Bloom, Benjamin S. *Human Characteristics and School Learning.* New York: McGraw-Hill Book Company, Inc., 1976.

Dale, Edgar. *Audiovisual Methods in Teaching.* New York: Dryden Press, 1946 (most recent edition, 1969).

Gagne, Robert M. and Leslie J. Briggs. *Principles of Instructional Design.* 2nd ed. New York: Holt, Rinehart and Winston, 1979.

Gardner, Howard J. *Frames of Mind.* New York: Basic Books, 1985.

Glasser, William. *Control Theory in the Classroom.* New York: Harper and Row, 1986.

Hancock, Alan. *Planning for Educational Mass Media.* London: Longman Group. Ltd., 1977.

Helm, Virginia. *Software Quality and Copyright.* Washington, D.C.: Association for Educational Communications and Technology, 1984.

Hermann, Ned. *The Creative Brain.* Lake Lurie, N.C.: Brain Books, 1989.

Kemp, Jerrold E. *The Instructional Design Process.* New York: Harper and Row, Publishers, 1985.

Knowlton, Daniel C. and Warren J. Tilton. *Motion Pictures in History Teaching.* New Haven, Connecticut: Yale University Press, 1929.

Lazer, David G. *Seven Pathways of Learning: Teaching About Multiple Intelligences.* Chicago: New Dimensions of Learning, 1993.

McLuhan, Marshall. *Understanding Media: The Extensions of Man.* New York: McGraw-Hill Book Co., 1964.

Meierhenry, Wesley C. *Enriching the Curriculum Through Motion Pictures.* Lincoln, Neb.: University of Nebraska Press, 1952.

Naisbitt, John and Patricia Aburedene. *Megatrends 2000.* Great Neck, New York: Morrow, 1990.

Nickerson, Raymond and Philip Zodhiates. *Technology in Education: Looking Toward 2020.* Hillsdale, N.J.: Lawrence Erlbaum Associates, 1988.

Office of Technology Assessment. *Informational Technology and Its Impact on American Education.* Washington, D.C.: U.S. Government Printing Office, 1982.

Roulton, Philip J. *The Sound Motion Picture in Science Teaching.* Cambridge, Mass.: Harvard University Press, 1982.

Roundtree, Derek. *Educational Technology in Curriculum Development.* 2nd ed. London: Harper and Row, Publishers, 1982.

Saettler, Paul. *A History of Instructional Technology.* New York: McGraw-Hill Book Co., 1968.

Skinner, B. F. "The Science of Learning and the Science of Teaching." *Harvard Education Review* 24: 86-97 (Spring 1954).

Skinner, B. F. *Verbal Behavior.* New York: Appleton-Century-Crofts, 1957.

Talab, R.S. *Copyright and Instructional Technologies: A Guide to Fair Use and Permission Procedures.* Washington, D.C.: Association for Educational Communications and Technology, 1989.

Travers, Robert M.H. *Research and Theory Related to Audiovisual Information Transmission.* Logan, Utah: University of Utah, Bureau of Educational Research, 1946.

Weisgerber, Robert A. *Instructional Process and Media Innovation.* Chicago: Rand McNally and Co., 1968.

Wiman, Raymond V. and Wesley C. Meierhenry. *Educational Media: Theory and Practice.* Columbia, Ohio: Merrill, 1969.

Wise, Harry A. *Motion Pictures as an Aid in Teaching American History.* New Haven, Conn.: Yale University Press, 1939.

Wittich, Walter Arno, and Charles F. Schuller. *Audiovisual Materials: Their Nature and Use.* New York: Harper and Row, 1987.

Wittich, Walter Arno, and John Gary Fowlkes. *Audio-Visual Paths to Learning.* New York: Harper, 1946.

GLOSSARY

Classroom Learning Centers: A self-contained station in a classroom where devices, activities, and materials are made available to a student and arranged in a manner that enables the student to use them to attain stated learning objectives through independent study.

Evaluation of Media: The process of determining the degree to which specific media items contribute to the attainment of desired instructional objectives.

Instruction: The act of planning, directing, and evaluating student learning.

Instructional Technology: A systematic process for designing, implementing, and evaluating learning. Involved are the development and use of specific objectives and the use of a variety of human and technical resources to attain them.

Interactive Media: Media designed specifically to involve the learner(s) in interaction with the media as learning progresses. May involve more than one form of technology, such as a microcomputer and videotape.

Learning: A process of acquiring and developing information, competencies and attitudes that starts before birth and continues throughout life.

Media (Educational or Instructional): Any item of material that may be used in teaching and/or learning and the devices needed to implement its use.

Media Center: A service unit in a school or school system that delivers a wide range of services, materials and equipment to students and teachers designed to enable them to attain desired learning objectives. May be called by various other names such as Learning Resource Center (LRC), Library, or Instructional Materials Center.

Multiple Intelligences: The concept that human intelligence is not a single capacity but a number of identifiable capabilities that are dynamic and can be learned and taught. The intelligences most commonly identified are (1) Verbal/Linguistic, (2) Logical/Mathematical, (3) Visual/Spatial, (4) Body/Kinesthetic, (5) Musical/Rhythmic, (6) Interpersonal, and (7) Intrapersonal.

Presentation Media: Media designed specifically to present information passively to an individual or to a group of learners, such as a film, videotape, or filmstrip.

Selection of Media: The process of investigating sources and availability of materials relating to desired instructional objectives, obtaining and evaluating available materials, and reaching decisions on the procurement and use of specific media items.

Utilization of Media and Technology: The process of systematically employing media and technology in teaching and learning activities.

Part II

Media Selection and Utilization Techniques

Video Systems and
Instructional Television

Audio Systems

Projection Principles

Overhead Projection

Slide Projection

Filmstrip Projection

Opaque Projection

Introduction

Selecting and using the various types of instructional media properly are critical skills facing today's educators. Each medium has unique features that can make specific contributions to the learning atmosphere. Today's educators must be thoroughly familiar with their possible media choices in order to choose among them intelligently. This section will acquaint you with the unique features of each type of media and demonstrate the techniques for proper equipment usage.

Design and engineering advances have helped to market instructional equipment that can be easily set up and used in a variety of learning and teaching settings. Miniaturization has enabled equipment to become highly portable equipment. Cartridges and cassettes have eliminated many complex threading chores. Automatic volume controls and similar advances have contributed to the ease of operation and improved production qualities of instructional equipment.

Despite these advances, instructors must still acquire special skills in operating instructional equipment. Teachers who can operate equipment effectively, can take advantage of the vast supply of materials available. These materials provide many new learning opportunities for students.

Equipment operation guidelines are included within each chapter. These instructions are intended to assist operators in developing skills and confidence with instructional equipment. Performance testing is an essential part of learning to operate instructional equipment. Checklists and diagrams are located at the conclusion of each chapter. They are designed for a self check, peer check and a final check by the instructor.

To use the Performance Checklists provided in the chapters, follow these steps:

1. Operate the equipment using the materials provided in your laboratory.

2. On subsequent operations of the equipment, continually rely less on the instructional materials until you can operate the equipment without using them.

3. Check yourself at least once on each checklist item as you operate the equipment.

4. Team up with another person who is about your same skill level. Check each other out using the checklist. Carefully correct each other's errors and emphasize strengths.

5. Use the space below the checklist to note any problems you have in operating the equipment or questions you want to ask the instructor.

6. Be prepared to operate the equipment with ease and confidence for your instructor. The instructor will use the checklist to evaluate your proficiency.

Marking Code	Skill Designation	Performance Criteria and Prescription
3	*Highly Proficient*	Operates the equipment with a high degree of proficiency, confidence, and speed. Prescription: No further practice is needed.
2	*Proficient*	Operates the equipment properly and with knowledge that the performance is accurately accomplished. Prescription: Limited practice to improve confidence/speed.
1	*Limited Proficiency*	Operates the equipment properly but is slow and unsure that the performance is accurately accomplished. Prescription: Additional practice to reinforce knowledge, increase speed, and improve confidence.
0	*Not Skilled*	Is not able to operate the equipment. Prescription: Use of programmed instructional manuals throughout the total process of operating the equipment, followed with extensive followed with extensive practice to develop knowledge, speed, and confidence.

Chapter 5

VIDEO SYSTEMS AND INSTRUCTIONAL TELEVISION

PURPOSES

▶ To recognize the value of instructional television and video systems in the classroom.
▶ To identify and describe various types of video technology.
▶ To become familiar with off-air copyright guidelines.
▶ To identify and describe basic video recording techniques.
▶ To acquire skills in operating a basic recording/playback video system.
▶ To acquire skills in operating a video laser disc player.

INTRODUCTION

During the past five decades, instructional television, video systems, and motion picture films have performed a major role in classroom activities. That span of time has seen a gradual evolution from using motion picture films to greater use of video-related technologies, such as satellite television, video cassettes, and laser discs.

Even though educators and media producers today place greater emphasis on video systems, many school districts still own and use extensive collections of motion picture films and projectors. Because some schools continue to use motion picture films, the skills of operating 16mm projectors may still be considered a necessity. Instructions for operating an autoload projector are included in Appendix B of this text for those who wish to learn to operate them. This chapter is devoted to video technologies that are being used as motion media in schools.

USE OF VIDEO PROGRAMS

Video programs stimulate sensory learning modes in a similar fashion to motion picture film and often provide many of the same types of special effects, so their educational uses may be handled in a similar manner. When they show video programs or films, educators should follow these general steps for optimal use:

1. Carefully review and plan the lesson's content, and be sure the program supports the instructional objectives.

2. Prepare students for the presentation by telling them what specific scenes to carefully watch, which ideas and content will be introduced, what important information to remember, and which activities will be used to follow up the program.

3. Plan follow-up activities that summarize the content and help students to meet lesson objectives.

There are numerous sources of professional television programs for classrooms, plus students and teachers are creating their own.

There are now several sources that produce professional-quality television programs for schools, such as Public Broadcast Television (PBS) Satellite Communications Systems and Channel One. In addition, teachers and students are becoming more competent with production of their own video programs and are finding many unique ways to use these video systems inside and outside of classrooms.

Video technology provides unique characteristics for teaching, such as instant production and playback. In addition, it provides some of the strengths of motion picture film, such as showing motion with sound, including footage of a variety of actual outside world events, recreating and dramatizing significant events, providing multiple replays of an event, or providing special visual effects such as animation.

Because of these reasons, teachers are starting to use more video systems:

▶ Many production companies are now producing more educational videotapes and laser discs for classroom use and moving away from film formats.

▶ Many schools can now access video programs via satellite, cable, public broadcasting TV, video rental stores, and numerous other sources that are making enormous collections readily available at relatively low costs.

▶ Teachers can control the delivery of information by videotaping programs off the air and adjusting schedules for playback at a more convenient time. Educators should note, however, the established copyright guidelines for duplicating videotapes and television programs. Videotaping is convenient for copying materials, but copyright laws must be followed for the protection of all concerned.

▶ Many teachers and students now have access to affordable video production equipment in their schools and homes that enables them to more conveniently produce their own video programs.

▶ Television has become a commonly used medium because it provides multisensory experiences through combined pictures and sound; thus, it has become a primary, effective teaching tool.

▶ Many remote or rural schools can now access video programming through some form of distance learning technology such as microwave transmissions, satellite programming, cable access channels, and educational broadcast stations.

TYPES OF VIDEO TECHNOLOGY

Basic Video System

Video cassette recorders (VCRs) are the most commonly used video equipment in today's classrooms. Many are table model VCRs that connect to a TV monitor mounted on a cart. These systems enable teachers to easily record, play, and control a variety of programming sources in numerous locations in the school. Teachers often use these systems to play prerecorded videotapes and

educational programming from cable or satellite connections. Increased availability of these systems at lower cost has enabled teachers and students to record and play programs at their convenience. In addition, some of these recorders and monitors may be connected to a separate portable camera so teachers and students may record class activities to play for instruction, presentations, and evaluation.

Camcorders

Camcorders are more portable than table model VCRs. Because they package the camera and recorder in a single unit, they can be carried around easily by one person and used for production virtually anywhere. Models of camcorders in the VHS-C or 8mm formats are the most portable, because their small size and weight mean easier storage and handling by even the youngest students. These smaller formats also require some special adaptations for playback on standard VHS recorders found in most classrooms.

Camcorders can be connected directly to a television set or monitor for playback. However, they are usually used for production only, with playback managed by a regular table model VCR mounted on a cart with a monitor.

Laser Discs

Laser videodisc technology is one of the newest video technology forms in classrooms today. Increased availability of software and the versatility of this medium has provided another valuable video form for classroom teaching. Its laser-created images are embedded in a plastic disc that can store regular motion video sequences, a combination of motion and still images, or at least 50,000 still images on each side of the disc.

The laser disc is gaining popularity because of its versatility. Unlike videotape, laser discs provide high-resolution images, rapid random access of information, and quality still image projection. The laser disc is not only more durable than a videotape, but the optical system of a laser disc player can hold a still image on the TV screen for several minutes without causing any damage to the player or disc.

Laser discs are available in two basic formats. The constant linear velocity (CLV) discs may provide up to one hour of motion video and stereo sound per side. The constant angular velocity (CAV) laser discs may provide up to 30 minutes of motion video or store several thousand still images on each side. CAV discs can be used to randomly select any single image almost instantaneously by a handheld remote control or a bar code reader. A laser disc player may also be interfaced with a computer to control the access of program information.

For level I interactive video, video discs are played much like classes would view a videotape or slides.

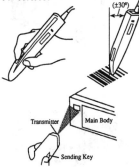

Level II interactive video involves a laser disc player with an internal microprocessor matched to the disc's software.

Students obtain individualized instruction with level III interactive video implementations.

Level IV interactive video involves the emerging multimedia technology being developed by computer vendors such as Microsoft and Apple.

In addition to their versatility and high-resolution images, laser discs provide two tracks of audio for stereo music or two separate audio tracks for bilingual use. Laser disc technology is emerging as a popular medium for interactive video applications in the classroom.

There are at least four different levels of interactive video use available to schools. In level I, the laser disc is played on a television monitor in a similar manner to a videotape. The disc can be used for group or individualized viewing, and the visual material is normally manipulated via a remote control pad, bar code reader, or controls on the player.

Level II interactive video involves the use of programs that have manipulative instructions embedded in the software material. Level II is not as popular in classrooms as level I or level III. Because Level II video discs are not fully compatible with all laser disc players, they must be played on specific machines that are designed for them. This limitation makes them less desirable for flexible activities in schools.

Level III involves interfacing a computer with a laser disc player to provide more sophisticated, learner-controlled lessons. This level combines the power of a computer's interaction and memory capabilities with the versatility of the laser disc player to create more individualized approaches to teaching. Level III equipment is capable of accessing several thousand still images, motion sequences, and multiple sound tracks almost instantly. Level III permits the learner to control the flow of the program and to determine the direction of the lessons, which may include testing, graphics, printed text, and a variety of multisensory experiences.

The emergence of level IV interactive video is not fully complete, but interfacing a variety of technology sources with computers appears to be approaching such a level in the *multimedia* products beginning to be marketed, such as Apple's Newton or a variety of other interfaced graphic, audio, video, and photographic devices. Figure 5.1 shows one configuration of a multimedia system.

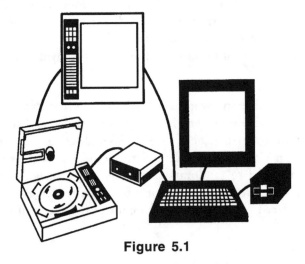

Figure 5.1

A Multimedia System Setup

The use of computer technology interfaced with a variety of video production systems is becoming more popular with schools. The advancement of video digitizing boards and video overlay boards has enabled teachers and students to create video productions that include fairly sophisticated special effects. Almost all computer platforms now have software and special video interface boards that school staff and students can use to produce motion video sequences directly on a computer or to transfer computer graphics onto video. Products like Amiga's Toaster are making school productions more affordable, professional looking, and exciting for students who want to create video presentations.

LCD Panels

Liquid crystal displays with active matrix color screens can now project motion video sequences for improved viewing by large audiences. This form of video projection is gaining popularity for displaying a variety of video and computer-animated programs.

LCD Panels are able to display large screen projections of a computer screen for larger groups to view.

LCD panels have been developed for computer technology and projection of computer displays on a large screen in conjunction with an overhead projector. They are available in gray tone or color models. Newer models of LCD panels can play realtime video images through their active matrix systems to display thousands or millions of colors in full motion. Active matrix LCD panels are preferable to passive matrix panels for showing true motion video images. The active matrix panels are bridging the gap between projecting analog video programs and digital computer images, so they could become popular within the next few years for multimedia presentations.

Video Projectors

Video projector devices have been available in the industrial and entertainment world for some time. However, simplified technology coupled with portability and reduced costs have enabled many schools to begin using video projectors to present video programs on big screens for large groups.

Video Editing Equipment

Many schools are beginning to purchase actual video editing systems to help create better quality productions. These editing systems usually include two recorders with an editing controller. This type of system enables students and educators to produce professional-looking, edited video programs. Editors can remove unwanted portions of a video scene electronically or allow for the insertion of additional video clips in the middle of different video scenes.

Students and faculty are editing their video productions for greater professionalism.

The use of video editing equipment provides for cleaner, smoother scene changes and visual transitions without the glitches created via more amateur forms of editing. Many schools are now preparing video programming for distribution through community cable systems and are using this type of video editing equipment to make their work appear more professional.

Distance learning is another area of video technology growing in popularity with schools. It involves accessing instructional information from a variety of sources such as those described here.

DISTANCE LEARNING VIDEO SYSTEMS

Satellite Systems

Using satellite communications, students and teachers can receive (*downlink*) video images from around the world in a matter of seconds. This medium provides large, widely dispersed audiences with access to a variety of up-to-date instructional programs. Even the most remote areas can usually receive satellite communications via a satellite dish. Many different types of educational programs are being provided for all levels of education by satellite. Many schools are purchasing their own satellite dishes to access these programs for classroom instruction, faculty inservice sessions, and community access.

Participants in the Jason Project can guide an exploration submarine in the ocean via remote control.

One example of a unique and popular distance learning program of the 1990s is the Jason Project. It enables students to explore the wonders of the ocean floor via a live satellite feed. The system connects remote classrooms throughout the country with an exploration ship sailing somewhere on the world's oceans. Each of the remote classrooms is equipped so students can actually guide an underwater exploration submarine by remote control from the classroom while viewing the ocean floor on live video feedback.

Adolescents are kept up-to-date through Channel One news.

Another example of a distance learning program is the Channel One news program that is being adopted by many school districts. It provides up-to-date, daily news programs to inform adolescents about timely events and other contemporary news items. The program has provided free satellite dishes, video equipment, and closed circuit cabling in participating schools so they may distribute programming to individual classrooms.

Higher education institutions, such as Oklahoma State University and Kansas State University, now administer distance learning courses via satellite. Many school districts are beginning to take advantage of these courses to improve or expand their curriculum.

Community Access Television (CATV)

Free access through CATV helps students inform their communities as well as other students about school activities and current events.

CATV is another growing segment of distance learning that is beginning to play an important role in many schools. Community cable companies often provide their local school districts with free access channels. These free channels enable schools to transmit programming from the school to the community or even among schools. Several schools produce their own news programs to inform the community of school activities, and many are playing their sporting and other special events over community access channels.

Public Broadcast Television (PBS)

Public broadcasting stations have been in existence for many years, and they still play an important role in providing educational television programming to many schools throughout the country. Schools that subscribe to PBS educational programming receive teachers' guides and are given permission to record and play back selected programs that are of value to classroom instruction.

PBS remains a widely used video tool in education.

Copying a PBS or any other station's broadcast should not be indiscriminate. Individuals and schools that break copyright laws by making unauthorized recordings or reproductions of programs transmitted over educational television may create a liability problem for the school.

Dramatic changes have occurred with video recording systems in the past several years. Miniaturization and sophistication of electronic systems have greatly improved video equipment by expanding its capabilities and making it lighter to carry and easier to operate. Most basic video recording systems include the items described in this section.

BASIC VIDEO RECORDING SYSTEMS

Camera

The camera converts visual images into electronic signals that are recorded on videotape. Teachers and students should learn about some of the general characteristics of camera controls to get the benefit of their production capabilities. Most video cameras used in school settings are lightweight and portable and have adjustments for the following processes:

Camera users should become highly familiar with the capabilities of the cameras available for their use.

- ▶ *Contrast*—The contrast feature is a lighting control that helps to obtain good image clarity. Many video cameras work extremely well indoors with available light or under low light conditions. This means special lighting is no longer required to create a fairly good image on video. Many newer cameras operate at light levels of three lux or less, which allows them to create good quality picture contrast in low light conditions.
- ▶ *Color Balance*—White balance is provided on many modern video cameras to help them adjust to the color balance of various types of lighting in different settings. This adjustment helps produce a more accurately colored image of what is being videotaped.
- ▶ *Focus Control*—Most of the modern portable cameras and camcorders have autofocus systems for image clarity that can automatically focus the image while the operator is moving the viewfinder from scene to scene. More versatile cameras provide a manual override on the autofocus so the operator can adapt to specific scenes by setting the focus manually. This manual override is desirable for better control in some taping situations.
- ▶ *Image Closeness*—Most cameras have telephoto lenses that zoom in from a distance position to provide a closer view of the subject. These zoom lenses will take close tight shots or can be zoomed back for wide-angle shots to show more of a scene. The degree with which a zoom lens can focus in on a subject is determined by the millimeter of the lens and its zoom ratio. Most cameras have a zoom lens with at least a 6:1 ratio. More

powerful zoom lenses usually have a ratio of 12:1 or 16:1 and can provide exceptionally close-up shots from greater distances.

▶ *Macro Lens*—A macro lens enables the operator to get extremely close to an object with the physical camera lens. The macro capability works like a magnifying glass to enlarge the image of a small object to completely fill the picture on a television screen.

▶ *Titling and Character Generators*—Electronic visual effects or titles can be produced right in the camera and stored in memory to be superimposed over live video images. These in-camera visual effects enable students and teachers to become more creative in producing professional-looking video programs without the major expense of editing equipment. Still, some schools are beginning to purchase complete editing systems for creating more professional-looking programs than are possible with titles created within a camera.

▶ *Clock*—Cameras usually provide a superimposed electronic image of a date and time clock that can appear on the live video at random by just pushing a button. This feature is often used to make a visual record of the timing of an event.

▶ *Fade Control*—A fade in/fade out control gradually brings an image into view or fades it out of view and is usually used at the beginning or end of a scene or transition point on the videotape.

Microphone

Better sound quality results from using an external microphone.

Microphones that are built into most portable cameras do a fairly good job of picking up sound under controlled conditions. A built-in microphone is convenient for portability and ease of recording, but the quality of its audio recording depends on the physical conditions of the recording site and the distance of the camera from the sound source being recorded. Many cameras allow external microphones to be attached via an audio cable and/or audio mixer. External microphones are sometimes preferable for better sound recording because they may be placed closer to the sound source than can the built-in camera microphone.

One popular type of external microphone for managing certain logistical problems in field recording is the wireless lapel mike that transmits signals to a receiver that can be attached to the camera. This type of microphone usually provides better sound recording of a subject being taped at some distance from the camera and eliminates the need for attached audio cables. The built-in microphone works fairly well for spaces the size of a normal classroom or smaller where the sound is fairly well controlled.

With dubbing, videotapes can be copied for use on machines with different formats.

Video recorders electronically record the visual and auditory information on a magnetic tape that can be immediately played back for review or demonstration. The most common recorder format found in schools is VHS, but some Beta, 8mm, and ¾-inch formats are also used. Video recorders with one- and two-inch tape formats are normally used in professional broadcast studios and are usually too expensive for most school operations. There are also Super VHS, Hi 8mm, and improved Beta formats that produce higher-resolution images than their more common counterparts, but the cost of these units still makes them prohibitive for many schools. These different formats are not interchangeable, but they can be dubbed from one format to another by attaching electronic audio and video cables between the different machines.

Figure 5.2 shows where video recorders normally record three types of electronic signals onto the magnetic coating of a VHS videotape. These three tracks produce the sound, visual image, and electronic control track. Some of the machines can record two separate audio tracks. Most newer machines allow audio dubbing, so narrative can be recorded over the original sound track at a later time. This enables other students or teachers to add an oral critique of activities on the videotape.

With audio dubbing, a narrative can be added to a recording's sound track.

In certain types of machines, the complete audio track can be replaced. The videotape does not determine how many audio tracks are recorded. The sync track is important for certain critical types of editing in which the producer wants to replace an unwanted clip with another clip.

A sync track enables the tape's producer to replace video clips, in what is called insert editing.

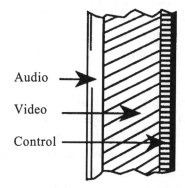

Figure 5.2

Location of the Audio, Video, and Control Tracks on a Videotape

Monitor/Receiver

A TV monitor/receiver is the television set used to view a video or television program. Television receivers are sets that enable the viewer to receive broadcast television through the airwaves via an antenna. Monitors are video tubes that allow the viewer to connect a camera, videotape player, or a CATV system for receiving closed circuit programming, but they have no channel tuner and cannot receive video transmissions broadcast over the airwaves. A monitor/receiver is capable of receiving both types of signals—closed circuit and airwave. Monitor/receivers are becoming more popular due to their versatility and ability to connect to a variety of new technology systems such as compact disc interactive (CDI), laser disc players, S-VHS video systems, and video cameras while they can also receive regular broadcast television programming.

BASIC VIDEO PRODUCTION TECHNIQUES

Due to greater presence of video recording equipment in homes and schools, an increasing number of students and teachers are producing instructional and informational video programs. A few basic techniques in operating video equipment for video production can prove to be valuable assets for the modern classroom teacher.

One key tip for producing instructional videos is to envision the material from the viewpoint of the learner when the photographer looks through the camera. This point-of-view will help the viewer see the activity as he or she would while performing it.

Camera Handling

Slower scanning and use of a tripod can prevent blurry, jerky images on videotape.

Handling and moving the video camera slowly, steadily, and smoothly is one skill many amateurs quickly discover to be essential for producing quality video programs. The typical beginner moves the camera too quickly when scanning a scene and create a blurry or jerky image with those abrupt movements. Slow, careful movements are desired in most productions, and the operator should take care to be braced for steady camera handling. The use of a camera tripod helps the photographer create steady shots. If a tripod is unavailable, the camera operator should try to brace against a solid object or surface to steady the camera.

Certain camera movements, as shown in Figure 5.3, are often necessary to acquire a better vantage point of a scene. *Panning* is the term for moving a camera from right to left or visa versa. *Tilting* the front of the camera up or down can also affect the view point of the observer. These two basic camera movements along with a few other adjustments for height or closeness to the subject can be helpful in creating a more effective instructional video.

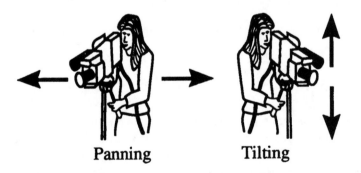

Panning   Tilting

Figure 5.3

Camera Movements for Panning and Tilting

Lens adjustments will vary according to the sophistication of the camera lens. More powerful zoom lenses such as one with a 12:1 zoom ratio can make distant objects seem much closer. This can be quite helpful for taping athletic events, nature scenes, or even dangerous scenes where distance is necessary. As is the case in regular camera movement, zooming should be done in a smooth and steady manner unless a fast zoom is required to catch a quick scene or for special effects. Zooming in close on a subject can provide better close-up details, and zooming back on a scene can provide for a panoramic view to provide an overall perspective of a setting.

Zooming movements should also be smooth and steady.

The macro lens permits the camera to be extremely close to small objects and create a magnified image on the video recording or TV monitor. This technique can be used to enlarge small objects for a whole class to see simultaneously when it would be difficult for several students to gather around the actual object.

Composition and Framing

Image composition through a variety of camera shots is also valuable to the operator. As shown in Figure 5.4, the basic shots are long, medium, and close-up. Long shots tend to provide lots of visual information, and unless they are used for a wide-angle shot of a scene such as a landscape, large group, or athletic event, they are not commonly used. This type of shot is usually achieved when the photographer is positioned fairly far from the subject and zooms the lens all the way back for a wide-angle shot. For a human figure, a wide-angle shot includes the entire body of the person in the scene. A medium shot with people in the scene is usually considered a waist-up shot, such as those often seen on television interviews. A close-up shot of a person includes primarily the head and shoulders in the scene; these shots are usually used for the anchor of an evening news program. Extreme close-up shots are usually used to convey the feelings of the subject to express anger, sorrow, fear or other emotions.

Photographers add to visual interest of their composition by mixing long, medium, and close-up shots.

Long Shot   Medium Shot   Close-up

Figure 5.4

Composition of the Wide-Angle, Medium, and Close-Up Shots

For proper framing, position a human subject's eyes one-third of the way from the top of the frame and slightly off center.

Framing an image refers to how the images are placed in a scene. A general guideline is to allow a small amount of subject headroom at the top edge of the frame. Too much headroom is almost always visually displeasing. Try to place a human subject's eyes approximately one-third of the way from the top of the scene. Have the subject slightly off center of the scene and always have him or her facing into the scene, as shown in Figure 5.5, especially if the subject is facing sideways. If you are not sure how far or which direction a subject may suddenly move, keep the lens zoomed back sufficiently to make adjustments for sudden movements of the subject so you don't lose the view.

Figure 5.5

Framing a Subject and Facing Him into the Scene

Transition Techniques

Scene transitions may be made through the camera by using a variety of techniques:

- ▶ Fade controls on many cameras allow the image to be electronically faded from or to a blank screen. Fading in or out is a common technique in professional productions; it keeps the scenes from changing too abruptly.
- ▶ Manually taking the scene in and out of focus is another simple technique for changing scenes.
- ▶ A good straight cut from one scene to another is accomplished simply by stopping the camera briefly and changing the perspective of the scene and restarting the camera. This technique creates a quick, clean transition to a different perspective of the same subject being viewed. The photographer should not just stop and restart the recording without any significant change in angle or visual conditions, or the scene will look like there is a mistake in the recording.

VIDEOTAPE CHARACTERISTICS

Some general characteristics of videotapes and equipment may affect their ability to record or be played back. As was mentioned earlier in the chapter, videotapes and equipment come in various sizes and formats. The size and format of the tape normally determine the type of VCR that can be used, but the recording speed can also make a difference. For example, VHS tapes are most commonly used in schools, but the following variations in VHS tapes can make a difference in their use.

Standard lengths of videotapes used in schools are 30, 60, and 120 minutes for recording and playback, but other lengths may be acquired for special circumstances. Tape length doesn't control recording and playing time entirely. Some VCRs will record and play at different speeds:

▶ Standard play (SP) is the same as the time identified on the tape.
▶ Long play (LP) doubles the length of recording time identified on the tape.
▶ Super long play (SLP) triples the length of recording time identified on the tape.

Consumer line VCRs normally record and play at all of these speeds, but industrial models sometimes play only at the SP speed. A tape recorded at the SLP speed on a consumer line VCR will not play on an industrial player that plays only at the SP speed.

In just the VHS format there are regular VHS, VHS-C, and S-VHS tapes and recorders. Each of these VHS formats may require special adaptations to play on another VHS player. Some regular VHS recorders will not play S-VHS tapes, and VHS-C tapes need an adapter to play on a regular VHS recorder. Similar issues of standardization also occur with other videotape formats.

CARE AND STORAGE OF VIDEOTAPES

Videotapes should not be stored in locations where there is high humidity and/or temperature. They should never be left in a closed car on a hot summer day or near a window that receives direct sunlight.

Keep tapes away from electromagnetic fields such as the front of a color TV screen, an electric motor, or microwave oven in operation. Make sure they are not near any type of magnet such as those found in stereo speakers. Keep them away from bulk tape erasers that are in use.

Do not open the cassette tape cover and disturb the tape or touch it with your bare hands.

Do not leave tapes in dusty areas where fine dust can seep into the cassette.

Avoid switching numerous controls on a recorder too rapidly, which may cause slack in the tape that will catch on the VCR spindles and break or badly wrinkle.

Avoid leaving a tape in the pause mode or still frame mode too long, because the player heads may cause tenting in the videotape. The VCR heads may also become encrusted with oxide from the tape and produce or play back a snowy picture or no picture at all.

Prevent accidental erasure of a videotape as it plays in a VCR by breaking the write-protect tab out of the back of the cassette, as shown in Figure 5.6. The missing tab will prevent users from accidentally placing the VCR in the record mode, thereby destroying the existing video program. If rerecording is desired at a later time, a piece of adhesive tape may be placed over the tab hole.

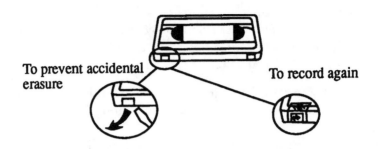

Figure 5.6

The Write-Protect Tab of a Video Cassette

COPYRIGHT GUIDELINES

Teachers now have opportunities to access vast collections of video programs through many sources. This easy access has the potential to exacerbate copyright infringement. Some teachers are tempted to duplicate copies of tapes or to record programs that are being played over one of the many distribution systems. These temptations can sometimes lead to abuse of the copyright laws. Following are guidelines for upholding video copyright laws:

▶ Off-air recordings can only be made at the request of an instructor for instructional purposes in the classroom. Programs may not be altered in any way.

▶ Some programs may be recorded off-air and then retained for a certain number of days, depending on the source and rights of the particular pieces of work. For example, if a program can be retained for 45 days, it must be shown during the first 10 days of the 45-day period. After the first showing, the program may be used only for reinforcement purposes.

▶ If a video cassette bears the label "For Home Use Only," it can only be used in the classroom as part of a teaching activity. Rented or purchased tapes must only be used for planned instructional activities. If a teacher decides to provide a "fun" day for students and show a rented video prior to a holiday, it could break the copyright laws.

COMMON VIDEO CABLE CONNECTIONS

Following are descriptions of common types of video cable connectors.

F Connector — This connector attaches to the antenna or VHF inputs and outputs of video equipment. The TV set should usually be set to channel 3 or 4 when the equipment is playing through this cable. It is sometimes called an RF connector.

RCA/Phono   The RCA/Phono plug normally connects to the audio and video in/out connectors. The TV should usually be set as a monitor when these cables are used for playback.

BNC Plug   The BNC is sometimes used instead of an RCA plug or an RF connector.

Mini Phone/Sony   This plug is often used for audio connectors or remote control cables.

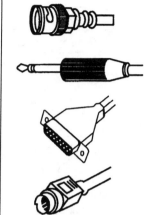

DB Connector   The DB connector is used to interface computers to laser disc players or to special RGB monitors. It is sometimes referred to as the RGB plug.

8 Pin Mini
DIN Plug   Sometimes referred to as a serial connector. It is used to connect to output ports for serial devices on a computer.

SUGGESTED ACTIVITIES

1. Use any available laboratory modules covering the operation of video recording equipment to guide you through learning to operating a camcorder. If these materials are unavailable, refer to appropriate operation manuals often furnished with the equipment.

2. Use the Performance Checklist at the conclusion of this unit to further guide you in the use of video recording equipment. After you complete a self check, demonstrate your skill to another person using the peer check on the Performance Checklist.

3. Watch public and broadcast television programs to observe some of the following production techniques: composition, scene transitions, camera movement, and shot selection.

4. Find out how schools and universities in your community are using distance education delivery systems for instructional activities.

5. Using the Performance Checklist at the conclusion of this unit to practice operations of a laser disc player, demonstrate your skill using a peer check on the Performance Checklist.

6. Locate a CAV and a CLV laser disc and play each of them on a laser disc player using the player, remote control pad, and bar code reader.

VIDEO CASSETTE RECORDER
Performance Checklist

Step	Description of Performance	Self Check	Peer Check	Instructor Check
	VIDEO PLAYBACK			
1.	Plug in power cords and turn on TV and VCR.			
2.	Check connect cable from "Video Out" of VCR to "Video In" on TV.			
3.	Set TV on Channel 3 or 4 according to VCR. If playback is to TV/Monitor, set switch on monitor to VCR.			
4.	Insert cassette into VCR.			
5.	Set VCR to play position.			
6.	Adjust TV for best viewing image (color, contrast, sound, etc.)			
7.	Use rewind, fast forward, slow motion, and still frame functions as necessary during playback.			
8.	Stop and rewind tape.			
	OFF-AIR RECORDINGS			
9.	Connect Cable from TV to recorder. It must be from an output on the TV to an input on the VCR.			
10.	If necessary, set VCR/TV switch on TV to TV.			
11.	Set input selector switch on VCR to TV.			
12.	Set and tune TV to proper channel.			
13.	Reset counter to 0000.			
14.	Set delayed timer on VCR if desired.			
15.	Begin recording by pressing the record button on the VCR.			
16.	Stop recording by pressing the stop button.			
17.	Press the rewind button and stop the tape at 000.			
18.	Press play and use slow motion, fast forward, and still frame functions as necessary.			
	RECORDING FROM CAMERA			
19.	Set up and attach camera to tripod (if appropriate).			
20.	Plug camera cable into recorder.			
21.	Set recorder input switch to "camera".			
22.	Turn on camera and make adjustments for focus, lighting, and/or color.			
23.	Load tape into recorder and set index counter to 000.			
24.	Set up the VCR to the record position.			
25.	Record a production.			
26.	Rewind the tape and play it back.			

Code for marking:
3 Highly proficient   **2** Proficient   **1** Limited proficiency   **0** Not proficient

Problem	Suggested Action	
No Power	Check all power cords, switches, and the timer switch.	**TROUBLE-SHOOTING TIPS FOR BASIC VIDEO SYSTEM**
No Image or Sound	Set the TV channel to channel 3 or 4 to match the VCR setting if the RF cable is being used. Set the TV to monitor if the separate audio and video cables are being used.	
	Make sure the VCR/TV switch on the recorder is set to VCR.	
	Make sure the tape is rewound to the beginning of the program and ready to play.	
Does Not Record	Check all cable connections among the camera, VCR, and TV on portable equipment.	
	Check the Camera/VCR switch on a camcorder.	
	Make sure the tab on the video cassette is intact.	
Cassette Tape Will Not Eject	Make sure the VCR or camcorder power is turned on.	
Cassette Ejects in Play or Record Mode	Make sure the tape was recorded at a speed that the VCR will play.	
	Check the record tab on the back of the cassette tape to make sure it hasn't been removed. If so, place a piece of adhesive tape over the hole.	
	Make sure the tape is the proper type for the recorder.	
Snowy picture (noise)	Adjust the tracking control.	
	Make sure the video heads are clean.	
	Make sure the videotape is not damaged or too old.	

**TROUBLE-
SHOOTING
TIPS FOR
LASER DISC**

No Power	Make sure power cords are plugged in for both the TV and laser disc player.
	Make sure the power is turned on for both the TV and laser disc player.
Laser Disc Won't Play	Be sure the laser disc was inserted in the machine.
	Be sure the disc is placed on the correct side. (It will usually give a visual cue on the monitor if it needs to be turned over.)
	Check whether a computer interface cable is connected to the disc player. On some models, this may disengage the manual controls.
	Be sure the batteries in the remote control or bar code reader are good.
No Picture or Sound	Be sure the VHF or audio cables are connected correctly between the disc player and the TV. If the VHF in/out connections are used, be sure the TV is set to channel 3 or 4. If the audio in/out cables are used, be sure the TV is set to monitor.
No Sound	Be sure the audio setting on the disc player is set to play sound. It may be set to play left speaker, right speaker, or stereo, or to turn speaker off.
	Be sure the volume control on the TV is turned up.
Two Sound Tracks Playing	Check the audio control on the laser disc player. See whether the control is set for stereo play. This would play both audio tracks on the laser disc. If the laser disc has two different audio tracks, it will play both sound tracks together. Set the audio on the laser disc to the left speaker or right speaker for desired sound track.
Laser Won't Play by Computer	Be sure the special interface cable is connected between the computer and laser disc player.
	Be sure the cable is the correct type. Different computer platforms require different wiring configurations of pin connections, even though they may use the same type of cable and plug.
	Be sure the computer software has been configured to control the type and model of laser disc player you are using. The laser disc player must be initialized by the software to start playing.
	Be sure the computer software is configured to control the laser disc player from the correct output port on the computer.

VIDEO LASER DISC
Performance Checklist

Step	Description of Performance	Self Check	Peer Check	Instructor Check
	LASER DISC PLAYING			
1.	Plug in the power cords and turn on the TV and Laser Disc Player.			
2.	Attach the connector cable from the disc player to the TV.			
3.	If using an RF cable, set TV to channel 3 or 4. If using AV cables, set TV to monitor.			
4.	Insert a CLV laser disc.			
5.	Use both the operational controls on the player and the remote control if available.			
6.	Operate the machine to do fast forward, reverse, still frame, and any other operations available on the controls.			
7.	Stop the player, remove the CLV disc, and replace it with a CAV disc, and repeat step 6.			
	BAR CODE READER			
8.	Insert a laser disc that has accompanying bar code information.			
9.	Use the bar code reader to read a bar code and search for a portion of a laser disc.			
10.	Stop the player and remove the disc.			
11.	Turn off the player and television.			
12.	Disconnect the cables and unplug the machines.			

Code for marking:
3 Highly proficient **2** Proficient **1** Limited proficiency **0** Not proficient

Chapter 6

AUDIO SYSTEMS

PURPOSES

▶ To describe the instructional value of audio recording systems in the classroom.
▶ To identify the differences between audio recording formats such as digital and analog.
▶ To identify newer technologies and their effects on audio recording systems.
▶ To be able to perform simple maintenance on audio tapes and recorders.
▶ To identify and/or solve common problems that cause poor sound quality in recordings.
▶ To be able to properly set up and operate audio recording equipment.

INTRODUCTION

Audio recordings can serve as critical teaching and reinforcement tools when teachers plan audible activities. Speech, drama, language, and music classes can use audio recordings extensively for evaluation or preservation of performances. A creative and imaginative teacher will discover many ways to produce and use audio recordings.

Students can make effective use of audio recordings for research and for giving reports. The simplicity of making audio recordings affords students an inexpensive means of producing recorded interviews within their community. Recordings of natural sounds captured from various locations can be used to enhance presentations. Many schools also have equipment that teachers and students use to synchronize audio recordings with slides for a presentation or promotional project.

Audio cassettes remain popular in educational settings, although newer audio media are emerging.

One of the benefits offered by audio technology is its wide range of available materials. Cassette tapes are still the most common format of audio used in schools, but many new audio formats are gaining recognition. Cassettes are popular because the equipment is readily available and the cost of tapes is relatively inexpensive. In addition, several companies still use cassette tapes to accompany commercially produced filmstrips and slide programs.

TYPES OF SOUND

Analog and digital sound are the two basic forms that are readily available in today's market. Cassette tapes are analog in nature. The recording is a measurable electromagnetic signal on the surface of a magnetic oxide tape. Fluctuation in quality of this signal depends on the quality of recording equipment and tape being used.

Compact disc and laser technologies minimize audio distortion on digital recordings.

AUDIO RECORDING AND PLAYBACK FORMATS

Digital sound is represented by numerical data and is normally recorded and/or played by a laser beam, such as on a compact disc (CD). The audio track is etched into a reflective aluminum and plastic disc. The use of laser beams eliminates the sound distortions that are commonly found with cassette tapes or records that require physical contact with recording heads or needles. CDs provide an hour or more of high-quality digital sound. Their encoded digital information creates an illusion of continuous sound that many listeners consider to be technically superior to analog types of sound systems.

Current audio recording and playback systems vary from small handheld microcassette recorders to sophisticated multicomponent analog systems and from small portable types of CD players to multicomponent, interfaced, computer-controlled, digital sound systems. Individuals use many of these audio technologies at home, so they are naturally extended into classrooms for educational uses. Interest is increasing in the digital recording and playback systems, but many schools still rely on older audio formats such as cassette tape recorders.

The focus of this chapter is primarily simple audio systems that are commonly used in today's classrooms, but a brief introduction to some of the evolving audio technologies is included to increase awareness of the emerging sound system technologies. Whatever the form of audio system, a number of benefits can be derived for educational applications. This section describes some of the current audio forms used in schools and the consumer market.

Compact Discs

The CD is a popular technology for playing high-quality digital music. CDs are quickly replacing cassette tapes in the consumer market for prerecorded music. The CD is recognized for its sound quality and its random access capabilities (it can quickly skip among recorded tracks to play tracks in whatever order the listener prefers). The 4¾-inch discs can hold an hour or more of recording. Laser beams are used to play the recording, so there is no friction on the system to cause wear as was a major problem for phonograph records. The current obstacle preventing CDs from playing a more important role in schools today is that they are "nonwritable": Teachers and students cannot produce them at an affordable price.

Music Instrument Digital Interface

One of the audio technologies gaining popularity in schools is the music instrument digital interface (MIDI). MIDI provides the ability to interface a microcomputer with a variety of electronic musical devices such as an electronic keyboard or a microphone.

The computer, along with a variety of available software editing programs, is a versatile tool for composing music or creating numerous types of sounds. The computer can receive analog signals from an electronic sound source via the MIDI device, which converts the sounds to digital signals. This digital information can then be altered into almost any imaginable form to be played back through speakers or a variety of sound devices. Teachers and students may use the MIDI system to compose their own music or may create sound tracks for other types of productions, such as video.

The introduction of the MIDI along with advancements in computer software for producing music have revolutionized many professional musicians' and music teachers' abilities for composing and/or altering audio recordings. Teachers and students are beginning to recognize the power of these interfaced devices and the versatility they provide for recording and creating musical compositions.

Sound Boards

In addition to the MIDI there are other types of interface devices for computers. Sound boards, such as the Audio Media board for the Macintosh computer, are available to purchase for nearly any computer platform. Users insert the circuit boards into computers to provide audio inputs and outputs that interface with almost any type of analog sound system. They allow up to four different audio tracks to be recorded or played back simultaneously—in addition to voice recordings via a microphone. The boards convert the analog signals to digital signals and vice versa.

Many of the software packages for recording with these devices are extremely sophisticated and allow a wide range of opportunities for altering, composing, and integrating many different sounds into new forms.

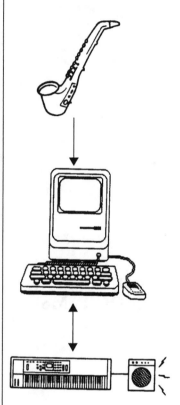

MiniDiscs

Another audio product that may impact schools in the future is Sony's MiniDisc (MD), an optical digital recording system. It records up to 74 minutes of stereo sound on a small, 2½-inch compact disc. The MiniDisc is one of the first digital optical systems available to the public in an approachable price range that allows the user to both record and play back digital sound. The disc resembles a 3.5-inch microcomputer floppy disk that is encased in plastic with a sliding shutter to protect it from dust, fingerprints, and scratches. The actual recording surface is more like a CD laser disc than the magnetic surface of a floppy disk. The small format is quite shock resistant.

The future of this form of audio technology in education remains to be determined. Current markets are aimed at the higher-priced consumer line of sales instead of schools, which have limited budgets. As is the case with many other forms of technology, once its prices begin to decrease and its versatility is fully recognized, many teachers and students may use the MD format.

Cassette Tapes

Even though advanced audio technologies provide a dazzling variety of audio formats—CDs, computer diskettes, and MDs among them—many schools continue to use cassette tapes or phonographic records that have been available for decades. Cassette tapes are still recognized as an important audio technology.

Cassette tapes are available in a variety of lengths. Cassette tape lengths are designated by the number of total minutes of recording time available. As the arrow to the tape length here shows, the number on the surface of the cassette label preceded by the letter C indicates the total recording/playback time available on the combined sides of the cassette when it is used at normal speed. Because some cassette recorders play at different speeds, the playing time can vary. Each side of the tape provides half of the time indicated by the number. Cassettes are available in lengths from a few minutes to two or more hours, and some are even available in continuous loop versions.

Cassette tapes are made from a variety of materials that meet different standards for durability and fidelity. The quality of the material affects the tapes' cost. Some tapes have special oxide coatings such as carbon dioxide, which helps eliminate background hiss ("noise"), but care must be used in playing these special tapes on recorders that are not designed to accept them. Extended play of special metal tapes may damage the recording and playback heads of a standard machine that was not designed to play them.

PRODUCING SOUND SYNC PROGRAMS

Sound-slide programs are popular projects for students and teachers to produce. Special audio cassette recorders can record sync pulses and combine them with narration on a cassette tape. The sync recorder can be attached to a carousel slide projector to play an automated program. Because most teachers and students have their own cameras for making slides and cassette tape recorders for producing regular sound recordings, production of these multimedia programs can be quite simple when a special sync recorder is used.

Sync types of audio cassette recorders are equipped to automatically advance slide projectors that have remote control capabilities. Some sync recorders even have stop/restart features that enable the program developer to include pauses in the audio recording and program. A special patch cord is attached from the recorder to the projector to cue the projector when to advance. An electronic pulse on the tape signals the slide projector to advance or tells the recorder to pause. Sound recording tracks on a synchronized cassette program record the audio message on the top, or Track 1, of the tape. The sync pulse is recorded on Track 2. By having these two separate sound tracks, students or teachers can edit either one without disturbing the other.

Production of sync recorded programs is not much different than making a regular recording on a cassette tape. The major difference is placing the sync part of the recorder into a record mode to create the automated pulses rather than placing the regular tape recorder in record. The basic process is as follows:

1. Connect the recorder and projector with the special patch cord.

2. Switch the sync button to the record mode.

3. As you listen to the regular narration on the tape, add pulses to the sound track without altering the original recording. Remember, pulses are placed on a separate track of the tape on the other half of the tape, so be sure to use a clean tape with nothing recorded on the other side.

   If you misplace a pulse, simply rerecord over that section of the tape. Be careful to use the sync pulse record switch and don't accidentally use the regular tape record switch, or you will erase the regular recording on the narrative side.

4. To play back the tape and slides, cue up the slide projector with the beginning slide and rewind the tape to the beginning. Be sure to set the sync selector to the PLAY mode on the audio recorder.

5. View the sound slide program, checking to ensure that the pulses are advancing the slides at the right moment. If a sync pulse is missing or is not in the proper location, simply rerecord pulses over that section of the tape.

AUDIO MEDIA MAINTENANCE AND CARE

It is good practice to keep all types of audio materials away from extreme heat, moisture, dust, abrasion, and warping due to uneven pressure. Any of these extreme physical conditions can damage audio media and render them unusable.

Compact discs normally require very little care with the exception of keeping them clean. They come with durable plastic storage cases, where they should be stored whenever they aren't in use. They should not be scratched by any sharp objects or by stacking several together in a pile so their surfaces may rub together. They should be handled by their edges so fingerprints and other foreign matter won't be left on the playing surface. Due to their relatively thin plastic coating, they should be carefully cleaned according to manufacturers' suggestions.

Handle CDs by their edges, store them in their cases, and clean the playing surface regularly.

Audio cassette tapes—as well as videotapes and computer floppy disks—are composed of plastic material coated with a magnetic oxide. The magnetic oxide is sensitive to any form of electromagnetic force field and is what stores the recorded information. It should be protected from all electronic, electromagnetic, or magnetic items or risk being partially or completely erased. Placing a tape on top of a large stereo speaker could jeopardize its safety, because stereo speakers often have quite large magnets in them.

Protect all magnetic media from erasure by keeping them away from electrical or electromagnetic fields.

To prevent accidental erasure, users should enable the write-protect tabs located on the back of each tape or computer diskette. The tab corresponding to the side of the audio or videotape to be protected can be punched out to prevent rerecording on the tape. Otherwise, an accidental erasure of existing material could occur by putting the machine in the record mode. If users decide to replace an existing recording and reuse the cassette, a piece of adhesive tape may be placed over the tab opening to permit overwriting the existing recording.

EQUIPMENT CARE AND CLEANING

Regular maintenance of video or audio cassette players includes cleaning the recording and erase heads and damp-wiping the outside of the case.

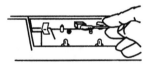

CD players require only removal of dust or lint with canned air.

CONNECTING CABLES

Be sure to match the monaural and stereo inputs and outputs properly during equipment setup.

Audio recording equipment must be kept clean to ensure proper reproduction of sound. Periodic cleaning of recording and playing heads contributes significantly to the quality of sound.

Commercial cleaning kits available for cassette tape players contain cleaning cassettes that can be inserted into the player and run through automatically. Some people prefer to use a manual form of cleaning with Q-tips and alcohol. A special head cleaning fluid can also be obtained from music or electronic stores.

A good procedure for cleaning is to apply a drop of fluid on one end of a Q-tip, rub the recording and erase heads briskly, and then use the other end of the Q-tip to remove any further residue or excess cleaning fluid. Heads can always be located by finding the shinny metal areas where the tape passes through the recorder. In some instances, users must remove the machine cover to clean the heads. In many machines the heads are openly accessible for cleaning. The case and all accessible parts of the recorder should be kept free of dust and lint at all times.

Because CD players use laser beams rather than a phonograph needle or tape head that physically touches the playing surface, they pick up no residue from the discs. They do, however, collect dust and lint that may affect the sound quality. This dust and lint may be cleaned off by air. There are some commercially sold air disk cleaners that can be played in a CD player to create blowing air and clear out the lint and dust.

Figure 6.1 shows common plug types used in connecting audio systems. The most common types of plugs are phone, mini phone, and phono. Some plug types are often referred to by more than one name. For example, ¼-inch standard phone plugs may use any combination of the descriptive words for identification. Mini phone plugs may also be identified by the diameter of the pin size, such as $\frac{1}{8}$-inch, $\frac{1}{16}$-inch, or $\frac{1}{32}$-inch mini phone plug. They may also be identified as a Sony plug. Phono plugs are sometimes referred to as RCA plugs.

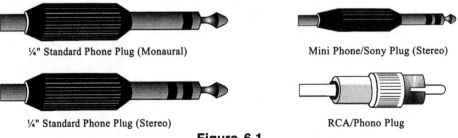

¼" Standard Phone Plug (Monaural)

Mini Phone/Sony Plug (Stereo)

¼" Standard Phone Plug (Stereo)

RCA/Phono Plug

Figure 6.1

Common Types of Audio Cables

Some of the mini phone and standard phone plugs have another special feature that is important to know to connect pieces of equipment properly. There may be one or two insulators (small little rings or washers) on the phone plugs. If there is one insulator, the plug is monaural or capable of transmitting a single audio signal. Stereo plugs include two insulators and are capable of transmitting two separate audio signals. Sometimes teachers and students mismatch the monaural and stereo inputs and outputs of audio equipment, which creates problems with the sound.

The standard ¼-inch phone and mini phone plugs are commonly found on microphones and headsets. The RCA phono plug is frequently used for speaker connections or input cables that attach one sound source to another, such as a tape deck, phonograph, or output on an amplifier. These common types of plugs are used on cables called patch cords that transfer sound between different pieces of audio equipment. If the plug on the mike, speaker, or patch cord will not fit into the input or output jack of an audio device, adapters similar to the one shown in Figure 6.2 are available that can convert the plug to the appropriate type or size.

Figure 6.2

Audio Plug Adapter (Left)

Problem	Suggested Action
Mushy Sound	Dirty playback heads on a tape recorder will cause audio tapes to sound mushy and indistinct. Alcohol applied to the heads will clean off deposits of metallic oxide that are causing the distortion.
Low Volume	Low volume results when the tape is not in full contact with the playback head. One of the following procedures should correct the situation:

1. Check the threading.

2. Check to be sure the wrong side of the tape is not in contact with the playback head.

3. Clean the heads of the tape recorder with head cleaner.

4. Make sure you aren't playing a monaural tape on a stereo tape player.

TROUBLE-SHOOTING TIPS FOR AUDIO TAPE RECORDERS

Voice or Music Too High Pitched	When a tape is played back at a faster speed than was originally used in recording, the recorded voice will be too high pitched (chipmunks effect) and can be corrected by lowering the speed on the recorder.
Tape Plays Too Slowly	If a portable recorder is being used with batteries, the batteries may be too weak. If an extended length tape is being used, it may drag in the cassette.
Background Hiss	After extensive use in the recording mode, a hissing sound can result from heads becoming magnetized. It is sort of like a buildup of static electricity. It is probably better to have a qualified technician correct this problem. The process is called *demagnetizing* or *degaussing*.
Two Sounds at Same Time	Make sure a stereo tape isn't being played on a monaural tape player.
Snarled Tape	Longer-length cassettes (such as a C-120) sometimes tend to get some slack and come out of the cassette, becoming snarled around the capstan on the recorder. Using shorter-length tapes (C-30, C-60) that are thicker will usually eliminate this problem.
Record Button Doesn't Stay Down	The write-protect tab on the back of a cassette may have been broken out, which prevents erasure of a particular tape. To rerecord on the tape once the tab has been removed, cover the tab opening with adhesive tape; the record button should function properly.

SUGGESTED ACTIVITIES

1. Locate a compact disc and play it on a disc player.

2. Use laboratory modules covering the operation of cassette tape recorders to guide you through your initial experiences with the equipment. If such materials are unavailable, locate and use the Operator's Manuals furnished by the equipment manufacturers.

3. Use the Performance Checklist in this unit to further guide you in the use of cassette audio recorders.

4. Look at the labeled parts of the generalized version of a portable cassette recorder in Figure 6.3 and learn to identify the importance of each part.

5. Have another person, preferably a peer who is also learning to use the recorders, check your equipment operations using the Performance Checklists.

6. Combine a sync pulse cassette tape recorder with a carousel slide projector and practice producing an automated tape that will advance the slides in the projector.

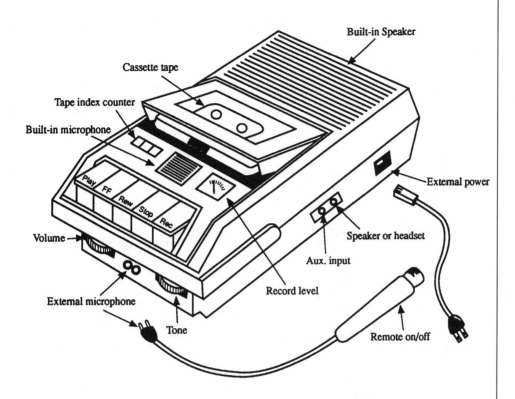

Figure 6.3

A Typical Audio Cassette Recorder

AUDIO CASSETTE RECORDER

Performance Checklist

Step	Description of Performance	Self Check	Peer Check	Instructor Check
	SET UP RECORDER			
1.	Open case and remove accessories.			
2.	Plug cord into power outlet.			
	MAKE A CONVERSATIONAL RECORDING			
3.	Load cassette into recorder.			
4.	Plug microphone into recorder.			
5.	Preset volume for recording.			
6.	Set tape index counter.			
7.	Switch into record mode.			
8.	Make conversational recording from mike.			
9.	Stop recorder at end of recording.			
	LISTEN TO THE RECORDING			
10.	Plug in listening headset.			
11.	Rewind to start point on cassette.			
12.	Switch into play mode.			
13.	Adjust volume and tone.			
14.	Stop recorder.			
	USE EQUIPMENT AS PUBLIC ADDRESS SYSTEM			
15.	Switch to PA position.			
16.	Plug in microphone.			
17.	Press play, record, and pause controls.			
18.	Adjust volume.			
	PUT EQUIPMENT AWAY			
19.	Rewind all tape to left side of cassette.			
20.	Remove and store cassette.			
21.	Remove and store microphone and headset.			
22.	Unplug and store power cord.			
23.	Close case and secure recorder ready for storage.			

Code for marking: **3** Highly proficient **2** Proficient **1** Limited proficiency **0** Not proficient

Chapter 7

PROJECTION PRINCIPLES

PURPOSES

▶ To become familiar with the essential skills necessary for projection of instructional materials.
▶ To identify and describe the components of a projection system.
▶ To develop skills in using projection screens to obtain maximum image legibility, brilliance, and image size for the viewing audience.
▶ To identify modifications to make in basic projection principles when teachers use liquid crystal display (LCD) and video projection devices.

INTRODUCTION

One of the basic skills in using instructional materials is the application of projection principles. Traditionally, projection principles have been applied to a variety of media: slides, filmstrips, 16mm film, and even opaque materials. Advances in technology now enable computer and video materials to be projected. The effective application of basic projection principles enables the instructor to direct the students' attention to visual images that are legible and easily seen.

BASIC PROJECTION SYSTEM

Prior to the operation of projection equipment, the instructor should regularly clean and maintain the equipment for dependable operation. When the projection equipment is to be used, the operator can use the following guidelines:

Following simple maintenance routines will ensure equipment is operational when needed.

▶ Operate the projection equipment properly.
▶ Project a legible and brilliant image on an appropriate viewing surface.
▶ Place the projection device and screen for optimum viewing by the audience.
▶ Control ambient light as necessary.

The basic projection system is composed of three major components, each of which is defined in Table 7.1 and illustrated in Figure 7.1.

Table 7.1 Definitions of Projection System Components

Major Element	Function
Projection Lamp	Provides a source of light for projection.
Lens	Controls the pattern of direct or reflected light through or from the material to the viewing surface.
Screen	Displays the projected image for viewing.

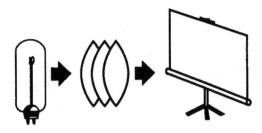

Figure 7.1

Components of a Projection System

Projector Bulbs

The projection lamp is a critical component of the projection system. The bulb usually has a life expectancy of 10 to 200 hours. There are a number of ways to increase the life of a projection bulb:

▶ Use the lower lamp position on a two-position switch (less power is also used).

▶ Replace a burned-out bulb with the type recommended by the manufacturer. Use the three-character code printed on the bulb to identify the correct replacement.

▶ Avoid touching new bulbs. Body oil left as a residue on the surface of the bulb condenses the heat of the lamp during operation and may result in premature bulb failure. To insert a new bulb, handle the lamp with a protective tissue or cloth. Check for proper base alignment of pins or flanges.

▶ Allow the bulb in a projector to cool before moving the device. While hot, the light element within the lamp is fragile. Jarring movement of a projector while the lamp is still hot may cause the element within the bulb to break.

Teachers should observe two safety precautions when replacing projection bulbs. A bulb that burns out during operation will be extremely hot for several minutes; it should cool before anyone attempts to replace it. To avoid electrical shock, the projector's operator should *always* unplug a projector before removing or inserting a bulb.

Projection Lenses

Projection lenses come in a variety of focal lengths. The focal length of the lens is the distance from the lens element to the film surface. This distance affects the image size projected on the screen.

General Rule: The shorter the focal length of a lens, the larger the image the projector will project in a given distance. For example, a lens with a 3-inch focal length will project an image 7 feet wide when the projector is placed 16 feet away from the screen. A lens with a 5-inch focal length, placed at the same distance from the screen, will project an image only 4 feet wide.

On some projection devices, a zoom lens enables the operator to alter the focal length of the lens. A common option for many slide projectors is a zoom lens; the focal length of the lens can be adjusted to a minimum of four inches or to a maximum of six inches by rotating the barrel of the lens. The zoom lens offers the operator the advantage of keeping the projector stationary while maintaining the ability to increase or decrease the size of the projected image.

Projection Screens

The third major component of a projection system is the projection screen. There are two general categories of projection screens: front and rear.

Front screen projection uses an image projected forward from a projector located in or behind the audience. Table 7.2 summarizes the characteristics of front projection screen surfaces.

Table 7.2 Characteristics of Front Projection Screens

Type	Advantage	Disadvantage
Matte White (White, nonglossy surface)	Most accurate image for sharpness and color across a wide area of the room.	Comparatively low light return.
Beaded (Tiny glass beads applied to a surface)	Brightness with high light return, especially in the center of the room.	Surface easily damaged because beads rub off. Narrower viewing angle than matte surface.
Lenticular (Many silver cylinder shapes on surface)	Returns light with brightness and sharpness equal to a beaded screen.	Some light "fall off" on side angles from screen.

Use glass-beaded or lenticular screens in long, narrow rooms for high light return to viewers. The matte white screen is a good general-purpose viewing surface except in rooms that have an extensive amount of ambient light that reflects off walls and ceilings or falls directly on the screen from windows or lighting fixtures.

Rear screen projection uses an image projected on the back surface of a semitranslucent screen placed between the viewer and the projector. Rear screen projection configurations usually require the use of a mirror to direct the image (in its proper orientation) to the screen. Figure 7.2 illustrates the need for such a mirror.

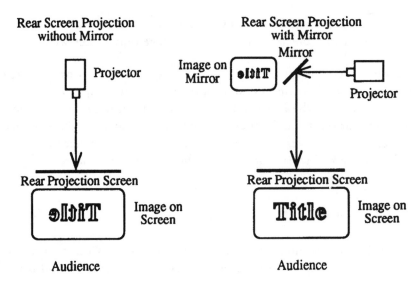

Figure 7.2

Rear Screen Projection with and without a Mirror

Table 7.3 summarizes additional issues concerning the size and proper placement of projection screens. Figure 7.3 illustrates these general rules.

Table 7.3 Application of General Rules for Projection Screens

Question	*General Rule*
How does one select the appropriate size projection screen?	The screen width should be at least ⅙ *the distance* between the projection screen and the viewer seated farthest from the screen. Example: If a student in the back of the classroom is seated 30 feet from the screen, the screen must be at least 5 feet wide; 30 feet divided by 6 equals 5 feet (⅙ the distance between the screen and the farthest viewer).
How close to the screen should one place the closest viewer?	The nearest viewer should be at least *two widths* from the screen to avoid eye fatigue and discomfort. Example: If the screen in the classroom is 5 feet wide, the closest viewer should be at least ten feet away; 5 feet multiplied by 2 equals 10 feet (two widths).
Where should one seat the viewers in relation to the screen?	The viewers should be seated in the optimum viewing area for the particular type of screen. Because screen reflection characteristics differ, the following viewing areas are recommended: *Lenticular and Glass-Beaded Screen*—seat viewers in an area 25 degrees on either side of the line of projection; *Matte White Screen*—seat viewers in an area 30 degrees on either side of the line of projection.

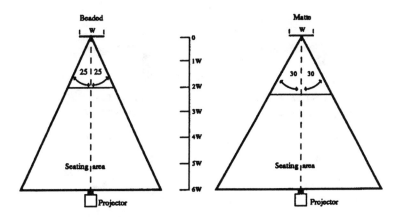

Figure 7.3

Optimal Screen Placement and Viewing Areas
for Matte and Beaded Screens

Once the proper equipment is selected and the instructor has ensured that the equipment works properly, the projection device and the projection screen should be placed for optimal viewing by the audience.

Projector Placement

In general, the projector should be placed at a distance that will fill the projection screen with the projected image. Depending on the focal length of the lens, slide projectors, filmstrip, and motion picture projectors should be placed in the rear of the classroom, whereas opaque and overhead projectors belong in the front of the classroom. A zoom lens may enable the projectionist to place equipment more easily in the classroom.

The Keystone Effect

Keystoning is a common problem in projection, especially when the overhead or opaque projector is used. The keystone effect is created when the projection device and the projection screen are not parallel. Figure 7.4 on the next page indicates the causes of and the solutions for the primary keystoning effects.

EQUIPMENT PLACEMENT

The image projected should just fill the screen and should be placed to avoid blocking students' view.

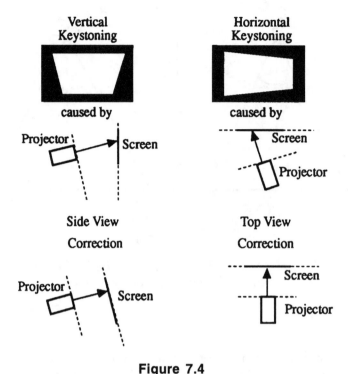

Figure 7.4

Causes of and Corrections for Keystoning

Screen Placement

It is essential to place the screen properly in the room. If a room can be well darkened, it is relatively easy to position the screen to obtain a brilliant and highly visible image. Consider the following recommendations for screen placement within the classroom.

▶ Consider the corner of the classroom, rather than the "front-and-center" screen placement. This is especially desirable when the overhead projector and chalkboard are to be used simultaneously.

▶ Position the screen where the minimum amount of ambient light from windows or room lighting will fall on the screen (that is, directly in front of windows).

▶ Place the bottom of the projection screen at the viewer's eye level. Be certain the projector is above the backs of viewers' heads to eliminate shadows on the screen.

In order to get the best possible image from the equipment, a projectionist must be thoroughly familiar with operating the equipment. Observing the following recommendations will further enhance the quality of projected images:

▶ Allow sufficient time to set up the projection equipment. Be familiar with how the equipment operates. Follow suggested threading diagrams or instructions imprinted on equipment cases. Review the operation manual for specific information.

▶ Make sure the height of the projection cart or table is adequate. It must be placed where there is an unobstructed view of the screen and where there are no shadows cast on the screen.

▶ If a power cord crosses an area where people may walk, secure the cord to the floor with tape to prevent accidents.

▶ If an external speaker is available, place it in front of the classroom or next to the projection screen. Sound will be more realistic when it comes from the same direction as the projected image.

▶ Always carry an extra projector bulb with the equipment. Be certain it is the correct replacement by checking the three-character code. If a bulb burns out during operation, turn the projector off, unplug the projector, and allow the lamp to cool before replacing the bulb.

▶ Always carry an extension cord when the classroom's outlet placement is unfamiliar. Also have a three-prong adapter available, because many older buildings do not have grounded outlets.

▶ Ensure that the room can be darkened for adequate projection. If window coverings are inadequate, place the screen in front of the windows that have the greatest light leakage. With the light coming from behind the screen, less light will reach the screen's surface to reduce image brightness.

EQUIPMENT MAINTENANCE

For maximum image brightness, the projection lens must be cleaned regularly. To clean lenses, use a soft camel hair brush, lens tissue, and special lens cleaning solution. To prevent damage to the lens surface, never clean it with strong or abrasive cleansers.

Cans of compressed air clean equipment nonabrasively.

Film gates and channels should be thoroughly cleaned on a regular basis to eliminate dirt, emulsion chips, and dust, any of which can damage the film surface. Clean these areas with soft brushes and lint-free dust cloths. Compressed air in disposable cans is also helpful for cleaning in tight corners or other hard-to-reach places.

MODIFICATIONS FOR LIQUID CRYSTAL DISPLAYS AND VIDEO PROJECTION

Advances in a variety of technologies have made it possible to project both computer and video images. The basic principles of projection systems generally apply to these new devices; however, it is worthy to note special requirements for such devices.

Liquid Crystal Displays

As mentioned earlier, among the most useful advances in projection technology is the development of LCD devices that can project computer and video images. These devices are now produced in a variety of models and configurations. Some are designed to be placed on top of an overhead projector; some are designed with a self-contained projection lamp; some are limited to data projection, whereas others project both computer data and video images; and some project in black and white, whereas others project in full color.

Active Matrix Versus Passive Matrix

Use passive matrix devices for computer-generated text or nonmoving art.

The primary distinctions among the various devices all concern the structure of the display area. Although it is beyond the scope of this text to explain the technical aspects of these distinctions, it is important for instructors to know that there are two common forms of LCDs: active and passive matrix. The chief characteristic of passive matrix devices is their slow operating speed. Passive matrix devices are generally good for displaying computer-generated text or static images.

Display moving images on an active matrix system.

Movement, detail, and high-quality color images generally require the use of active matrix devices. They can display moving computer images and, in some cases, video images.

Modification of Projection Principles

The use of LCD projection devices requires greater attention to some of the basic principles previously stated in this chapter. It is always important to provide a bright image on the screen; however, when an instructor uses liquid crystal devices, producing a brilliant image becomes more critical and more difficult. The three major modifications for using LCD devices are related to the following areas:

▶ increasing the brilliance of the projected image
▶ increasing control over the lighting within the classroom
▶ altering the placement of the projection unit

The first modification that should be made to the projection system is to increase the brightness of the lamp used in the projection device. Sometimes this is a matter of simply replacing the bulb with a high wattage lamp. However, instructors must verify that the projector was designed to work with that high a wattage.

The typical overhead projector produces approximately 1,000 lumens (a measure of the flow of light). Most manufacturers of LCD devices recommend using a projector that will produce between 3,000 and 6,000 lumens. Therefore, the use of LCD projection devices generally requires the use of a more expensive projector. When LCD devices were first marketed, heat buildup from a projection unit could cause the liquid crystals to malfunction. Although virtually all manufacturers have now installed fans in their LCDs, instructors making recommendations or purchases should attempt to identify the projector that produces the brightest light source with the least heat.

The second modification requires the instructor to gain greater control over the lighting within the classroom. Even after increasing the amount of light passing through the LCD, an instructor may find it necessary to dim the classroom's lights. Some light may be necessary for student note-taking. Because most current classrooms are not equipped with dimmers, it may be necessary to provide a small source of light—such as a desk lamp or partially opened curtain—when all of the lights are turned off. Whatever is used, the source of light should be located behind the screen so that the light provided does not fall on the surface of the screen.

The final modification for using LCD devices has to do with placement of the projection unit. Whether an LCD device is self-contained (contains its own projection unit) or is placed on top of an overhead projector, it should be located so that the projected image fills the screen. Generally, this is not a problem with self-contained units. However, because the display area of an LCD unit that is used in conjunction with an overhead projector is frequently smaller than the display area of the overhead projector itself, it may be necessary to move the overhead projector farther away from the screen. This movement may affect audience seating arrangements and the position that the instructor assumes during the presentation.

The ability to set up and operate projection equipment with confidence and skill is essential to effective instructional communication. Once educators master these skills, a wealth of resources awaits use in classroom instruction.

SUMMARY

1. Identify a number of instructional areas (classrooms, labs, auditoriums, and so on), obtain the dimensions of the areas, and determine optimum screen type, screen size, screen placement, and seating arrangement for each.

SUGGESTED ACTIVITIES

2. By seeing a projector and screen that are misaligned or by viewing the shape of the projected image, indicate how a projection unit should be moved to eliminate keystoning.

3. Viewing a variety of pieces of projection equipment, identify the components of the projection system (lamp, lens, screen).

4. Obtain product information on a wide range of LCD projection devices. Create a chart that summarizes such features as price, type of matrix (active or passive), number of colors displayed, types of input received (data and/or video), manufacturer's recommendations concerning light source, and so on.

Chapter 8

OVERHEAD PROJECTION

PURPOSES

▶ To identify the advantages of using overhead projectors in the classroom.
▶ To describe a variety of presentation techniques for using the overhead projector.
▶ To become skilled in setting up and operating overhead projection equipment.
▶ To perform user maintenance tasks such as cleaning overhead projection equipment.

INTRODUCTION

Overhead projection provides a convenient and effective means of presenting visual materials to a variety of audience sizes. The overhead projector derives its name from the fact that students can view the information "over the head" of the instructor. For proper overhead usage, the total facility—room, seating, screen, and projector—must be properly placed and arranged.

Equipment Placement

The overhead projector is one of a relatively few projection devices designed to be used from the front of the classroom. This position has both advantages and disadvantages. From the front of the classroom, an instructor can maintain eye contact with students—an obvious advantage. However, because the projector may be placed relatively close to the projection screen, the effects of keystoning are more pronounced, and instructors tend to neglect filling the entire screen. These disadvantages can easily be overcome by proper equipment placement. The overhead projector should be placed far enough from the screen that the focused image of the transparency fills the entire screen. As discussed in Chapter 7, keystoning can be eliminated by making the projection lens of the projector and the projection screen parallel.

Although the overhead projector is designed to work in a lighted classroom, ambient light falling on the screen can degrade the projected image significantly. The projection screen should never be placed directly underneath overhead lighting. When possible, place the screen directly in front of windows so that light that enters the room through the windows falls on the rear of the screen rather than the projection surface.

Ambient light must be controlled when classes use an overhead projector.

Some projectionists advocate placing an overhead projector in the corner opposite to the presenter's right or left hand. If the presenter is left-handed, the

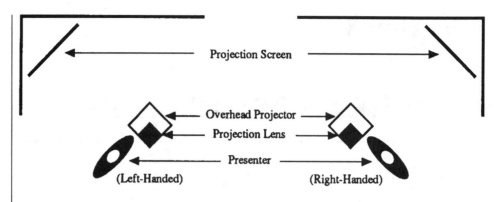

Figure 8.1

Corner Placement of Overhead Projection Screen

screen should be placed in the corner to the presenter's right; if the presenter is right-handed, the screen should be placed in the corner to the presenter's left (see Figure 8.1 above). Advocates of this screen placement argue that it provides enhanced light control (corners are usually the darkest areas of any room); larger image size (the angle to the corner generally provides a longer distance than to the front of the classroom); and less obstruction of the presenter's view (the projector head is located away from the audience).

Once the projection equipment is properly placed, overhead projection has the following advantages:

▶ Overhead projectors present large, visible images in a fully lighted room. The light of the overhead helps focus attention and gives all students a front-row seat in learning.

▶ The instructor faces the audience and maintains eye contact while presenting information.

▶ Equipment is lightweight, readily available, and easy to operate.

▶ The equipment is adaptable to any size audience and grade level.

▶ Overheads enable the teacher to build concepts in a step-by-step manner in front of the classroom.

▶ Materials are easy to prepare and reproduce. Teachers can easily create their own transparencies that meet a specific need with basic skills and materials.

▶ Overhead transparency materials are durable and are easy to store for future use.

TYPES OF OVERHEAD TRANSPARENCIES

A wide variety of instructional materials can be locally produced or are commercially available for overhead projection. Chapter 23 contains step-by-step procedures for creating common types of overhead transparencies. The usual formats include the following:

▶ Handmade transparencies are prepared by drawing and writing directly on sheets of clear or colored plastic film often referred to as acetate. The presenter can easily write or draw on transparencies spontaneously. The instructor can modify the visual as students view it, so they see the changes taking place. By writing on individual sheets or a roll of plastic attached to the side of the projector, the instructor can use the projector as a substitute chalkboard. A wide variety of colored markers and types of plastic film are available for handmade transparencies.

▶ Thermal transparencies are prepared by using special heat-sensitive film and a carbon-based master. Carbon masters may be created with pencils, photostatic copiers, and laser printers. An infrared copier is used to transfer the image from the carbon-based master to the transparency film. A variety of color film is available for this process. Because the image is permanently burned into the surface of the film, it cannot be washed or wiped clean as can handmade transparencies.

▶ Photocopier transparencies are produced by a copy machine when special transparency film instead of paper is placed in the photocopier's paper bin. This method is rapidly replacing the thermal process as the most convenient method for transparency production, but because most photocopiers produce only black images, the thermal process is still preferable for color materials. As color laser copiers become more readily available, full-color transparency production will also become more readily available.

▶ Computer-generated transparencies can be produced by teachers and students who have access to the appropriate computer equipment. Graphics programs can be used to produce and edit original artwork for transparency production. High-quality images can be printed on laser printers, and transparencies can be produced using the thermal or photocopier methods mentioned earlier.

Some laser printers accept certain types of acetate loaded directly through the paper tray or paper bypass. Because some acetate can melt under the heat produced by a laser printer, check the Operator's Manual or contact the manufacturer of the laser printer to verify what type of acetate is required. Prevent damage to the laser printer by using only the type of material recommended by the manufacturer. Newly developed color ink jet and color laser printers can also produce full-color transparencies. Verify in the Operator's Manual or with the printer's manufacturer what type of medium to use to produce transparencies in the specified printer.

Color transparencies can be produced on color ink jet or laser printers.

A relatively new form of overhead projection is making its way into a number of classrooms: LCDs. These display devices (discussed in greater detail in Chapter 7) are placed directly on top of the overhead projector and are used to project images generated by computers, and in some cases video images. Desktop presentation packages have been developed that help educators to create presentations using the computer's text, color, sound, and graphics capabilities. Many of these packages provide special transition effects and special development tools that make the production of desktop presentations graphically pleasing as well as efficient.

LIQUID CRYSTAL DISPLAYS (LCDS)

UTILIZATION TECHNIQUES

Turning the projector off and on can refocus students' attention.

Each new layer focuses attention on material being added.

The Impact of the Power Switch

One of the most neglected features of the overhead projector is the Power switch. Many instructors turn the projector on and leave it on during an entire presentation, frequently without any image displayed, so that a blank white screen glares from behind the instructor. This practice not only diminishes the effectiveness of the overheads, it may distract students and shorten the life of the projection bulb. Instructors should turn the projector off when it is not being used, thus redirecting the students' attention to the instructor.

Many projectionists advocate turning the projector off while one transparency is replaced with another and turning it on again only after the new transparency is in place. The flash of the projection lamp is almost guaranteed to attract and focus student attention on the new material.

Disclosure and Revelation Techniques

One of the advantages of locally produced transparencies is the greater control over content that they afford the instructor. Not only can local instructors produce content- and curriculum-specific material, they can maintain greater control of how students receive that information. A carefully planned and well-designed transparency can help the instructor make a more effective presentation. Chapter 23 covers the design and production of the types of overhead transparencies described here.

Overlays involve placing information on separate transparency sheets and hinging them in layers to a base cell (shown in Figure 8.2) so instructors may move through the presentation in steps. The audience's attention is directed to the newly presented material. The overlay technique enables the instructor to sequence information to meet students' needs.

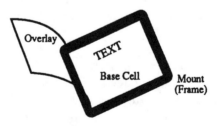

Figure 8.2

Example of Transparency with Overlay

Cover sheets can be used to hide any part of a transparency until the instructor is ready to present the material. At the appropriate time, the instructor moves the cover sheet to reveal the previously hidden information. Any opaque piece of paper can be used as a cover sheet. As Figure 8.3 shows, this technique is especially useful for presenting a list of items. The instructor moves

Figure 8.3

Example of Transparency with Cover Sheet

the cover sheet to reveal each line of text; audience attention is focused on the new information as it is revealed and discussed.

Masks are usually attached permanently to the overhead transparency with tape hinges. The mask is opened like a door (see Figure 8.4) when the information under it is to be shown. Usually associated with graphic rather than text images, masks are a dramatic and effective means of focusing attention on the specific information being presented.

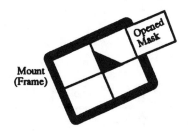

Figure 8.4

Example of Transparency with Masks

Manipulatives

A variety of items can be manipulated on the stage during the presentation. These items may be simple construction cutouts used as silhouettes to dramatize a story, glass or clear plastic containers used to show changes over time, or transparent rulers and other measuring devices used to illustrate a procedure. Specially designed materials can be prepared that feature motion to demonstrate processes.

Enlargement

Occasionally, a transparency or some form of transparent material may contain an image the instructor would like to use in a drawing for a bulletin board or some other surface. The overhead projector can be used to enlarge the image. The original must be transparent or must be made into a transparency using one of the techniques described in Chapter 23. The basic procedure for using the overhead projector to enlarge visuals is described in the following steps and is illustrated in Figure 8.5.

1. Follow the basic instructions for operating an overhead projector given earlier in this chapter. Rather than aiming the projector at a projection screen, however, aim the projector at a piece of posterboard or butcher paper securely taped to a wall or tacked to a bulletin board.

2. Place a transparency, transparent object, or an opaque object (if only an outline is desired) on the overhead projector.

3. Adjust the image size by moving the projector either closer or farther away.

4. Focus the image occasionally to keep the image clear until the desired size is obtained.

5. Draw the projected image on the appropriate surface.

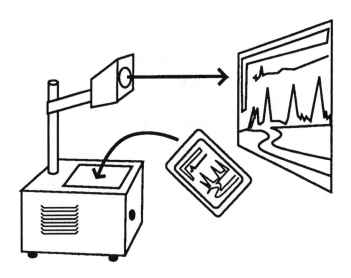

Figure 8.5

Enlarging with an Overhead Projector

MAINTENANCE

Overhead projectors continue to function well only when staff take care to keep the equipment clean and properly stored. The projector has a cooling fan that draws a large amount of air through the machine to dissipate the heat generated by the lamp. As air moves through the machine, dust, lint, and other pollutants are brought into the interior of the projector. The projector should be opened and the interior thoroughly cleaned with compressed air or a vacuum cleaner at least once a year. Exterior metal or plastic parts should be cleaned frequently with a clean damp cloth or paper towel. A mild cleaning agent may be used to remove stubborn deposits of dirt from these surfaces.

All parts of the optical system should also be kept clean. The optical system includes the Fresnel lens assembly, the projection stage glass, any mirrors or lamp reflectors in the projector, and the projection lenses. Lenses have highly polished glass surfaces and should be cleaned with lens cleaning fluid and lens tissue, which can be obtained from camera and photography shops and many department stores. As the projectionist cleans the Fresnel lens, he or she should follow the circular pattern of the lens, do not clean across the rings. The glass projection stage is not highly polished and can be cleaned with ordinary household glass cleaner. Reflective surfaces should be cleaned with a damp, lint-free cloth or paper towel.

Cleaning supplies include lens cleaning fluid, glass cleaner, and a lint-free cloth.

The bulb in a typical overhead projector has an average life of 25 to 40 hours; therefore, the average classroom instructor will most likely need to change the bulb in an overhead projector several times, depending on the frequency and duration of projector use. It is wise to become acquainted with the procedures for changing bulbs so that instruction can continue after a bulb burns out with as little interruption as possible. All overhead projectors will have an opening leading to the lamp assembly. The procedure for removing the bulb depends on the type of mounting used; some projectors provide an ejection lever that will dislodge the lamp; other projectors may have a spring release. Consult the Operator's Manual of the identified projector for specific instructions. Always replace the bulb with a new one of the same three-character identification code printed on the lamp. A spare bulb should be available at all times. Be sure to observe the guidelines for changing lamps discussed in Chapter 7.

Instructors should know how to change projector bulbs on the spot.

SUMMARY

The overhead projector offers many advantages compared with other projection devices: It is used in front of the audience so that the instructor can maintain eye contact; it is designed to be used in a lighted room; and it has a horizontal stage that permits the use of manipulatives. These advantages, combined with the ease of operating an overhead projector and the ease of producing curriculum-specific instructional materials locally, make the overhead projector an important piece of classroom equipment. Liquid crystal display devices have increased the importance of the overhead projector in today's technological classroom. Teachers can use the Performance Checklist at the end of this chapter to acquire skill and confidence in operating the overhead projector.

SUGGESTED ACTIVITIES

1. Use laboratory modules covering the operation of the overhead projector to guide you through initial experiences with the equipment. If such materials are not available, locate and use the Operator's Manual furnished by the manufacturer of your projector for instructions on its operation.

2. Use the Performance Checklist in this unit to further guide you through the operation of the projector. Make use of the diagrams in this unit that show the various controls used in operating the projector.

3. Have another person—preferably a peer who is also learning to use the projector—check your operation of the equipment by completing the Performance Checklist.

4. Practice operation of the overhead projector until you can operate it with confidence and skill and without hesitation. Write down any questions or problems you have with the equipment and discuss them with your instructor. Your instructor may also evaluate your projection skills using the Performance Checklist.

5. Observe the use of overhead projection in a variety of instructional situations. Note both proper and improper techniques and record which communicate most effectively. Write a brief paragraph describing the elements of successful presentations you observed. Write a second paragraph indicating how less successful presentations could have been improved through the proper use of overhead projection.

6. Given an overhead projector, projection screen, and an empty classroom, place the equipment for optimal viewing of an overhead transparency. Complete this activity in a variety of instructional settings.

7. Plan a brief presentation to demonstrate one of the utilization techniques described in this chapter. Share your presentation with a small group of your peers who have also prepared presentations. Discuss the specific preparations required for incorporating the selected technique.

OVERHEAD PROJECTOR
Performance Checklist

Step	Description of Performance	Self Check	Peer Check	Instructor Check
	SET UP PROJECTOR			
1.	Turn projector toward screen.			
2.	Plug cord into electrical outlet.			
	USE THE PROJECTOR			
3.	Turn projector on.			
4.	Adjust image to screen horizontally.			
5.	Adjust image to screen vertically.			
6.	Place transparency on screen.			
7.	Focus.			
8.	Move through a series of transparencies.			
9.	Mark on transparencies during showing.			
10.	Show transparency overlays.			
11.	Use cover sheets and masks.			
12.	Project transparent objects.			
13.	Project silhouette of opaque objects.			
14.	Turn projector off.			
	PUT EQUIPMENT AWAY			
15.	Remove and store materials.			
16.	Unplug and store power cord.			
17.	Change bulb.			
18.	Secure projector for storage.			

Code for marking:
3 Highly proficient   **2** Proficient   **1** Limited proficiency   **0** Not proficient

Chapter 9

SLIDE PROJECTION

PURPOSES

▶ To identify the typical size of instructional slides.
▶ To describe alternate ways in which instructional slides can be produced.
▶ To discuss the advantages of using instructional slides.
▶ To become familiar with setting up and operating slide projection systems.
▶ To develop troubleshooting and user maintenance skills related to the use of slide projectors.

INTRODUCTION

A *slide* is a small, positive transparency (usually a photographic transparency) mounted in a sturdy frame. Mounting frames are typically white cardboard but may also be made of plastic and glass. The 2" x 2" slide is considered the standard size for instructional purposes. When produced by a 35mm camera, the image produced appears in either a vertical or horizontal orientation, as shown in Figure 9.1.

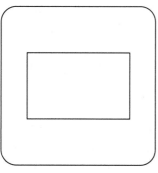
Horizontal Orientation

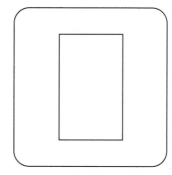
Vertical Orientation

Figure 9.1

Orientation of 35mm Slides in 2" x 2" Mounts

Effective use of instructional slides offers the following advantages in the classroom:

▶ Slides offer full color and photographic detail in projected images. They provide maximum realism for instruction, because a wide variety of photographic techniques can be used to capture unique visual images.
▶ Slides can be adapted easily for use in small or large groups; slides also fit well into individualized learning programs.

▶ Slides are easy to store and are convenient to use in slide trays. The equipment is considered easy to operate.

▶ Slides are fairly inexpensive to produce locally. Teachers and students can produce slide programs that meet specific curricular needs. Student-produced programs afford classes an excellent means of developing visual literacy skills while exploring new content areas.

▶ Slides are readily combined with audio recordings to provide valuable multimedia learning materials.

PRODUCING SLIDES

New technologies enable anyone to produce professional-looking photographs.

New autofocus, autoexposure cameras have eliminated much of the complexity of producing high-quality photographs. In addition to traditional photographic processes, teachers should be aware of alternatives provided by technological advancements in both camera and film technology.

Commercial developers offer perhaps the easiest and most accessible means of slide production. The photographer can purchase slide film (which, regardless of brand, usually ends with the suffix chrome) at most locations where print film is sold. After shooting the roll of slides, photographers take the exposed film to any of a number of commercial developers for processing. In some instances the process may take 3 to 5 working days, depending on available service, though some developers may offer 24-hour service or even one-hour service for a higher fee.

Instant development is also available. Instant slide film (there are four varieties) can generally be purchased at professional photography supply stores. Instant slide film is packaged with the chemicals necessary for development contained in a small kit.

With a film processing kit, instant slides are developed in about five minutes.

The film can be loaded into any standard 35mm camera. However, because some varieties of instant slide film require a slow film speed setting (ISO 40) and because, to date, the film canisters are not DX coded, instant slide film may be difficult to use in autoexposure cameras that do not provide a way to set the film speed manually. The DX coding is printed on film canisters so cameras can automatically read the coding.

In addition to the chemicals that come packaged right with the film, developing instant slide film requires the use of a film processing kit (a small black box about the size of a shoe box), which retails for less than $200. The film processor provides the means for chemical interaction with exposed film. The entire process takes about five minutes. After development is complete, the slides must still be cut and mounted. This process can be done by hand, or the photographer can purchase an additional slide mounting unit.

Instant slide film offers the obvious advantage of rapid ("instant") development. With an appropriate camera, a copy stand, and some advanced planning, it is possible for a student or instructor to shot, develop, mount, and present a slide show within a limited amount of time. Last-minute changes to existing slide shows can be made relatively easily and inexpensively.

Film recorders are new devices that bring the power of computer-generated images to film. In general, film recorders enable the user to send images generated by a wide variety of graphic software packages to a device that "records" the image on film. Depending on the manufacturer, the film recorder may be connected directly to a microcomputer or may be an independent unit. If the film recorder is independent, it has the capacity to "read" the computer images stored on a diskette and transfer the image to film. After the film in a film recorder is exposed, it is developed in the traditional manner (instant slide film can be used in some film recorders).

Images created with graphics software can be stored on diskettes using a film recorder, then transferred to slides.

IMAGE ORIENTATION

One aspect of slide production that may not be apparent to novice producers is the orientation of finished slides. Because most slides are produced on 35mm film, the final images appear either vertical or horizontal rectangles. Most of these images are then projected on a square projection screen. If the projection equipment is set so that a horizontal slide fills the screen from side to side, when a vertical slide is projected, the image will fall off either the top or bottom of the screen. If the projection equipment is placed so that a vertical slide fills the screen from top to bottom, then a horizontal slide will not fill the screen from side to side.

Slide sets with a single orientation—all vertical or all horizontal—look more professional.

To avoid this problem, most experienced slide producers make sure that all of the slides within a particular presentation maintain a consistent orientation—either all vertical or all horizontal. It may take some advanced planning and some creative photography, but it will give the finished product a more professional quality.

SLIDE PROJECTION SYSTEMS

Two types of slide projection systems are available in most classrooms:

▶ Slide projector only systems are used when an instructor lectures or narrates while slides are projected.

▶ Sound-slide systems use an audio tape to deliver the narration while slides are projected. Depending on the equipment used, the slides may be advanced automatically when an inaudible impulse recorded on the tape is transmitted to the projector. (Review the section entitled Producing Sound Sync Programs in Chapter 6 for more detail on producing sound-slide programs.) This system requires the slide projector to be connected to a special sync tape recorder. Commercially developed programs frequently include the same narration on the second side of the audio tape. This narration includes audible tones that indicate when the operator should manually advance to the next slide.

Sound-slide systems are used with a sync tape recorder.

PROJECTOR CARE AND MAINTENANCE

The optical and mechanical parts of the slide projector should be kept free of dirt, lint, and other foreign deposits at all times. Follow these steps for cleaning the major components:

1. Always unplug the projector and turn the projector upside-down to open the panel on the bottom of the projector for access to the internal lenses.

2. Loosen the wire retainer lever to free the lenses and a glass heat shield.

3. Carefully remove and clean the lenses with lens cleaning fluid and lens tissue.

4. While the lenses are out of the projector, use compressed air or a vacuum cleaner to remove dirt and dust from the interior of the machine.

5. Replace the lenses in exactly the same way they were found in the projector by reversing the sequence used to remove them. The guides on the side of the lens area should help properly orient the lens and the heat shield.

6. Make sure the wire lever and the panel door are securely fastened before the projector is turned upright.

7. Remove the projection lens assembly for cleaning by pushing the focus knob to the side and pulling the lens toward the front and out of the projector.

TROUBLE-SHOOTING TIPS FOR SLIDE PROJECTORS

Slides that have jammed in front of the lamp must be removed on the spot.

Damaged and Jammed Slides

Occasionally, a slide mount becomes bent or frayed and the slide does not feed properly into a projector. If a slide will not load, first try to straighten or slightly trim the edges of the slide mount. If the slide still does not load freely, it may be necessary to remount the slide. Various slide mounting frames are available from camera and photography stores.

Sometimes a slide will jam within the projector, making it impossible either to advance or remove the tray by normal means. If this occurs, follow these steps to remove the tray:

1. Place a coin or screwdriver in the slot at the center of the circular slide tray. (Some newer models use a "pinch" release as opposed to the "screw" release.)

2. Turn the screw counterclockwise (or pinch the release).

3. Hold the screw counterclockwise (or pinch the release) and lift the tray from the projector.

4. Make sure the slide tray lock ring is secured and turn the tray upside-down. Place the upside-down tray aside.

5. Remove any jammed slide(s) from the projector and lay it (them) aside.

6. Pick up the slide tray and continue to keep it upside-down. Turn the metal rim on the bottom of the tray until the rim engages in its locked position.

7. Turn the tray upright, remove the slide lock ring, and reload the loose slide(s).

8. Replace the tray on the projector and advance the tray to the appropriate point in the presentation.

The most common slide projector is the carousel-type, named for the round slide tray that rotates atop the projector. Because they are used so extensively, carousel projectors are used here to illustrate the operation and care of slide projectors. The projectionist must pay particular attention to the procedures used in loading slides into the circular trays. Slides can be properly loaded into a tray by following these steps and checking the illustrated process in Figure 9.2:

LOADING SLIDES INTO A TRAY

1. Set the tray down as it will be positioned on top of the projector. When the operator is sitting directly behind the projector, the notch in the tray and the slot marked "1" should be on the right.

2. Remove the slide lock ring (also called the retaining ring) from the tray.

3. Select a slide and hold it so that the image on the slide appears as it should when the slide is projected. Any text on the slide itself (not on the mount) should be readable left-to-right.

4. Turn the slide upside-down and drop the slide into slot "1." (Do not turn the slide around!)

5. Follow the same procedure for each slide in the presentation.

6. Replace the slide lock ring to ensure that slides do not fall out of the tray.

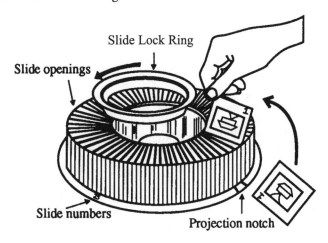

Figure 9.2

Loading Slides into a Carousel Tray

The projectionist should always preview the slides alone before a public showing to ensure that each slide is loaded properly. If the slides are to be retained and shown in the same order, they should be numbered. Placing the number near the upper right corner of the mount (as it is arranged in the tray) will provide a reference as to how the slide is to be placed in the tray. This will save time when slides are reloaded subsequently.

Plan to preview the display of a slide set to check that they are not "flipped" or out of sequence.

SUMMARY

Slide projection provides an effective and relatively inexpensive means of integrating visual materials into instruction. Slide presentations may be produced locally and can be readily revised and updated.

SUGGESTED ACTIVITIES

1. Use laboratory modules covering the operation of the slide projector to guide you through initial experiences with the equipment. If such materials are not available, locate and use the Operator's Manual furnished by the manufacturer of your projector for instructions on its operation.

2. Use the Performance Checklist in this unit to further guide you through the operation of the projector. Use the diagrams in this chapter that show the various controls used in operating the projector.

3. Have another person—preferably a peer who is also learning to use the projector—check your skills at projection using the Performance Checklist.

4. Practice the operation of the slide projector until you can operate it with confidence and skill and without hesitation. Write down any questions or problems you have with the equipment and discuss them with your instructor. Your instructor is likely to evaluate your operation of the projector using the Performance Checklist.

5. Given 10 randomly selected slides, load them into a carousel slide tray properly. Project the slides to verify that each was loaded correctly.

6. Investigate the alternative forms of slide development available in your area. Is instant slide film available? If so, what is the cost? How does the cost of instant slide film compare with the cost of commercial development? How fast can slides be developed commercially in your area?

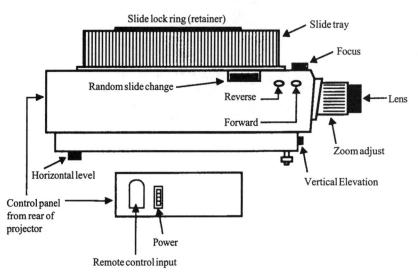

Components of a Slide Projector

AUTOMATIC SLIDE PROJECTOR
Performance Checklist

Step	Description of Performance	Self Check	Peer Check	Instructor Check
	SET UP PROJECTOR AND LOAD SLIDE TRAY			
1.	Remove power cord and plug in.			
2.	Load and lock slides in tray.			
3.	Turn on and test the fan and lamp.			
4.	Load slide tray on projector.			
5.	Advance to first slide in series.			
6.	Adjust image to screen horizontally and vertically.			
7.	Change image size with zoom lens.			
8.	Fine focus.			
9.	Cool lamp and turn projector off.			
	USE THE PROJECTOR			
10.	Turn on lamp and fan.			
11.	Move through slide series in forward direction.			
12.	Move through slide series in reverse direction.			
13.	Randomly select slides.			
14.	Attach remote control.			
15.	Remotely control the projector for forward, reverse, and focus functions.			
16.	Connect to sync tape recorder.			
17.	Return slide tray to "0" and remove tray.			
18.	Remove slide tray without returning tray to "0" position.			
19.	Cool lamp and turn projector off.			
	PUT EQUIPMENT AWAY			
20.	Unplug and store cords.			
21.	Store slide tray.			
22.	Change lamp.			
23.	Secure projector for storage.			

Code for marking:
3 Highly proficient   **2** Proficient   **1** Limited proficiency   **0** Not proficient

Chapter 10

FILMSTRIP PROJECTION

PURPOSES

▶ To recognize the advantages of using instructional filmstrips.
▶ To be able to perform simple equipment maintenance and filmstrip handling techniques.
▶ To become skilled in setting up and operating filmstrip projectors and viewers.

A filmstrip is a series of transparent pictures on a strip of 35mm film that are projected vertically through the optical system of a filmstrip projector. Filmstrips are most commonly in a single-frame format. The image runs horizontally across the width of the film.

Filmstrips offer the following advantages for instruction in the classroom:

▶ Presentations can be carefully planned because images are always in a fixed sequence. Once the filmstrip is properly loaded, images cannot be projected upside down or jam up like slides.
▶ Filmstrips are inexpensive to purchase and are available in most conventional subject areas. Filmstrips with audio recording are very popular.
▶ Filmstrip projectors are commonly found in schools and are easy to set up and operate. Equipment systems are available for individual viewing and listening, or for large group presentations. Many projectors have synchronization for audio cassettes.
▶ Filmstrips are a versatile medium that can be used in a variety of ways by the creative teacher. They work extremely well for individual study in a library media center. In addition, they are excellent for visualizing still images to large groups of students.

A wide variety of equipment is available for use in projecting and viewing filmstrips. Filmstrip projectors range from those with low-level outputs for small groups to projectors capable of showing images to large audiences.

FILMSTRIP HANDLING AND CARE

Silent Filmstrip Projectors

Silent filmstrip projectors are only capable of projecting the visual image. The presenter narrates and/or discusses while projecting the images. A script or teachers guide is often available for these programs.

Sound Filmstrip Projectors

Sound filmstrip projectors are designed to show the image and play an accompanying sound track, most often on an audio cassette. A large assortment of sound filmstrip projection equipment is available for individual/small group use or large audiences.

Preventive Maintenance

Filmstrips have a rather long life if properly handled and maintained. Care should be taken to avoid scratches and prevent contamination by dust. They should always be stored in a regular filmstrip container. When you remove a filmstrip from its container, place your finger inside the roll and turn slightly to loosen the roll. Always handle it by the sides to avoid fingerprints on the picture area of the filmstrip. When you place the filmstrip back in storage, roll tightly, starting with a roll about the size of a pencil. Should you end with a roll too large to fit into the container, start over making a smaller, tighter roll. (see Figure 10.1). Never pull or cinch the filmstrip to produce a smaller roll. This causes scratches that will appear as vertical lines on the screen.

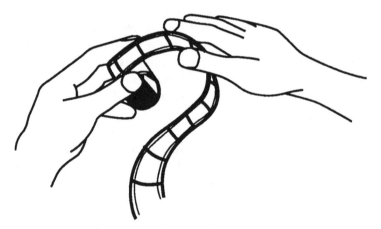

Figure 10.1

Proper Technique for Rolling a Filmstrip

Threading

When you thread a filmstrip into a projector or viewer, never force the film or the advance lever. Should the filmstrip be forced, damage to the sprocket holes on the sides will likely occur. Learners who use filmstrips for individual viewing should be thoroughly trained in the care and handling of the materials and equipment.

Materials Repair

Any organization that has a collection of filmstrips should have repair and maintenance supplies needed for the upkeep of the materials. Special tape is available for repairing cuts, tears, and enlarged sprocket holes. Splicing blocks, cutters, and additional film leader are also essential in the proper maintenance of filmstrips.

Care and Maintenance

Filmstrip equipment should be kept clean and properly maintained to insure proper operation over a long period of time. Most projectors have an opening at the top of the projector to give access to the lamp and internal lenses. The projection lens on most projectors can be pulled forward to remove it for cleaning. Projectors and viewers should be placed in a case or enclosed in plastic covers when stored. As with all such equipment, they should be stored in a dust-free area.

Troubleshooting

An inverted image will appear on the screen if a filmstrip is improperly threaded. The first frames of a filmstrip must be inserted in the filmstrip carrier upside-down.

When a line appears across the top of the image, cutting off the bottom of the visual, or vice versa, the filmstrip is out of frame. Locate the framing knob or lever and move it either up or down until the line disappears.

1. Use laboratory modules covering the operation of the filmstrip equipment to guide you through your initial use of the equipment. If such modules are not available, locate and use the Operator's Manual furnished by the manufacturer of your equipment for instructions in its operation.

2. Use the Performance Checklist in this unit to further guide you through the operation of the equipment. Make use of Figure 10.2 which shows the various controls used in operating the equipment. Both the diagram and the checklist refer to a combination filmstrip-slide projector. If you are operating a filmstrip viewer, be alert to the fact that you will need to skip some steps and substitute others, and that controls will be located at different places on the machine.

3. Have another person, preferably a peer who is also learning to use the equipment, check you out using the Performance Checklist. Practice

EQUIPMENT MAINTENANCE & TROUBLE-SHOOTING

SUGGESTED ACTIVITIES

**Rear Screen
Projector**

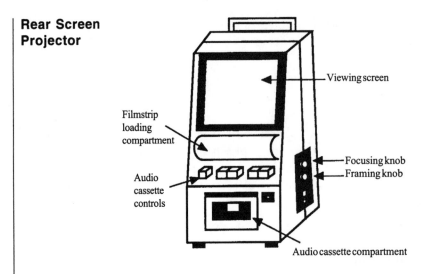

Viewing screen

Filmstrip
loading
compartment

Focusing knob
Framing knob

Audio
cassette
controls

Audio cassette compartment

**Front Screen
Projector**

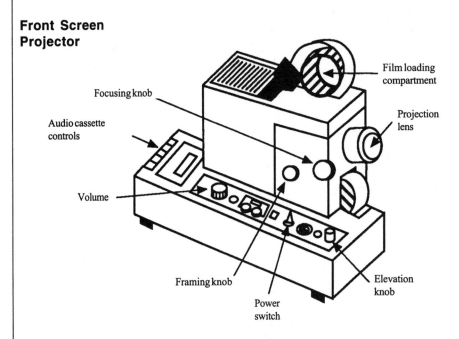

Film loading
compartment

Focusing knob

Projection
lens

Audio cassette
controls

Volume

Framing knob

Elevation
knob

Power
switch

Figure 10.2

Components of a Filmstrip Projector

operating the equipment until you are able to operate it with confidence and skill without the use of printed material or assistance.

4. Proceed through all activities just indicated. Practice the operation of the filmstrip equipment until you are able to operate it with confidence, skill, and without hesitation. Write down any questions or problems you have with the equipment and discuss them with your instructor. Your instructor will likely want to evaluate your operation of the equipment using the Performance Checklist.

SOUND FILMSTRIP PROJECTOR
Performance Checklist

Step	Description of Performance	Self Check	Peer Check	Instructor Check
	SET UP PROJECTOR			
1.	Open case and remove accessories.			
2.	Plug cord into power outlet.			
3.	Test fan and lamp.			
4.	Adjust image to screen.			
5.	Prefocus.			
	LOAD CASSETTE AND FILMSTRIP			
6.	Insert cassette into compartment.			
7.	Rewind cassette to begin.			
8.	Set and play back to automatic advance.			
9.	Check filmstrip for start and proper rewinding.			
10.	Insert filmstrip into loading compartment.			
11.	Thread filmstrip through projector.			
12.	Advance filmstrip to begin frame.			
13.	Adjust filmstrip frame.			
14.	Adjust focus.			
	SOUND FILMSTRIP PLAYBACK			
15.	Start cassette for automatic advance of filmstrip.			
16.	Project filmstrip.			
17.	Adjust volume control.			
18.	Synchronize filmstrip with sound.			
19.	Turn off filmstrip projector and audio cassette.			
	PUT EQUIPMENT AWAY			
20.	Rewind cassette and filmstrip.			
21.	Unplug and store power cord.			
22.	Store accessories in case or projector compartment.			

Code for marking:
3 Highly proficient   **2** Proficient   **1** Limited proficiency   **0** Not proficient

Chapter 11

OPAQUE PROJECTION

PURPOSES

▶ To be able to recognize potential uses of opaque projectors in the classroom.
▶ To be able to perform simple equipment maintenance on the opaque projector.
▶ To become skilled in setting up and operating the projector.
▶ To learn how to enlarge visuals for a variety of applications.

INTRODUCTION

Opaque projectors are considered old technology in terms of the length of time they have been available in schools, but they remain a valuable tool for many classroom teachers and students. The opaque's method of projection, as shown in Figure 11.1, differs from most other types of projectors. Most projectors create an image by passing light through transparent materials directly onto a screen. Opaque projectors create images of opaque materials such as books, maps, real objects, and three-dimensional items by reflecting light from the surface of the materials onto a mirror that directs the image toward the screen.

Due to its unique method of projecting images, the opaque must be used under relatively dim light for optimal viewing. The low-light conditions must be considered when teachers require students to take notes or the teacher must monitor the class closely.

Opaque projectors require a low-light environment for good contrast.

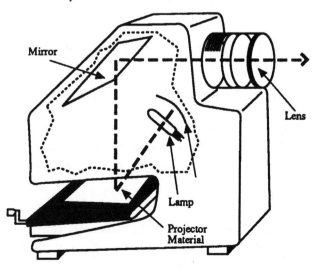

Figure 11.1

Projection Path of an Opaque Projector

To improve image brightness on the opaque projector, a high-wattage lamp is often used. This may cause heat buildup, so the projectionist must watch for heat damage to the materials being projected. Thermal transparencies and other heat-sensitive objects should not be used in the opaque projector.

USES OF OPAQUE PROJECTION

Opaque projection offers a variety of potential uses, and its value can be greatly enhanced by the imagination and creativity of teachers and students. Images of relatively flat materials, such as fabrics, collections of small rocks or leaves, measuring instruments, and other three-dimensional objects, can be projected quickly and easily in their real form. Other types of projectors would require some modifications of the real materials into graphic representations for projection. Not only would this graphic conversion take up valuable teacher time, but the graphic representation is not always as effective as seeing the real object projected from the opaque projector.

Technical forms, writing samples, or small works of art can be presented to an entire class for discussion or critique.

The opaque projector can create its own works of art on walls, bulletin boards, or stages.

The opaque is a popular tool for enlarging images for displays or for decorative purposes. A small drawing, picture, or object may be placed into the opaque and projected onto a sheet of poster board or large sheet of paper to be traced. The enlarged image may be used for displays such as bulletin boards, charts, stage props, murals, or promotional items for special events. It can be used for creating life-sized images of people or large murals for the wall of a classroom or hallway to gain attention. Enlargements are often used to decorate spaces for school parties or open house. Pep clubs often use it to produce large murals or banners for ball games.

PROCEDURES FOR ENLARGEMENT

Follow these steps to prepare enlargements with an opaque projector:

1. Prepare the surface you wish to use for an enlarged visual. It could be the chalkboard, poster board, a large wall, or a large piece of paper that is attached to a wall.

2. Load the visual material to be reproduced into the projector and project the image onto the desired surface.

3. Adjust the distance between the projector and reproduction surface to achieve the desired image size. Moving the projector farther away makes the image larger and closer will make the image smaller. Continue to focus the visual with the focus knob as you move the projector back and forth to make the appropriate sized image as clear as possible.

4. Trace the projected image of the visual.

Other projectors such as overhead or slide projectors can be used for image enlargement, but the opaque is unique in being able to project detailed images of opaque items.

If an instructor wishes to use a visual that is in a copyrighted publication, copyright laws may allow the production of a single copy of the visual such as a diagram; cartoon; graph; or picture from a book, periodical, or newspaper if it is to be used for teaching in a class. Be familiar with the copyright laws to determine what is appropriate.

Maintenance tasks for the opaque projector vary only slightly from those for other projectors. Most opaque projectors have a side or rear panel door that provides access to the projection lamp and internal parts that may need replacement or cleaning.

Because this machine has an extensive amount of interior space and surfaces, a small vacuum cleaner attachment is recommended for interior dust removal. It is important not to touch the projection lamp and reflective mirror surface with bare hands, abrasive materials, or cleaning materials that could scratch them or leave a residue on them.

1. Use laboratory modules covering the operation of the opaque projector to guide you through your initial experiences with the equipment. If such materials are not available, locate and use the Operator's Manual furnished by the manufacturer of your projector.

2. Use the Performance Checklist in this unit to further guide you through the operation of the projector. Make use of the diagrams in Figure 11.2 that show the various controls used in operating the projector.

3. Have another person, preferably a peer who is also learning to use the projector, check your operational skills using the Performance Checklist.

4. Practice operating the projector until you are able to operate it with confidence and skill and without the use of printed material or assistance from someone else.

5. Write down any questions or problems you have with the equipment and discuss them with your instructor.

6. Find a small visual or opaque object and place it on the opaque to see how easy it would be to create an enlarged image.

COPYRIGHT LAW

PROJECTOR MAINTENANCE

The mirror surface of the projector must be kept free of dust and fingerprints.

SUGGESTED ACTIVITIES

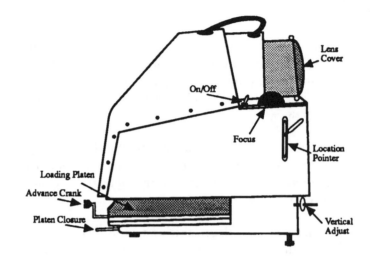

Figure 11.2

Components of Opaque Projector

OPAQUE PROJECTOR
Performance Checklist

Step	Description of Performance	Self Check	Peer Check	Instructor Check
	SET UP PROJECTOR			
1.	Turn projector with lens toward screen.			
2.	Open lens cover.			
3.	Plug power cord into electrical outlet.			
	USE THE PROJECTOR			
4.	Turn the projector on.			
5.	Load a picture into the projector.			
6.	Focus.			
7.	Adjust image to screen horizontally.			
8.	Adjust image to screen vertically.			
9.	Show a series of pictures.			
10.	Show a picture in a book.			
11.	Use location pointer.			
12.	Turn projector off.			
	PUT EQUIPMENT AWAY			
13.	Remove and store pictures.			
14.	Unplug and store power cord.			
15.	Secure projector for storage.			

Code for marking:
3 Highly proficient   **2** Proficient   **1** Limited proficiency   **0** Not proficient

Recommended Readings

Brown, James W., Richard B. Lewis, and Fred F. Harcleroad. *AV Instruction: Technology, Media, and Methods.* 5th ed. New York: Mcgraw-Hill Book Co., 1983.

Bullough, Robert B., Sr. *Creating Instructional Materials.* 2nd ed. Columbus, Ohio: Charles E. Merrill Publishing Co., 1978.

Coburn, Peter et al. *Practical Guide to Computers in Education.* Reading, Mass.: Addison-Wesley Publishing Co., 1982.

Gerlach,Vernon S., and Donald P. Ely. *Teaching and Media: A Systematic Approach.* 2nd ed. Englewood Cliffs, N.J.: Prentice Hall, Inc., 1971.

Henich, Robert, Michael Molenda, and James D. Russell. *Instructional Media and the New Technologies of Instruction.* New York: John Wiley and Son, 1989.

Kemp, Jerrold E., and Deane K. Daytin. *Planning and Producing Instructional Materials.* 5th ed. New York: Harper and Row, 1985

Knirk, Frederick G., and Kent L. Gustafson. *Instructional Technology: A Systematic Approach to Education.* New York: Holt, Rinehart and Winston, 1986.

McInnes, James. *Video in Education and Training.* London: Focal Press, 1980.

Minor, Ed. *Handbook for Preparing Visual Media.* 2nd ed. New York: McGrawHill Book Co., 1978.

Minor, Ed, and Harvey R. Fry. *Techniques for Producing Visual Instructional Media.* 2nd ed. New York: McGraw-Hill Book Co., 1977.

Nichols,Herbert L., George H. Culp, and Linda G. Polin. *The Practical Apple.* Pacific Grove, Calif.: Brooks/Cole Publishing Co., 1988.

Percival, Fred, and Henry Ellington. *A Handbook of Educational Technology.* New York: Nichols Publishing Co., 1984.

Pohlmann, Ken C. "Sony MZ-1 Portable MiniDisc System." *Stereo Review,* 58, No. 3 (March 1993), pp. 53–56.

Price, Robert V. *Computer-Aided Instruction: A Guide for Authors.* Pacific Grove, Calif.: Brooks/Cole Publishing Company, 1991.

Purdy, Leslie Noble. *Reaching New Students Through New Technologies.* Dubuque, Iowa: Kendall/Hunt Publishing Co., 1983.

Schwartz, Ed. *The Educators' Handbook to Interactive Videodisc.* Washington, D.C.: Association for Educational Communications and Technology, 1987.

Sleeman, Phillip J., Ted C. Cobun and D.M. Rockwell. *Instructional Media and Technology.* New York: Longman, Inc., 1979.

Van Horn, Royal. *Advanced Technology in Education.* Pacific Grove, Calif.: Brooks/Cole Publishing Company, 1991.

Vockell, Edward, and Eileen Schwarts. *The Computer in the Classroom.* Santa Cruz, Calif.: Mitchell Publishing Co., 1988.

VORT Corporation. *Guide to Instructional Materials.* Palo Alto, Calif.: VORT Corporation, 1980.

Wittich, Walter A., and Charles F. Schuller. *Instructional Technology: Its Nature and Use.* 6th ed. New York: Harper and Row, 1979.

Woodbury, Marda. *Selecting Materials for Instruction.* Littleton, Colo.: Libraries Unlimited, Inc., 1979.

GLOSSARY

Active Matrix: A construction scheme for liquid crystal display devices generally used when movement and color images are displayed.

Ambient Light: Light from a source other than a projector that falls on the surface of a projection screen and degrades the projected image.

Analog Recording: The type of recordings or electronic signals usually associated with audio tapes, videotapes, and telephone transmissions.

Bar Code Reader: A small handheld laser scanner, similar to grocery store checkout scanners, used to read preprinted bar codes for programming a laser disc player.

Beaded (Glass-Beaded) Screen: A highly reflective projection screen surface made of tiny glass beads. This screen normally provides the brightest image from a narrow viewing angle.

Camcorder: A handheld video camera and recorder combined into one unit.

CATV: Community antenna television or cable TV.

CAV: Constant angular velocity; a form of laser disc that allows rapid random access of any one of 54,000 images. Each frame is assigned a unique index number that can be used to access it.

CD: Compact disc; a medium that provide a high-quality digital sound played by a laser.

CDI: Compact disc-interactive; a self contained CD player marketed by Philips that attaches to a television set for still, animated, and full-motion video aimed at the home consumer market.

Channel One: News network program, established by Chris Whittle, that is providing many schools with video equipment and closed circuit cabling to view daily news programs.

CLV: Constant linear velocity; laser discs that are primarily designed to play motion video programs; frames are not individually indexed, but segments of a disc may be randomly selected by seconds of time that are on the disc.

Control Track: An electronic signal on a videotape recording that keeps it in sync when it is playing or recording.

Digital Recording: A type of recording created by converting analog electronic signals into numbers to create a soundfile that consists of many number samples.

Distance Education: The delivery of instructional programs outside the traditional classroom environment via satellite, cable television, fiber optics cable, microwaves, or another remote means.

8mm Video: A small, compact videotape format.

Film Loops: The slack in 16mm film provided above and below the lens on a motion picture projector that are necessary for proper threading of the projector.

Focal Length: The distance between a projection lens and the film surface. The shorter the focal length of the lens, the larger the projected image.

Framing: Adjusting a projected image so only one full frame will show at any given time.

Front Screen Projection: Projection system placement where the projector is in or behind the audience projecting an image on an opaque screen placed in front of the audience.

HI 8mm Video: High-resolution form of 8mm video format.

Illusion of Motion: Sense of motion created when a series of still images are shown quickly, such as on a 16mm film.

Instructional Television: Any television programming that is planned and used in an instructional setting to help students achieve learning objectives.

Interactive Video: Normally refers to the use of video laser discs in activities that require the viewer to perform certain functions while viewing the video at levels I, II, III, or IV.

Keystone Effect (Keystoning): Distortion of a projected image that occurs when the projection screen is not parallel with the vertical and/or horizontal axis of the projection lens.

Laser Disc: Usually referring to 12" or 8" laser video recording on a plastic disc.

LCD Panel: Liquid crystal display unit used to project computer images via an overhead projector.

Lens: Highly polished and shaped glass used to focus the pattern of direct or reflected light through or from the material to the viewing surface.

Lenticular: A projection screen surface made of many cylindrical mirrors that run from the top to the bottom of the screen. The surface is an aluminum color, and it provides a more uniform image over a wide horizontal angle and narrow vertical angle to the viewing audience.

Level I Interactive Video: Basic level of playing laser discs manually or with a remote control pad.

Level II Interactive Video: A level of use in which laser discs are used with embedded video commands and controls.

Level III Interactive Video: The interfacing of a computer and a laser disc player for interactivity and possible lesson development.

Level IV Interactive Video: Evolving term referring to multimedia extensions of computer and laser technology interfaced to create new presentation techniques.

Line of Projection: The imaginary line drawn directly from the projection lens to the projection screen.

Liquid Crystal Display (LCD): A technology used to create low power consumption display devices for a wide variety of applications including portable computer displays and projection devices.

Lumens: A unit of measure for the flow of light from a light source.

Macro Lens: A special lens or an adjustment on a regular lens that allows video or photographic cameras to get extremely close to an object to create a magnified image.

Matte White: A nonglossy, white projection screen surface used for even reflection across a wide viewing area. This screen is considered the most universal for image brightness and viewing angle.

MD: New MiniDisc marketed by Sony that enables the user to record and play up to 74 minutes of digital sound on a small disc.

MIDI: Musical Instrument Digital Interface; a system that enables musical and other electronic sound instruments to be connected to a computer for manipulation.

Monitor: A video screen usually associated with computers or special video editing equipment that is only capable of showing directly connected video sources.

Monitor/Receiver: A television set capable of receiving broadcast television signals as well as connections for direct or closed circuit video signals.

Optical: Sometimes used to refer to recordings that are read by laser beams and require no physical contact for playing, such as CDs.

Pan: Video camera movement referring to movement from right to left or vice versa.

Passive Matrix: A construction scheme for liquid crystal display devices generally used when relatively static images are displayed.

PBS: Public Broadcast System; the broadcasting system that is associated with educational television stations to provide instructional programming.

Projection Lamp: The light source in a projection device.

Rear Screen Projection: Projection system placement where the projector is in front of the audience projecting an image on a translucent screen placed between the audience and the projector; this scheme generally requires the use of a mirror to properly orient the projected image.

Satellite Communications: The transmission and/or reception of audio and/or video images through satellites and receiving dishes.

Screen: A generic term used to refer to the surface on which a projected image is displayed.

Sound Sync Programs: Sound filmstrip or slide program with audio sync pulses recorded on audio tape to automatically advance the visual images.

SP/LP/SLP: The recording and playback speeds of consumer line VCRs; SP stands for standard play, LP for long play, and SLP for super long play.

S-VHS: Super VHS recordings that have a higher resolution than normal VHS images.

Thermal Copier: A device that can be used to make transparencies and other thermal types of instructional materials by exposing a carbon-based master to heat-sensitive film.

VCR: Video cassette recorder.

VHS-C: Compact VHS format that uses a cassette of 1/2" videotape that is smaller in overall dimensions and provides less recording and playing time than standard-sized VHS equipment and cassettes.

Video Disc: *See* Laser Disc.

Video Projector: A projector that enlarges a video image and projects it on a normal projection screen.

Videotext/Teletext: Text information delivery via cable, telephone lines, satellite, or some other means, so that it can be presented to the user on a video display monitor.

White Balance: A color control usually found on portable video cameras that helps adjust the camera to the different color temperatures of light.

Wide-Angle Lens: A lens that produces a wider field of view. On cameras, this lens shows more visual information in the picture by including more to each side. On projectors, this lens type allows the projector to be closer to the screen and still fill up the screen with an image, which is useful for areas in which projection distance is short.

Zoom Lens: A lens with an adjustable focal length. On photographic and video cameras, a zoom lens allows the camera to make distant objects appear closer. On projection equipment, a zoom lens allows the operator to vary the size of the projected image without moving the projector.

Part III

Microcomputers in the Classroom

Introduction to
  Microcomputers

Microcomputer Operation

Models for
  Microcomputer Use

Word Processors

Spreadsheets

Database Managers

Graphic Applications

Networking and
  Telecommunications

Software Selection
  and Utilization

Multimedia

Introduction

The microcomputer is an exciting instructional resource for the classroom teacher. It is extremely important for teachers to become thoroughly acquainted with the microcomputer. This instructional tool can only be used to maximum potential when the user is comfortable and confident with uses of microcomputers in the classroom.

Part III includes an introduction to microcomputers, operating tips for using them; ways to make instructional applications of this technology; procedures for using word processors, spreadsheets, and database managers; and valuable information regarding graphic applications, software selection, and software package evaluation. This part also features a chapter on telecommunications and a chapter on multimedia.

Persons using this book are encouraged to complete the suggested activities at the end of each chapter. It is important that computer novices experience hands-on exercises with microcomputers involving applications such as word processors, database managers, and spreadsheets.

Illustrations of computer screens in this portion of the text are designed to reflect the general principle being discussed rather than illustrating the specifics of any software package or platform.

Chapter 12

INTRODUCTION TO MICROCOMPUTERS

PURPOSES

- ▶ To provide a working definition of "computer literacy"
- ▶ To describe the historical background of microcomputers
- ▶ To identify basic hardware components of a computer
- ▶ To identify layers of computer software

INTRODUCTION

According to the U.S. Office of Technology Assessment, during the decade of the eighties, the percentage of American schools with one or more computers intended for instruction increased from 18 percent to 95 percent. The proliferation of computers has been fueled by the general perception that all students must become "computer literate" in order to achieve success in an increasingly technological society. As a result, teachers must be familiar with what constitutes "computer literacy" and the nature of the technology itself.

"COMPUTER LITERACY" CONTINUUM

Though the debate for a single definition of "computer literacy" has subsided, it is important to recognize that this debate is the root of most computer activity in public schools. In general, computer literacy is meant to describe what an individual knows about and can do with a computer. Many states now have students demonstrate computer competencies as graduation requirements. However, there is little agreement about what knowledge and which skills should be mastered. The central issue is that no one body of knowledge and no single set of skills adequately describes all the levels at which an individual might be considered "literate." Descriptions of individuals with computer knowledge and abilities tend to spread along a continuum rather than falling into discrete categories (see Figure 12.1).

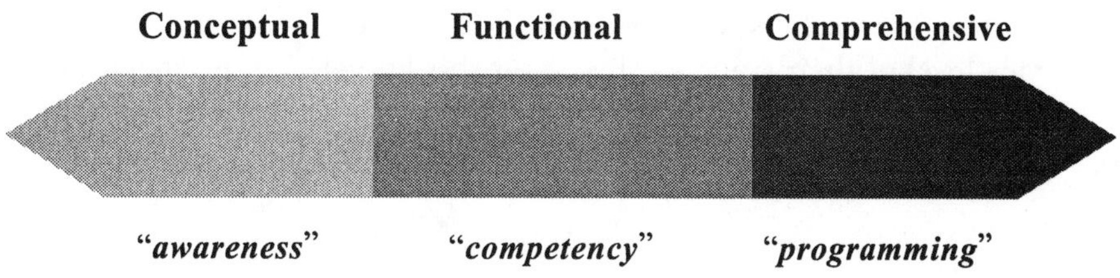

Conceptual   Functional   Comprehensive

"awareness"   *"competency"*   *"programming"*

Figure 12.1

Computer Literacy Continuum

Conceptual Literacy (Awareness)

At one extreme of the continuum are individuals who know *about* computers. They know computer terminology and concepts. Generally, they are aware of the impact computers have on society and may be able to discuss legal, philosophical, and ethical issues related to computer use. This end of the continuum is labeled "conceptual literacy" because individuals in this position have developed knowledge-based concepts *about* computers. A common title for courses that are taught at this end of the continuum is "Computer Awareness." However, many educators believe that knowledge about computers is not adequate, students must also be able to *do* something with the computer.

Functional Literacy (Competency)

The addition of some operational skills usually marks a shift toward the center of the continuum. In figure 12.1, this region is labeled "functional literacy." Individuals who fall within this area are able to use the computer to complete some task. Their skills may be limited to properly starting a computer and running a preprogrammed activity, or their skills may be so well developed that they are able to use a number of applications such as word processors, database managers, and spreadsheets to complete complex tasks. Many courses dealing with this area of the continuum have titles similar to "Computer Competence." However, some educators still believe even this level of knowledge and skill is inadequate. They would require all students to learn to program a computer.

Comprehensive Literacy (Programming)

Using the computer to complete a desired task is one level of computer literacy.

The ability to write a computer program that correctly completes a desired task would characterize an individual on the end of the continuum labeled "comprehensive literacy." These individuals are not constrained by limited options available in preprogrammed activities. Such individuals are in control of the computer, unlike individuals in other regions of the continuum who are controlled by another's design. Proponents of this position advocate that individuals achieve computer literacy only when they can understand and complete the programming process.

Computer activities should be matched to students' level of literacy.

It is important for teachers to know both their own computer literacy level and the literacy level of their students. Based on this knowledge, teachers can make appropriate decisions about their own professional development and about appropriate computer-related instructional activities for their students.

HISTORY OF COMPUTERS

Rationale

Although the study of computer history is not essential for computer operation, it is essential for understanding the nature of the technology and its implications for instruction. Historical knowledge of computers is also a critical element in a "conceptual literacy" foundation. Studying the historical development of computers also reveals two characteristics of computer technology:

▶ Computer technology is *synergistic*
▶ Computer technology is *centripetal*

Synergism generally expresses the concept that "the whole is greater than the sum of the parts." Computer technology is synergistic because it incorporates a number of other divergent technologies. Computer technology is also centripetal because it has a tendency to draw other technologies toward a common center—the computer—that offers automated control. In the review that follows and in Figure 12.2 note the number of devices and concepts developed independent of the computer that were incorporated into more efficient, more reliable, and less expensive computers.

ANCESTORS	FIRST GENERATION	THIRD AND FOURTH GENERATIONS
500 BC–Abacus	1946–Mauchley and Eckert's ENIAC	1975–Altair 8800 First micro announced
1575–Napiers's Bones	1947–Bardeen, Brattain, and Shockley invent transistor at Bell Labs	1976–Apple founded
1642–Pascal's "Pascaline"		1977–Apple II introduced
1676–Liebnitz's "Step Reckoner"	1949–von Neumann's EDVAC 1951–UNIVAC commercially available delivered to U.S. Census Bureau	1979–VisiCalc first commercially successful micro program for business
1801–Jacquard's Automated Loom	1954–General Electric First private firm to buy a computer-UNIVAC I	1981–IBM PC introduced
1822–Babbage's Difference Engine	1958–Kilby at Texas Instruments builds first integrated circuit	1984–Apple introduces Macintosh
1833–Babbage's Analytical Engine		1988–Jobs introduces NeXT
1890–Hollerith's Tabulating Machine	**SECOND GENERATION**	**FIFTH GENERATION**
1924–IBM founded from Hollerith's Tabulating Machine Co., Int'l Time Recording Co., & Dayton Scale Co.	1959–First integrated circuit chip 1960–COBOL developed	**?**
1939–Atanasoff and Berry develop a small special-purpose electronic computer	1964–BASIC developed 1967-Logo language developed	
1944–Aiken's Harvard Mark I	1972–PONG begins video game "craze"	

Figure 12.2

Computer History Highlights

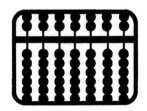

Early Ancestors

Technically, computers have been in existence less than 50 years, though their roots can be traced to humans' earliest attempt to use some device for calculating numbers. Among the most crucial contributions that illustrate the synergistic and centripetal nature of computer technology are the work of Joseph Jacquard, Charles Babbage, Ada Lovelace, Herman Hollerith, and Howard Aiken. A number of other individuals, devices, and contributions are identified in Figure 12.2.

In 1801, Joseph Jacquard, a Frenchman, developed a system for controlling the woven pattern on a textile loom. His system used a series of stiff cards, each with a different pattern of punched holes, which when used sequentially, allowed only certain threads to pass through during each step. In essence the loom, by use of the punched cards, controlled its own operation. The concept of machine control was later incorporated into the designs of an Englishman named Charles Babbage.

In the late 1800s, Charles Babbage designed a machine that contained many of the elements of modern computers.

During the 1800s Babbage designed two machines, the difference engine and the analytical engine. The designs contained many of the elements of today's computers: an input device, a storage area, a number calculator, a control unit, and an output device. For this reason, Babbage is known as the "Father of the Computer." Ada Lovelace has been called the first computer programmer for her work with Charles Babbage. Lovelace kept extensive notes on the operations of Babbage's machines and helped develop the instructions for completing calculations on the analytical engine.

Sixty years later, an American, Herman Hollerith adapted punch card technology to an electric tabulating machine, with which he completed the 1890 census for the U.S. government. Hollerith, noting the commercial applications of his tabulating device, founded the Tabulating Machine Company, which later merged with two other companies to become the International Business Machines Corporation, or IBM. In 1936, IBM would sponsor the work of Harvard professor Howard Aiken. Aiken's desire was to construct a modern equivalent of Babbage's analytical engine. In 1944, the Harvard Mark I was announced and became the first electromechanical computing device.

First Generation

While early computer developers worked on improving previous designs, researchers were developing an improved electronic switch, the vacuum tube. John Mauchley and J. Presper Eckert are traditionally credited with constructing the first fully electronic computing device, ENIAC (Electronic Numerical Integrator and Calculator), based on the new vacuum tube technology. In 1974, a federal court ruled that the Atanasoff-Berry Computer, the ABC, developed by John Vincent Atanasoff and Clifford Berry in 1939, was actually the first digital computing device.

The first generation of computers, characterized by vacuum tube switches, had many problems:

- ▶ high heat production
- ▶ great electrical consumption
- ▶ low reliability
- ▶ little flexibility

Changing the operation of the device actually called for rewiring the machine. This final fault was corrected when John von Neumann designed and built EDVAC (Electronic Discrete Variable Automatic Computer), the first computer to incorporate an internally stored program concept. Many believe that the computer age began when the first commercial computer, UNIVAC (Universal Automatic Computer), was delivered to a client on June 14, 1951.

Second Generation

Another improvement to the electronic switch ushered in the second generation of computers. William Shockley, John Bardeen, and Walter H. Brattain, working for Bell Telephone Laboratories developed the *transistor*, a switching device that would allow Bell to create a national telephone network. The device also happened to be the key for a more reliable and efficient computing device.

The launch of the Russian satellite Sputnik spurred the U.S. government to allocate considerable funds to all technologies that could support an expanded space program. It was the effort to organize and miniaturize computer technology for the confined quarters of a space capsule that lead to the next significant changes in computer design.

Third and Fourth Generations

Integrated circuits, an organized collection of transistors and other electronic circuitry on a silicon chip, became standard switching units for the third generation of computers. At the same time, the process of large-scale integration, organizing integrated circuits, made it possible to place all the circuits necessary to construct a computer on a single chip. This collection of integrated circuits became known as a *microprocessor* and is the "heart" of the current microcomputer.

Fifth Generation

No one is quite sure what will distinguish the next generation of computers. Potential traits of fifth generation computers include these, among others:

- ▶ Artificial intelligence, the computer's ability to mimic human tasks involving intelligence, imagination, and intuition

▶ Natural language interfaces that would allow the computer to understand common "everyday" language

▶ Expert systems, software that stores the knowledge and rules for applying the knowledge about a specific discipline

▶ Simultaneous processing, the machine's capacity to complete two instructions at the same time rather than sequentially

COMPUTER SIZES

Distinctions between computer categories are fading.

Sizes of Computer Systems

Computer systems are organized into three primary categories. As Table 12.1 shows, the categories are based on processor speed, memory size, number of simultaneous users, and cost. Each of the two extreme categories have splintered into additional variations. It should also be noted that distinctions between categories are fading; processor speeds and memory capacities, especially at the low end, are increasing constantly.

Table 12.1 Comparison of Computer System Characteristics

Size Designation	Processor Speed	Memory Size	Number of Users	Cost
Supercomputer	fastest	unlimited	50+	$2 million+
Mainframe	extremely fast	unlimited	50+	$1 million+
Minicomputer	very fast	limited	2–50	$.5 million+
Microcomputer	fast	very limited	1	$1,000+
Laptop/ Notebook	fast	very limited	1	under $1,000

Mainframe computers are the first primary category. These computers have the fastest processing speeds, use such techniques as "virtual memory" to give all users what appears to be limitless memory, are designed to be used by large numbers of users, and cost millions of dollars. *Supercomputers* are the fastest mainframes with the most processing power. Mainframe computers and supercomputers require special working environments including additional air conditioning and electricity.

The term *minicomputer* actually refers to computer systems that fall within the middle category. Minicomputers use somewhat slower processors than do mainframes; have extensive but limited memory, are designed to support a moderate number of users (around 50 users, depending on the application), and generally can be purchased for less than $1 million.

Microcomputers are the third primary category. They generally use slower processors than do minicomputers, have limited amounts of memory, are designed for a single user, and can be purchased for about $1,000. Currently, microcomputers are designed to facilitate direct networking among users. A subdivision of the microcomputer category includes *laptop*, *notebook*, or *palmtop* computers (also known as "personal digital assistants"). These computers have the same features of microcomputers with the added benefits of portability and battery power.

Clear distinctions between computer categories will continue to blur due to technological innovations; however, the microcomputer—the first computer designed for a single user—has revolutionized the way people think about and work with computers.

The mechanical and electronic components of a computer system are called *hardware*. Regardless of size, a computer system contains five basic hardware components:

▶ central processing unit
▶ internal memory
▶ input device
▶ output device
▶ storage device

HARDWARE COMPONENTS

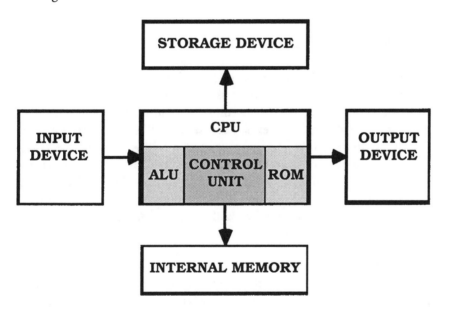

Figure 12.3

Computer Hardware Components

Central Processing Unit (CPU)

The "brain" of any computer system is the CPU. The CPU is the center of all the computer's activities. It consists of three primary parts: the control unit, which gives directions to all other parts of the computer; the arithmetic/logic unit (ALU), which is used for completing mathematical operations and logical comparisons; and read only memory (ROM), which contains permanent instructions built into the computer by the manufacturer. ROM cannot be changed by the user and is not lost when the user turns off the computer.

Internal Memory

Computer storage is measured in kilobytes and megabytes.

Closely related to the CPU is the computer's internal memory, a number of electronic switches (integrated circuits) that allow the computer to temporarily store data, intermediate calculation values, and instructions. Often referred to as random access memory, RAM, the size of this area is one way to measure the capacity and power of a microcomputer. Computer storage is measured in *kilobytes* (K) or *megabytes* (MB). A megabyte is 1000 kilobytes. A kilobyte or 1K of memory would store about 1,000 characters or numbers; therefore, a computer with 640K RAM has less capacity and less "power" than a computer with 4MB RAM, which has less capacity and less "power" than a computer with 16MB RAM, and so on. One other characteristic of RAM is that it is *volatile,* which means it is only temporary, the information stored in RAM is lost when the user turns off the computer.

Input Devices

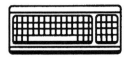

The primary function of a computer system's input device is to allow the user to communicate with the central processor, to enter data or instructions, or to respond to computer directions. The most common input device on a microcomputer is the keyboard. However, because the CPU is primarily a collection of electronic switches, any operation that can be converted to an electronic impulse can be entered. For example, speech can be converted to electronic impulses through a microphone, so special input devices designed for speech input have been developed. Other devices such as joysticks, light pens, touch-sensitive screens, and graphics tablets have been created to facilitate input.

One of the most popular input devices is the *mouse*, a device that converts physical movement into computer input. A mouse contains two important components: the rolling ball, which translates the user's movement of the mouse on the desktop to a pointer (generally an insertion point displayed on the computer monitor) for movement on the computer monitor; and one or more mouse buttons, which the user presses to indicate a selection.

Basic mouse activities include *pointing*—moving the mouse until the pointer on the computer monitor is appropriately oriented; *clicking*—pressing and releasing the mouse button while the pointer is located on the desired element; *double clicking*—two "clicks" of the mouse button in rapid succession; and *dragging*—pressing the mouse button down and holding it down while the user moves the mouse. Each of these activities may have multiple effects, depending on the software installed on the computer.

An adaptation of the computer mouse, popular on portable laptop, notebook, and palmtop computers, is the *trackball*. Basically an inverted mouse, the trackball may be installed directly into the keyboard area of the computer. Because the housing must remain stationary, the rolling element is exposed for direct user manipulation. The movements of the trackball are translated to pointer movement on the computer monitor. Buttons are located in close proximity to the trackball to replicate the functions of mouse buttons. Trackballs are especially popular on portable computers intended for use in tight spaces.

Output Devices

Converting electronic impulses from the CPU into some form that the user can understand is the primary function of a computer system's output device. The output device shows the user what is happening. Two output devices most commonly associated with microcomputers are monitors and printers.

Computer monitors are usually classified according to the number of colors and the resolution displayed. Resolution has to do with how well defined and how sharp the images appear on a screen; the higher the resolution, the clearer the image. **CRTs** (cathode ray tubes) are generally low-resolution monochrome displays of white, green, or amber characters on a black background. **VDTs** (video display terminals) are generally high-resolution full color displays.

Printers also fall into categories. Two popular categories describe the method used to create the printed image—impact and nonimpact printers. Dot matrix and daisy wheel printers are good examples of impact printers. They create the printed image by striking the paper. *Dot matrix printers* strike the paper with small pins, placing dots of ink in a grid pattern to produce the desired character, similar to the way lights on a scoreboard are used to display numbers. *Daisy wheel printers* create images in much the same way that a typewriter creates images. The entire shape of the character is created with a single strike of the printing device. Due to the mechanical nature of moving both the printing element and the striking element, impact printers tend to be noisy and slow.

Nonimpact printers, such as laser and ink jet printers, do not require a print head or daisy wheel to strike the paper. As indicated by the name, *laser printers* use a high-intensity light source to create a high-quality printed image. Because of their print quality, speed, and quiet operation, laser printers are the "printer of choice" today. A lower-cost alternative to a laser printer is an *ink jet printer*, which is similar to a dot matrix printer, but rather than striking the paper, ink jet printers spray small dots of ink onto the paper. Ink jet printers also offer more affordable color printing than is currently available through color laser printers.

As with input devices, special output devices have been developed to meet the unique needs of specific users. Braille printers, large print displays, and speech synthesizers have been developed for the visually impaired. Color laser printers and multicolored plotters have been developed for high-quality color and graphics production.

Storage Devices

Because the computer's internal memory is volatile and limited, some kind of external or bulk storage device is usually connected to a microcomputer to facilitate the permanent storage of programs and data. Data and programs are stored on magnetic surfaces in a diskette or hard disk format. These devices, called *drives,* come in three primary forms: the most common form is the floppy disk drive, which "reads" and "writes" information on a 5.25" diskette (a 3.5" diskette is popular with newer microcomputer models); the second form is a hard disk drive, which stores many megabytes of data on a rigid surface completely enclosed in an airtight environment. Cartridge drives, a magnetic drive system that uses removable hard disks, are becoming more affordable and more common. The third form of bulk storage today is a CD-ROM drive, which reads data by laser, similar to an audio CD. Compact disc-read only memory (CD-ROMs) can store large amounts of data but lack a means to be modified. Other optical formats, such as write once, read many (WORM) drives, are being developed for microcomputer use. Optical drives currently available are expensive, but prices are being lowered as technology continues to advance. The tape drive is no longer used extensively with microcomputers except to make a backup copy of the contents of a hard disk drive.

SOFTWARE COMPONENTS

In order for the hardware components of a computer system to operate properly, instructions must be given; that is the function of software. It is helpful for teachers to understand that the instructions given to computers via software work in layers (Figure 12.4). Each succeeding layer is dependent on the previous layer for completing its designed task. Certain specific activities are performed within specific software layers. Knowing the purpose of each layer and the types of errors likely to occur there helps teachers determine what activities should be accomplished at each layer and helps teachers comprehend error messages, diagnose problems, and (in some instances) correct minor malfunctions.

Read Only Memory (ROM)

In some ways, ROM, the first layer of software illustrated in figure 12.4, is a hybrid of hardware and software. Although it is permanently "wired" at the time of manufacturing, which makes it hardware, it contains instructions, which makes it software as well. In most cases, the instructions contained in ROM are limited and are normally invisible to the operator. However, some manufacturers place other instructions in ROM. Many laptop and notebook computers have application programs in ROM. Because ROM is essentially electronic, the possibilities for error and malfunction are minute. The primary function of ROM is to give the CPU the initial instructions for getting the system started and for locating the next layer of instructions, usually located on a hard disk or on a diskette in the first disk drive.

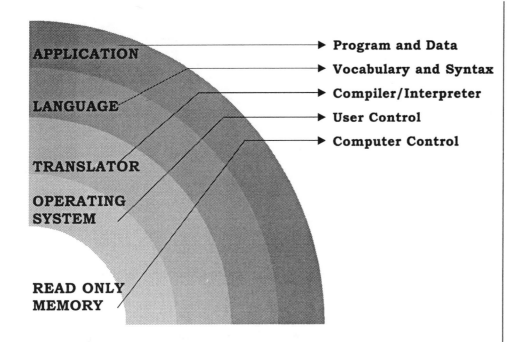

Figure 12.4

Layers of Software

Operating System

Because this layer of software usually resides on either a hard disk or diskette, it is sometimes called the *disk operating system* (DOS). The primary function of this second layer of software is to give control of the system to the user. Preparing blank diskettes for use (a process called *formatting* or *initializing*); copying diskettes; and copying, deleting, and organizing files are the most common activities completed at this software layer. The important task of organizing files on a hard disk is discussed in the next chapter.

Operating systems have taken two primary forms. The first form, the command-driven system, requires an operator to enter an appropriate command when the computer displays a *system prompt*. Users have to memorize or refer to lengthy manuals to select appropriate commands. Command-driven operating systems, such as the original versions of PC DOS, MS-DOS, and systems such as UNIX, are illustrated in Figure 12.5.

A computer's operating system performs basic tasks for the user.

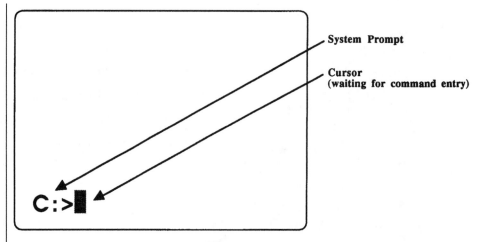

Figure 12.5

Sample Screen for Command-driven Operating Systems

Apple's Macintosh computer dramatically altered operating system design and popularized the second form of operating systems. The Macintosh computer introduced an operating system incorporating a *graphic user interface (GUI)*. The GUI uses representative graphic images displayed on the screen, called *icons*, to manage various components of the system. The operator uses the mouse to move the icons on the screen to symbolically execute a desired activity. What can't be displayed graphically is usually handled through a menu of options. A sample GUI screen appears in Figure 12.6.

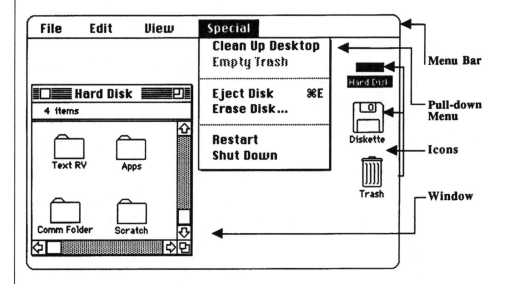

Figure 12.6

Sample Screen for GUI-based Operating Systems

The popularity of GUI-based operating systems inspired the Microsoft Corporation to create software that would work in conjunction with command-driven operating systems to implement the functionality of GUI-based systems. The software, known as "Windows" (or the newer version, "Windows NT"), actually functions as the operating system. Icons, pull-down menus, mouse input, and multiple applications working in multiple windows simultaneously are some of the GUI features that are incorporated into the Windows environment. Figure 12.7 shows a sample Windows screen.

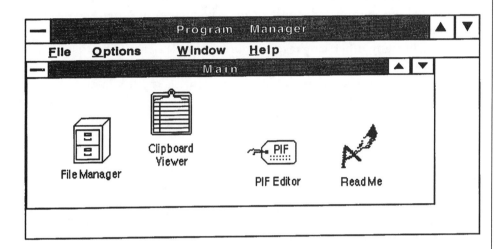

Figure 12.7

Sample Windows Screen

Errors at the operating system layer, referred to as *system errors*, are among the most troublesome because it is frequently necessary to restart the computer to overcome the system error.

Translators

If an operator desires to start or write a computer program, the program must be translated. The instructions for completing this task are contained in the software layer known as the translator. There are two primary types of translators:

▶ Interpreters translate one instruction, complete the instruction, and then translate the next instruction.
▶ Compilers translate all of the instructions first and then begin to complete the instructions from the beginning to the end.

The type of translator used depends on the programming language selected and each type of translator has its advantages and disadvantages. A program translated by an interpreter is usually easier to debug because the translator stops the program at the first instruction that can't be completed; however, because the translator must translate each instruction every time the program is repeated, these programs take longer to run.

Interpreted programs debug easily, but compiled programs run faster.

Compilers on the other hand, have already translated all of the instructions so they run much faster; the primary disadvantage of compilers is that the debugging process tends to be more complicated because the operator must correct all possible problems before any of the program will work.

Languages

All instructions given to a computer by an operator are entered in a particular *language* and the appropriate translator must be present in order to convert the programming language into instructions the CPU can complete. Programming languages, like any other language, comprise two elements. The first element is a defined *vocabulary*. Each computer language has a set of words and symbols that when translated provide the computer with specific instructions. Although all languages have basically the same structures, identical vocabulary words may not be used. The second element of a computer language is the rules that govern how the vocabulary must be organized for accurate communication: *syntax*.

One of the most frequent and frustrating error messages for novice programmers is the ambiguous *syntax error*. Usually this message means that one of the language's rules concerning spelling, spacing, punctuation, and/or organization has been broken, but it does not indicate exactly what the problem is, leaving the user to determine the actual error.

High-level programming languages are easier for novice users to learn.

Computer languages are divided into categories based on their similarity to natural language:

- ▶ **High-level** languages use common words and have fewer syntax restrictions.
- ▶ **Low-level** languages use more abstract vocabulary and have very precise syntax patterns.
- ▶ **Machine-level** language is what the CPU can recognize, all languages are eventually translated to this form.

There are many programming languages and there are many dialects for some of the more popular languages. Each computer language has unique characteristics and capabilities. Selecting the appropriate programming language often depends on the type of application being created.

Many teachers and students wanting to learn programming have used *BASIC* (Beginners All-Purpose Symbolic Instruction Code) because it was designed to be a relatively simple language to learn and use. Other educators have advocated the use of *Logo*, a language that facilitates experimentation and is noted for its procedural orientation and graphic "turtle." *Pascal* has been adopted in many educational settings because it is considered a structured high-level language; that is, its syntax is somewhat more stringent than other high-level languages, yet it retains the use of familiar and descriptive vocabulary. And students who want to program in the business world often learn the C language, or its newer version, C++.

Applications

The final layer of software is called the *application*. This layer performs tasks that the user actually wants to accomplish by using the computer; it may be an educational game, a word processor, calculations, or a tutorial program. Some teachers and students will learn to program a computer that will require them to become familiar with the other software layers, but most teachers and students are better acquainted with application software. Though all of the layers are present, most commercial packages are designed to move the user directly from the operating system to the application, making the intermediate layers virtually invisible.

Most teachers and students spend computer time running application packages.

All application packages comprise two integral parts. The first is the program itself, the instructions the computer follows to complete the desired application. The second part is the unique data entered by the user, including everything from joystick movement in an arcade-type game to multipage text documents created using a word processor.

SUGGESTED ACTIVITIES

1. Using a scale from 0 to 10 (0 would mean absolutely no "conceptual literacy" and 10 would indicate that one has "comprehensive literacy," meaning one is competent in using a least one programming language), rate your own level of computer literacy and justify your rating. What steps do you need to take in order to improve your own computer literacy? What level of literacy should be required of all teachers? What level should be required of all students?

2. Research and report on one of the major historical developments of computer technology (Figure 12.2 and your instructor can provide topics) or compile a list of current and anticipated developments. Do the developments illustrate either the synergistic or centripetal nature of computer technology?

3. Review the product literature of several popular microcomputers used in education. Compare characteristics of the five hardware components of each system. How do prices and capabilities compare?

4. Identify and read about a computer programming language. For what special applications was the language designed? What are its unique characteristics? Is it interpreted or compiled?

5. Compare two operating systems available for microcomputers. How does each allow the user to complete the following tasks: format or initialize a blank diskette, copy a diskette, copy and delete a file, and organize files? What are the unique characteristics of each system?

Chapter 13

MICROCOMPUTER OPERATION

PURPOSES

- ▶ To review the hardware components of a microcomputer system and to identify how they are connected
- ▶ To load and use the operating system to complete the following tasks: obtain a display of the contents of a disk, initialize or format a blank diskette, copy a diskette, copy and delete a file
- ▶ To load and run preprogrammed diskettes

INTRODUCTION

Many brands and models of microcomputers are being used in public schools. Among the most popular are computers manufactured by Apple, IBM, and Tandy/Radio Shack. Many other compatible computers are designed to work like any one of the major brand-name computers. Unfortunately, no two systems are exactly alike, which makes it virtually impossible to give step-by-step instructions for each activity for each system. However, with the following generic instructions, a manual for the particular computer system, and a little patience, a novice user should be able to complete all of the tasks described in this chapter. For later reference, educators may want to write the specific instructions for a particular computer in the margins beside the generic instructions.

CHECKING THE SETUP

It is always a good idea to become familiar with the physical arrangement and connections of a microcomputer system. Microcomputers are similar to home entertainment centers: They can be purchased as a single unit with all elements housed in a single cabinet, or they may be purchased as individual components that must be properly connected in order to operate correctly. Take a few moments to locate, identify, and check the items described in this section.

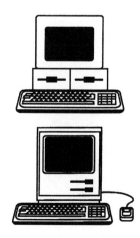

Central Processing Unit (CPU)

Usually located in a flat rectangular cabinet, the CPU may also contain the keyboard and/or disk drives. Regardless, this unit contains the microprocessor, internal memory, and usually a speaker. It will have a power cord, which may be detachable, and a Power switch. In addition, any other pieces of equipment that must be connected to the computer system are usually connected to this unit; consequently, on the back of this unit one should find a number of different kinds of connection points. When connecting new equipment or moving the CPU, it is best to unplug all devices to prevent damage to the electronic components of the system.

Monitor

A computer monitor usually sits on top of or behind the CPU. Monitors are usually connected to the processor through a single cable. Possible labels for this connection would be "video in" on the monitor and "video out" on the processor cabinet. Some monitors draw their power directly through the CPU; however, most monitors have independent power cables that are plugged into an electrical outlet. If this is the case, these monitors also have an independent Power switch to operate when the system is powered on. Most monitors also have brightness, contrast, horizontal, and vertical controls.

The instructor should check cabling connections of the CPU, monitor, keyboard, disk drives, and printer.

Keyboard

If the keyboard is not housed with the CPU, it is usually connected by means of a coiled expansion cable that looks similar to a telephone cord. This permits maximum flexibility to position the keyboard relative to the user, monitor, processor, and other devices.

Disk Drives

Most computer systems are configured with at least one floppy disk drive, others may have two floppy disk drives, and still others may have a single floppy disk drive and a hard disk drive. If these units are not housed in the cabinet with the CPU, they are usually connected to the processor via a multi pin cable. Some external hard disk drives that do not reside in the CPU housing may also have an additional power cord and Power switch.

When more than one disk drive is present without a hard disk, it is important to know which drive the computer will access first, that drive is called the *default drive*. It is the drive in which the operating system disk should be placed. Most manufacturers label the drives 1 and 2 or A and B. If the disk drives on a computer are not labeled, it is common practice to configure systems so that the default drive is oriented on top of or to the left of the other disk drive. It is also common practice to configure computer systems to access a hard disk drive before accessing any connected floppy disk drives, so the operating system and other major programs are stored on the hard disk.

Printer

Not every microcomputer system will be connected to a printer; however, if a printer is part of the system, be sure the cable between the computer and printer is securely attached. All printers have independent power cables and power switches. Most printers have another button labeled Select or On-line that users press to temporarily disconnect the printer from the computer without physically removing the cable. When the operator wants the printer to perform independently from the computer the Select/On-line button is off. Then the operator can use other buttons on the printer to advance the paper few lines or to the top of the next page. When the operator wants to resume printing from the computer, the Select/On-line button is switched on.

Computer keyboards are similar to typewriter keyboards in appearance; however, it is beneficial to know the unique characteristics of the computer keyboard.

KEYBOARD ORIENTATION

Return/Enter Key

Usually a large key located to the right of the alphabetical character keys, the Enter or Return key has two functions depending on the software being used. In most instances, pressing the Return/Enter key indicates that the user has entered a command or has responded to a computer prompt and is ready for the computer to continue. In some programs, particularly word processing programs, pressing Return/Enter moves the cursor to a new line and to the left-hand margin, just like the carriage return of an electric typewriter.

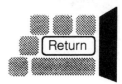

Space Bar

Located on the lowest row of keys, the Space Bar moves the cursor one position to the right; however, unlike a typewriter, computers consider the space created by using the Space Bar a character. Therefore, spaces can be inserted and deleted just like other computer characters.

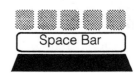

Shift Key

Identical Shift keys are located on each side of the alphabetical keypad. Pressing and holding this key while pressing another key prints the uppercase character on alphabet keys or the upper character on keys that display two characters. On most computers, the Caps Lock key, usually located on the left side of the alphabetical keypad, only locks the alphabetical characters; for two-character keys, the Shift key must still be pressed in order to obtain the upper character. This is not the way most traditional typewriters function. Some older model microcomputers do not have upper- and lowercase capabilities.

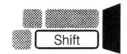

Cursor Movement Keys

Left, Right, Up, and Down arrows are generally located on the lower right side of the keyboard. Pressing these keys moves the cursor in the direction of the arrow. Generally, this cursor movement does not affect the data entered. On some keyboards, these keys are incorporated into the numeric keypad. If this is the case, another key (usually the Number Lock key) will have to be pressed in order to activate and/or deactivate the cursor movement function.

Delete/Backspace Key

Usually located in the upper right-hand corner of the alphabetical keypad, the Del or Backspace key may also use a left arrow as part of the label. Unlike the cursor movement keys, this key deletes or removes a character each time it is depressed.

Escape Key (Esc)

Usually located in the upper left-hand corner of the alphabetical keypad, this key is generally used to stop or interrupt computer processing. Frequently, computer programs use the ESC key to return the user to a menu of choices.

Control (Ctrl)/Alternative (Alt)/Option Keys

All of these keys may not be present on a single keyboard; however, it is common to have at least one. These keys represent nonprinting characters that give the computer special commands. These keys function in much the same way that the Shift key functions; the operator must press and hold the Control key down while pressing a second key.

For example, holding the Control key down and pressing the S key usually stops a program listing; and holding down the Control key and pressing the C key is frequently used to give the computer the signal to continue. The other two keys function exactly the same way. Usually the computer's manual or the program's manual provides a list of these multi key commands.

Reset Key

Because of the nature of the Reset key, it is usually located away from the central keyboard configuration. This key is generally used to restart the computer once a malfunction has occurred. It is used as a last resort when all other options for making the computer program operate correctly have been exhausted. Any data previously entered into the computer's temporary memory (RAM) is lost when this key is pressed.

Function/Programmable Function Keys (F/PF keys)

Some keyboards provide an additional row of keys located above the alphabetical keypad. These keys, usually labeled F1-F15, are known as *function keys*. Some software packages provide the user with single keystroke shortcuts for various commands, the shortcuts are activated by pressing the appropriate function key. When the software permits the user to assign specific activities to a desired key, the keys are called *programmable function keys*. In conjunction with the Shift, Control, Alternate (Alt), and Option keys described previously, these 15 keys can make as many as 75 commands available from the keyboard.

Confusing Keys

All microcomputers expect precise input; therefore, certain practices that are acceptable when typing are not acceptable when using a computer keyboard. Avoid using the following typewriter equivalents:

- ▶ Capital letter I for number one
- ▶ Lowercase L for number one
- ▶ Capital letter 0 for number zero

The process of starting the computer and loading the operating system is called "booting DOS" or "booting the system." Because most microcomputer systems are now sold with internal hard disks, it is common practice to load the operating system on the hard disk and designate the hard disk as the default drive or the startup device (usually drive C for PC compatibles). The operating system is automatically loaded when the microcomputer is turned on. However, on occasion, the hard disk may become damaged, preventing normal startup procedures; therefore, all educators should also know how to start their microcomputers from diskettes. Whether an instructor starts the system from a hard disk or a diskette, two general procedures may be followed.

BOOTING THE OPERATING SYSTEM

Cold Boot

Starting the computer and operating system when the power to the central processing unit is off is called a *cold boot*. Follow these steps for a cold boot:

1. Turn on all peripheral equipment (monitors, printers, and so on).

2. Turn on the CPU. The system prompt or opening screen should appear shortly. The *system prompt* is a special character displayed by the computer indicating that the operating system is loaded and waiting for a command.

The operating system manual will identify the appropriate system prompt. Some newer operating systems will display a menu of choices available, rather than a system prompt. Other operating systems will use graphics to indicate available choices; a flashing cursor on the screen indicates that the computer is waiting for the user to enter the next instruction.

If the system is being started from a diskette:

1. Select a diskette that contains the operating system for the computer to be started. These disks have names such as "system master," "system disk," "startup disk," and "DOS disk."

2. Turn on all peripheral equipment (monitors, printers, and so on).

3. Verify that the *In Use* light of the disk drive is off. Never insert or remove a diskette while the light is on.

4. Open the disk drive. If the microcomputer system has two floppy disk drives, use the default drive marked 1 or A (usually located to the left of or on top of the second disk drive). Generally, 3.5" drives do not have to be opened.

5. Remove the diskette from its envelope or holder.

6. With the label facing upward and your thumb on the label, gently insert the diskette into the slot of the disk drive. The open oval of a 5.25" diskette or the metal part of a 3.5" diskette should enter the drive first. Do not force or bend the diskette.

7. Once the diskette is inside, close the disk drive.

8. Turn on the CPU. The system prompt or graphic display should appear shortly. (Some manufacturers instruct the user to turn on the CPU before inserting diskettes. Check the operating system manual for specific instructions.)

Warm Boot

Restarting the computer and operating system while the power to the CPU remains on is called a *warm boot*.

1. If the system is being started from a diskette, be sure that a diskette containing the operating system for the computer to be restarted is in the default drive marked 1 or A. Verify that the *In Use* light of the disk drive is off. Never insert or remove a diskette while the light is on.

2. The second step must be performed using instructions from the operating system manual. Some systems require the user to press two or more keys simultaneously, for example: the Control, Alternate, and Delete keys (PCs) or the Control, Command (Open Apple), and Reset keys (Apples). Other systems may allow the operator to directly enter a command,

whereas still other systems permit the operator to press a single reset button.

3. The system prompt or opening screen should appear shortly.

As mentioned in Chapter 12, a crucial task of the operating system is to help users to organize data stored on hard disks and diskettes. All data stored by a computer are stored as files, either *application files* (lists of commands to be executed by the computer), or *data files,* such as a document created by a word processor. The operating system is responsible for the actual physical storage of these files on hard disks or diskettes. Likewise, the operating system is responsible for the logical organization of the files. All operating systems provide methods for listing the names of the files stored on a hard disk or diskette. The 100⁺ megabyte hard disks currently popular could contain thousands of files. Listing the titles of thousands of files would be a logical nightmare for most users; therefore, both command-driven and GUI-based operating systems have created hierarchical organization systems for files stored on hard disks and diskettes.

ORGANIZING FILES ON HARD DISKS AND DISKETTES

Directories and Subdirectories

Command-driven operating systems organize hard disks and diskettes into logical units called *directories*. Directories can contain files and other directories, creating a hierarchical directory/subdirectory structure. The operator enters a command to list the contents of a specified directory. Other commands are available to make, change, and remove directories. Users should be careful when they remove directories to avoid accidentally deleting important files. Because the microcomputer will only access a single drive at any one time, the operator will usually have to enter the command and a special designated drive number or letter in order to view the contents of diskettes or directories in other drives. A sample directory display is shown in Figure 13.1.

```
Volume in drive a has no label
Directory of a:\

PARENT      LTR       1234          9-9-93        8:32 p
CONFIG      SYS      38554         10-13-92       9:40 a
LOTUS       <DIR>
FORMAT      COM      12206         10-13-92       9:43 a
SYS         COM       5045         10-13-92      10:00 a
HMWK1       TXT       2468         12-7-93       11:00 a

5 File(s)      667648 bytes free

c:>dir a:
```

Figure 13.1

Sample Directory Display from a Command-Driven Operating System

Folders and Files

GUI-based operating systems use the icon of a folder to represent the logical units of hard disks and diskettes. A folder is the same logical structure as the directory in a command-driven operating system. Folders can contain files and additional folders, creating a hierarchical organization of files. GUI-based operating systems generally provide pull-down menu or keyboard options to create new folders. Files are placed inside or removed from folders by dragging the appropriate file (or folder) icons into or out of the folder, the operating system makes the necessary adjustments to the logical organization of the hard disk or diskette. Individual files or entire folders can be removed by dragging the appropriate icon to the trashcan icon. Exercise caution when folders are removed to prevent the accidental removal of important files.

To view the contents of a hard disk, diskette, or folder icon, the user generally moves the mouse until the pointer is directly on top of the desired icon, then presses the mouse button twice in rapid succession (double-clicks it). This action selects the icon and then issues an open command. The contents of the icon are displayed in a window on the monitor. Figure 13.2 shows a sample display.

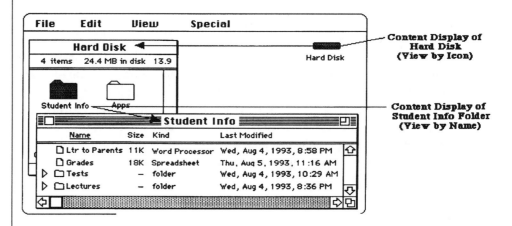

Figure 13.2

Sample GUI-based Display of a Folder's Contents

Current operating systems allow the user to specify a variety of ways to view the contents of hard disks and diskettes, or directories and folders: by name, by type of file, by size of file, by date of last modification, and others. As mentioned earlier, the Windows environment developed by Microsoft provides many of the GUI-based operating system features for command-driven operating systems.

BACKING UP A HARD DISK

Because of the critical nature of the files stored on hard disks, operating systems provide the user with commands, menu options, or other methods of making a copy of the entire contents—a *backup*—of a hard disk. The copies may be made to another hard disk, multiple diskettes, or even magnetic tape or cartridges. The primary difference between a hard disk backup and copies of all the files on a hard disk is that a hard disk backup retains the organizational structure of the original and can be created or restored with a single command or operation. The backup command also improves the efficiency of the backup operation by providing the user with various options including, but not limited to, selecting files created since the last backup or selecting files modified since the last backup, or both.

Frequently users choose not to back up application files, which tend to be large and can be reinstalled easily. Generally, it is a good idea to include in a backup any file that the user would not want to recreate and to make multiple backups of critical files. Never work with a file's backup copy. Use the backup copy only to restore the original file or to make a copy of the file. After experiencing a program or hard disk failure, many users have resorted to working on their backup copies, without making additional backups, only to experience a subsequent program or hard disk failure that destroys their only remaining copy.

General Backup Procedures

Using a second external hard disk, removable cartridge drive, magnetic tape drive, or optical drive is becoming more popular with microcomputer users because of the increased capacity of hard disks and the decreased cost of the additional equipment required. Currently, due to hardware and funding limitations, most educators back up hard disks to diskettes. Prior to initiating the backup procedure, the user should prepare (format) an adequate number of blank formatted diskettes. Once the command or menu-option is selected and the files to be included in the backup are identified, the computer will begin copying files from the hard disk to diskettes. The computer will indicate when the current diskette is "full" and will instruct the user to insert another blank formatted diskette. It is helpful—sometimes critical—to identify the sequential order of the diskettes and the date of the backup on the diskette labels. Backup diskettes should be locked or "write-protected" (discussed later in this chapter) to prevent accidental erasure.

Despite the large capacity of today's hard disks, diskettes are still a popular medium for transferring data between nonnetworked computers and for making backup copies of important files. Educators should learn to prepare blank diskettes for use.

Diskette Density

Technology continues to improve the efficiency of storing data on magnetic surfaces. As a result, diskettes must be designed to work with the most current hardware capabilities. One of the first changes made to 5.25" diskettes was a change from *single-sided* (SS) to *double-sided* (DS) diskettes. The DS designation certifies that both sides of the diskette surface meet industry standards for data storage. The computer operator must manually remove, flip, and reinsert a double-sided diskette to allow the computer to read data stored on the second side.

A second change for 5.25" diskettes was that from *single-density* (SD) to *double-density* (DD) capacities. The DD designation certifies that the magnetic surface meets industry standards for increased data storage capacity and increased reliability. Unless specified by the manufacturer, it is prudent to use double-sided, double-density (DSDD) 5.25" diskettes.

Disk drives for 3.5" diskettes have changed also. Originally designed to hold approximately 800 kilobytes of data, 3.5" diskettes have been redesigned to hold almost 1.5 megabytes of data because of improved disk drive design. The new diskettes, called *high-density* diskettes, have an additional square hole in the corner opposite the "write-protect" lock and an "HD" embossed in the diskette housing.

The multiple forms of diskettes have created some compatibility problems. Generally, older disk drives cannot read diskettes formatted with the high-density structure; however, the new drives are able to read both the low- and high-density structures. The most frustrating problem is when a high-density diskette is formatted in an older drive as an 800K diskette, then is inserted in a newer drive. The new drives are designed to "read" the second square hole in the high density diskette housing and look for the new high-density structure on the surface of the diskette. Because the diskette has the older 800K format, the computer fails to recognize the diskette. The computer may indicate that the disk is unreadable and ask the user to reinitialize. Placing a small piece of tape over the second square hole opposite the "write protect" lock is a simple solution to the problem; the new drive can no longer "read" the second hole and will expect to find a diskette with the lower 800K structure.

INITIALIZING OR FORMATTING BLANK DISKETTES

The process of preparing the magnetic surface of a diskette for use by the microcomputer system is called *initializing* or *formatting* a diskette. When a user purchases blank diskettes, the diskettes may be used in any disk drive that will accept that particular size. However, each operating system, and some disk drives, prepare the magnetic surface of the diskettes differently. That is why diskettes prepared for use on Apple computers cannot be read by PCs and vice versa.

If diskettes are reformatted for the proper operating system, they may be used in a different machine, but the reformatting process completely erases the contents of a diskette. Microcomputers that use the same operating system can usually read diskettes created on different machines. Recent developments in both disk drive hardware and operating system software are making it possible for a single drive to read multiple formats.

Various operating systems have different ways of starting the initialization process. Menu-driven systems list formatting as a menu option. Command-driven systems usually have a Format or Init command. The Macintosh's operating system automatically recognizes an unformatted diskette and prompts the user for directions, as illustrated in the dialog box in Figure 13.3.

Specific instructions for each operating system should appear in the user's manual. Some programs create unique data diskette formats. When this is the case, formatting a data diskette is one of the program's options.

There are two primary purposes for copying diskettes:

▶ the legal duplication of purchased software to create a "working copy" as described in the program's documentation
▶ to create a second copy of valuable data called a backup

The illegal duplication of computer software for distribution among other users, either teachers or students, is a critical issue that must be addressed by computer-using educators.

CAUTION! READ LICENSE AGREEMENTS

Most commercial programs include printed license agreements containing terms which govern the number of copies which can be made. In general, most packages are sold to be used on a single machine, even if multiple copies of the program can be made. Many software publishers interested in the public school market are making it more financially feasible to purchase multiple copies of a single program. However, educators should not compromise the issue; they should not use, nor should they allow their students to use, illegally duplicated software.

COPYING DISKETTES

Like music, books, and films, computer programs are copyrighted and should not be copied illegally.

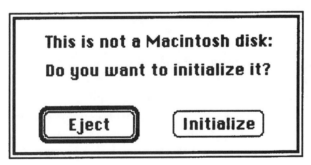

Figure 13.3

Sample of an Initialize Diskette Dialog Box

General Procedures

To complete the copying process, the operating system must know which diskette, folder, or directory contains the material to be copied and which will receive the copy. The diskette, folder, or directory to be copied is usually called the "source" and the receiving one is called the "target." Through a typed command, selected menu option, or a manipulated icon, the operating system is instructed to copy the contents of the source diskette to the target. In single disk drive systems, this procedure will require the user to "swap" or insert

Diskettes, like video and audio cassettes, have write-protect tabs to prevent accidental deletions.

source and target diskettes alternately into the same disk drive. Care should be taken not to confuse the two diskettes during the process.

One way to prevent the accidental erasure of the source diskette, regardless of the number of drives used in the copying process, is to write protect the diskette. Write protecting a diskette is a simple procedure (see Figure 13.4). When a 5.25" diskette is placed in its protective sleeve so that the label is visible, on the right-hand side of the diskette about an inch below the upper right-hand corner is a small square notch. When this notch is open, as it customarily is, material on the diskette can be erased. When this notch is covered with one of the "write-protect" tabs packaged with new diskettes, the material on the diskette cannot be altered or erased.

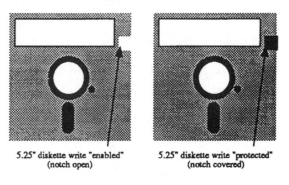

5.25" diskette write "enabled"
(notch open)

5.25" diskette write "protected"
(notch covered)

Figure 13.4

Write Protecting a 5.25" Diskette

Write protecting a 3.5" diskette is equally simple (see Figure 13.5). Looking at the back of the diskette with the metal portion of the diskette closest to the operator, a small black plastic square appears in a rectangular track in the upper left-hand corner. When the small plastic square is in the lower half of the rectangular track, material on the disk can be erased. When the small plastic square is moved to the upper portion of the rectangular track, exposing a hole that passes through the entire diskette, material on the diskette cannot be altered or erased.

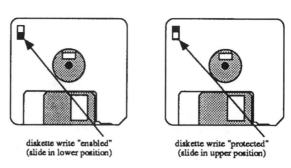

diskette write "enabled"
(slide in lower position)

diskette write "protected"
(slide in upper position)

Figure 13.5

Write Protecting a 3.5" Diskette

Two other operating system commands that are extremely helpful have names such as Copy or Duplicate and Delete, Erase, or Remove. These commands make it possible for the user to deal with individual files or groups of files. Material that is no longer of value can be removed from a diskette, creating more space for current activity. Important files can be copied to a backup diskette in case the original file is damaged or lost.

Copying a file usually requires identifying the name of the file to be copied and the disk drive or directory in which the diskette containing the file resides. Then the user must designate which disk drive contains the diskette on which the copy should be made. Frequently, a user may alter the filename during the copying process.

Deleting a file is generally as simple as selecting or naming the file, entering a Delete command, and indicating the appropriate disk drive or directory. Many operating systems will ask the user to verify the command before completing the operation. Care should be exercised, once a file is deleted it is difficult for a novice user to restore.

Although diskettes make it relatively easy to store large amounts of data and working copies of programs, like cassettes, they are a vulnerable medium. Inside both 5.25" and 3.5" diskettes is a thin plastic disk coated with magnetic material that is similar to the surface of recording tape.

The main difference between the two types of diskettes is storage capacity, the 3.5" disk can hold almost four times the amount of data. Although the rigid construction and metal slide provide better protection for the 3.5" diskette, the following suggestions are offered for handling all forms of magnetic disks.

- ▶ Make regular backup copies of important diskettes.
- ▶ Handle diskettes by the jacket and label. Never touch the exposed magnetic surfaces.
- ▶ Use a felt tip pen to write on a diskette. Do not press hard. It is best to write on a separate label and then attach it to the diskette.
- ▶ Keep diskettes away from magnetic fields or electrical devices like televisions, motors, or telephones which use magnets.
- ▶ Store diskettes upright and covered in a diskette holder, paper sleeve, or even a shoebox.
- ▶ Keep diskettes away from direct sunlight and extreme hot or cold temperatures.
- ▶ Keep diskettes dry.

1. Locate the operating system manual for the computer you will be using. Identify the instructions for and practice the following tasks:

   start the computer using a cold boot process
   start the computer using a warm boot process
   initialize a blank diskette
   list the contents of a diskette, directory, or folder
   copy an entire diskette, directory, or folder

COPYING AND DELETING FILES

Even with today's commands for undeleting files, it's wise to erase with caution.

CARE OF DISKETTES

SUGGESTED ACTIVITIES

copy single files from one diskette, directory, or folder to another
delete files from a diskette, directory, or folder
backup a hard disk

2. Read about microcomputers and copyright or software piracy in public schools. What steps will you take as a professional educator to deal with the issue of illegal software duplication?

3. Research some health and comfort issues about microcomputers, including subjects such as risks of eye strain, miscarriages, or carpal tunnel syndrome. Learn what is being done in the field of *ergonomics*, the science of designing machines for optimal comfort of users and intuitive use.

Chapter 14

MODELS FOR MICROCOMPUTER USE

PURPOSES

- ▶ To describe computer-assisted instruction (CAI) and computer-managed instruction (CMI) as a model for microcomputer use
- ▶ To describe integrated learning systems (ILSs) as a model for microcomputer use
- ▶ To describe the tool approach as a model for microcomputer use

INTRODUCTION

Once educators realized the capabilities of the computer, they started looking for ways to use the technology for instruction. There is great diversity in how educators have chosen to integrate technology and instruction; however, three broad categories—each with multiple variations and some hybrids—encompass most approaches.

COMPUTER-MANAGED INSTRUCTION AND COMPUTER-ASSISTED INSTRUCTION

The concepts of computer-managed instruction (CMI) and computer-assisted instruction (CAI) developed during a period when schools were attempting to adapt large mainframe computer technology to classroom instruction. CMI began as an approach to use computers to direct the entire instructional process. It did not involve the computer in the actual teaching of material. CMI promised the elimination of many important but repetitive and tedious chores in the areas of recordkeeping and testing that consumed time otherwise devoted to teaching. Software packages were developed for grade reporting, attendance, IEPs (individual education programs), inventorying, as well as programs for diagnostic/prescriptive purposes.

Goal of CMI

The primary goal of CMI was, and continues to be, to lessen the clerical and managerial load of educators by using the computer to perform the "house-keeping" tasks just described. Because educators spend considerable time preparing, administering, and grading tests; keeping records; and filling out required forms, CMI had and continues to have great appeal.

With CAI, students progress through instructional material at their own pace.

Because CMI was developed as a teacher-oriented application of computer technology, a related approach, computer-assisted instruction (CAI) developed as a student-oriented application of computer technology. CAI uses the computer technology for direct instruction. Generally, CAI presents instructional material in an individualized environment for each student.

Goal of CAI

The concept of CAI developed around the use of computer technology to enhance learning in the traditional classroom setting. CAI comprises many important technology-based features: the computer's ability to individualize the instructional process; the computer's ability to keep students informed of their progress through immediate feedback and achievement summaries; the necessity for systematically prepared, sequenced, tested, and revised curriculum that could be delivered electronically; and many others. These computer-based interactive modes of instruction are usually grouped into categories such as drill and practice, tutorials, games, simulations, and problem solving.

Types of CAI Software

Drill and practice programs take advantage of the computer's endless patience and ability to provide immediate feedback and reinforcement, which can be tailored to a student's individual needs. Typically, drill and practice programs reinforce basic skills and assume that the concept or skill being presented has previously been taught. These programs are structured in various ways to provide, as much as possible, a nonthreatening learning situation for students. The greatest selection of educational software currently available is in the drill and practice mode.

Tutorials have the primary goal of teaching new concepts to students. A tutorial program assumes that the student has little or no prior knowledge of the particular subject matter involved. A well-designed tutorial begins at point zero and carefully guides the learner through all steps required to understand the concept. Most tutorials primarily display text on the screen, but some incorporate graphics to explain and illustrate certain concepts, as the Project Zoo screen in Figure 14.1 shows. Tutorials also give explanations of why answers are wrong, as well as branch students to easier or more difficult materials as their performance dictates.

Instructional games are classified as games because they employ a definite set of rules and a strategy for winning. Instructional games appeal to a student's sense of play in meeting educational goals. They address the area of basic skills but also provide situations in which problem-solving skills must be utilized to win. The power of the computer allows most games to be more complex than noncomputer games, resulting in the teaching of multiple skills and concepts in a way that learners find enjoyable. Figure 14.2, Math Blaster, is an example of an instructional game.

Drill and practice programs help students practice material previously covered.

New content and instruction adapted to each student's competence is characteristic of tutorial software.

Instructional games offer an appealing way to practice problem solving.

Figure 14.1

Sample Tutorial with Graphics: Adventures with Charts and Graphs:
Project Zoo (National Geographic Society, 17th and M Streets NW,
Washington, DC 20036, 800-368-2728)

Figure 14.2

Sample Instructional Game: Math Blaster (Davidson & Associates, Inc.,
P.O. Box 2961, Torrance, CA 90509, 800-545-7677)

Simulations help students pretend and explore safely.

Simulations generate environments for the learner that otherwise might be impossible to provide in the classroom, because of their expense, danger, time limitations, or impracticality. Simulation programs allow the learner to change variables, repeat procedures, and explore and role play various situations. Simulations enabling the learner to role play presidential campaigns, stock market procedures, moon expeditions, or archaeological digs are examples of possible simulations that could provide powerful learning experiences for students. Figure 14.3 gives a sample simulation from the popular geography package, Where in the World Is Carmen San Diego?

Figure 14.3

Sample Simulation: Where in the World Is Carmen San Diego?
(Broderbund Software, P.O. Box 6125, Novato, CA 94948, 800-521-6263)

Students practice strategic thinking with problem-solving programs.

Problem-solving programs, such as The Factory shown in Figure 14.4, create a special environment for the learner by using general algorithms common to one or more problems. Students must investigate, plan strategies, and calculate to solve instructional problems created by the computer. Problem-solving environments are often featured in tutorials and instructional games.

Many educators believe that the true benefits and best uses of CMI and CAI are yet to be realized. Among the rationale offered for lack of full development is technological change. The full vision of well-developed CMI and CAI depended on extensive computer power, which was quite expensive initially. However, as the technology developed, microcomputer prices plummeted. Early microcomputers could not support elaborate software that could both manage and deliver instruction; therefore, the functions seemed to split and develop along separate paths. Many stand-alone educational (CAI) packages were developed. Few stand-alone management (CMI) packages were developed. Recent improvements in the processing power, speed, and networkability of microcomputers have rekindled the vision of CMI and CAI.

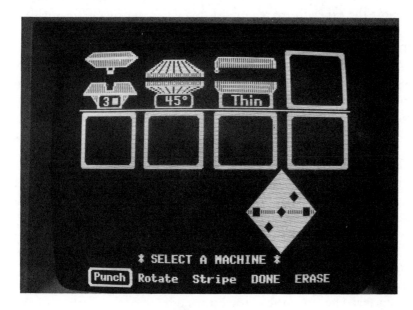

Figure 14.4

Sample Problem-Solving Program: The Factory: Strategies in Problem Solving (WINGS/Sunburst, P.O. Box 660002, Scotts Valley, CA 95067, 800-321-7511)

INTEGRATED LEARNING SYSTEMS (ILSS)

The rekindled vision is cast in the form of *integrated learning systems* (ILSs). The now-familiar CMI and CAI are at the heart of integrated learning systems. Today's ILSs are based on today's microcomputers' increased networking capabilities, described more completely in Chapter 19. ILSs enable students to work at their own pace in a variety of subject areas and at a variety of levels. All work is monitored by the system and reported to both student and teacher. The system documents achievement and/or may indicate areas for additional work. Many ILSs incorporate all the forms of CAI in some way, providing a wide range of student activities.

Many schools provide computer labs where entire classes of students may work simultaneously; however, each student works at an individually appropriate level. Frequently, the labs are monitored by personnel who are specially trained to operate the ILS hardware and software. Recently, many of these installations have adopted a "distributed" approach to the technology. Rather than placing all of the computers in a single lab, a limited number of computers are distributed to each classroom. The distributed implementation provides greater teacher control over the integration of the computer-based curriculum and the classroom-based curriculum.

Research on the effectiveness of ILSs is inconclusive. The use of ILSs appears to improve achievement for some students. Most studies conclude that the ILS approach to microcomputer use is at least as good as the traditional classroom

Integrated learning systems incorporate both student management and instructional delivery.

181

MICRO-COMPUTERS AS TOOLS

approach. Many educators believe that the lackluster performance of ILSs does not support the expenditure required to establish and maintain such a system.

In response to the personal empowerment symbolized by the microcomputer, the first computer designed for individual use, educators looked for a model of microcomputer use that would de-emphasize the control and management issues that grew out of CMI, CAI, and ILSs. In the early 1980s, R. P. Taylor proposed that educators divide microcomputer applications into three functional areas: tutor applications, tutee applications, and tool applications.

Tutor applications are programs that deal with the delivery of instructional content. This is a new label for all of the activities previously described as CAI. Although this form of software continues to dominate the software market, it should be noted that many educators do not believe that tutorial applications are the best use of computer resources.

Tutee applications reverse the traditional roles of student and computer. In tutee applications, the student "teaches" the computer by learning to use a programming language. The student can teach the computer to perform new and complex tasks that it could not perform prior to "instruction." Proponents of comprehensive computer literacy advocate this form of microcomputer application. Programming offers the user ultimate control over the microcomputer's resources. Chapter 12 lists the programming languages most popular in education, and Figure 14.5 shows a sample use of Apple Logo.

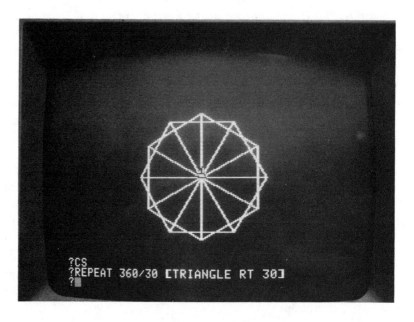

Figure 14.5

Sample Tutee Application: Apple Logo (Apple Computer, Inc., 20525 Mariani Avenue, Cupertino, CA 95014, 800-776-2333)

Tool applications are computer uses that enable the student, within the parameters of the software, to store, organize, and manipulate subject matter in a personalized manner. When students learn to use application packages such as a word processor, spreadsheet, or database manager, they are learning skills similar to learning to use a pencil or pen, typewriter, or calculator. The tool doesn't teach, but it facilitates student involvement with content. There are many reasons for the shift toward application-oriented computer instruction:

Current models of microcomputer use focus on teaching students to use the computer as a tool.

▶ It more closely models microcomputer use outside the educational setting.

▶ It emphasizes higher-order reasoning and problem-solving skills.

▶ It offers more teacher control over curriculum applications than do tutor or tutee applications. Software packages such as word processors, spreadsheets, and database managers are considered "curriculum independent"; they can be used in virtually any curriculum at any level, which is not true of the other two categories.

▶ It provides a more financially feasible approach to software acquisition. Purchasing tutor-oriented packages for each subject area at each grade level can be quite expensive, not to mention use of applications adopted in conjunction with textbooks, which must be discarded when new textbooks are adopted. Application packages enable students to be introduced to simple uses of the tool in elementary grades and to discover more complex uses of the same tool in intermediate and secondary grades. The tools don't change; the uses of the tools become more complex.

▶ It facilitates training. Greater numbers of users of a single program make training more economical. Grade-, school-, or district-wide use of a particular application creates a cooperative support system for users discussing the program's curriculum applications, troubleshooting routines, new and advanced techniques, and other areas of common concern.

Word processors, spreadsheets, and database managers are the three applications that dominate this category. Two additional applications are gaining in popularity: telecommunications and graphics. Two reasons should compel teachers to become "functionally literate" in the use of these five application types: They can increase personal productivity, allowing a teacher more time to teach; and they can facilitate student interaction with subject matter. The remainder of Part III is devoted to identifying basic features of and to suggesting personal and instructional uses for each of the application types.

1. Interview a practicing professional currently using microcomputer software for instruction. Classify the use as one of the three models presented: CMI and/or CAI approach, integrated learning system approach, or tool approach.

2. Locate and read an article from educational literature about the effectiveness of CAI. Is CAI more effective than other computerized methods? Is CAI more effective than noncomputerized methods? Is CAI more effective under certain conditions?

3. Observe a class of students using an ILS. What are the advantages of the observed system? What are the limitations? How is the computer-based

**SUGGESTED
ACTIVITIES**

curriculum, delivered by the ILS, coordinated with the classroom-based curriculum delivered by the teacher? Does the ILS require specialized training and/or operators?

4. Examine a number of software publishers'/producers' catalogs. How are their programs categorized? Based on the information provided, attempt to locate one program in each of the categories (drill and practice, tutorial, game, simulation, and problem-solving) described in this chapter. Are any categories not represented? Are any categories represented more than others? List some reasons that might affect the number of software packages available in a given category.

5. Interview a practicing professional who uses one of the five applications (word processor, spreadsheet, database manager, graphics, or telecommunications) to provide instruction. What did the teacher have to learn before the application could be integrated into the curriculum? What did students have to learn in order to complete the assignment? How did the assignment enable the student to interact with the content being studied?

Chapter 15

WORD PROCESSORS

PURPOSES

▶ To identify the basic features of word processing software
▶ To describe teacher use of word processing programs as a personal productivity tool and as an instructional device

INTRODUCTION

Word processing refers to the use of the computer and accompanying word processing software for entering, editing, formatting, printing, and storing text. Essentially, word processing software creates a blank electronic page on which the user enters text by typing on the keyboard. The monitor displays the contents of the electronic page. The electronic page is stored on disk for later retrieval and/or modification. A printer can be used to create a hardcopy of the electronic page. Word processors have been popular since the early days of microcomputers and have come to include features found in other applications

TEXT EDITING FEATURES

Two text entry features are generally critical for educational applications. The most useful word processors are capable of entering and displaying both upper- and lowercase letters and they are capable of displaying 80 characters across a single line of the monitor without "scrolling" to the right when the customary size of text is used.

Because the text entry page is electronic, it can be easily altered or edited by using commands available in the word processor. Usually these commands are given by moving the cursor to a particular location and then pressing a specific key combination, manipulating an icon, or clicking a mouse button on a menu option. The following are among the most popular text editing commands used in documents.

Delete

The Delete function removes the designated character, word, sentence, paragraph, block of text, page, or entire document from the display. Text following the deleted material is repositioned to occupy the space created.

The Delete or Cut function removes the highlighted text.

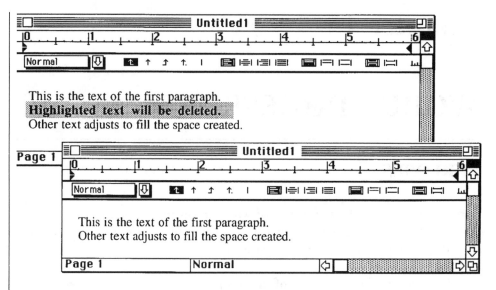

Figure 15.1

Highlighting Text for Deletion (Above) and Text Remaining
After the Block Deletion

Insert

The Insert or Paste function places a previously marked block at the current location.

The Insert function allows text (character, word, sentence, paragraph, etc.) to be placed between existing text elements. As in Figure 15.2, text following an insertion point is repositioned, *not* removed.

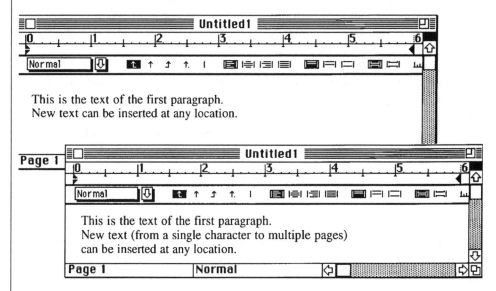

Figure 15.2

Text Before and After New Material Is Inserted

Copy

The Copy function allows the user to identify a portion of text, generally referred to as a *block,* and instructs the program to duplicate the block of text in another location, either in the same document or perhaps a different document. The original block of text is not affected, as shown in Figure 15.3.

The Copy function duplicates a block.

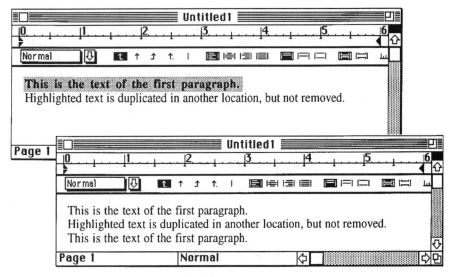

Figure 15.3

When Highlighted Text (Above) Is Copied to a New Location,
It Remains in Its Original Location

Move

The Move function allows the user to remove an identified block of text from its current location and to insert the text at a newly specified location. Text around both the original location and the new location are repositioned after the block is transferred, as in Figure 15.4.

The move function transfers a block to a new location.

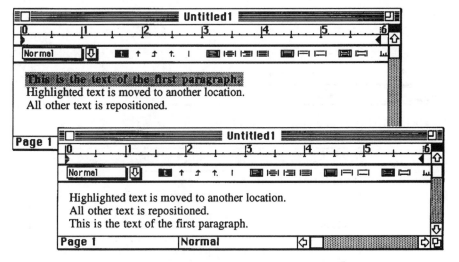

Figure 15.4

When Highlighted Text (Above) Is Moved to a New Location,
It Is Deleted from Its Original Location

Search or Find

The search function finds specific characters or whole words in a document.

The Search function enables the user to enter the desired text to be located. When a search is started, the program finds the first occurrence of the text; when the appropriate commands are given, subsequent occurrences of the text are located. Most word processors with a search or find option enable the user to indicate whether the specified text should be located when it appears only as an entire word or whether the text should be located when it appears within a word. Using the second option and the text *the,* the program could locate such words as *other* and *there,* as well as the specified characters. Figure 15.5 shows a common dialog box for initiating the Search of Find function.

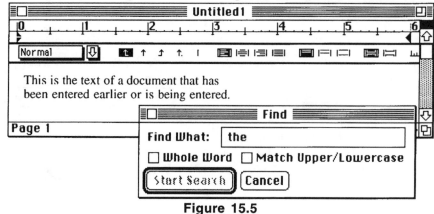

Figure 15.5

Example of a Typical Search or Find Dialog Box

Find and Replace

The user can replace all occurrences of text or view each instance using the Find and Replace function.

The Find and Replace function enables the user to specify a certain text element (character, word, phrase, and so on) to be located by the computer and replaced with a second text element specified by the user, see Figure 15.6. Generally, the user has the option of allowing the program to make all of the changes automatically, or the user may preview each change and either accept or reject it.

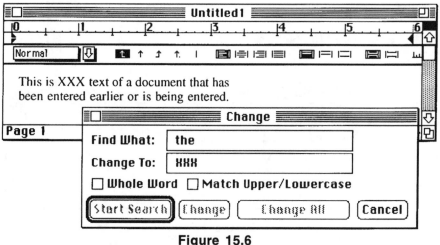

Figure 15.6

Example of a Typical Search and Replace Dialog Box

Once text is entered and edited, the next major function of word processing software is to format the text. Formatting has to do with the appearance of the document when it is eventually printed. Most word processors provide standard text formatting operations, such as these:

▶ margins
▶ justification
▶ line spacing
▶ character modification
▶ pagination
▶ headers and footers

TEXT FORMATTING FEATURES

Margins

Left, right, top, and bottom margins may be adjusted for an entire document or may be adjusted for individual paragraphs or sentences within a document, as illustrated in Figure 15.7. One of the interesting features of word processors that works in tandem with the margins established by the user is a feature called word-wrap. This feature, when activated, automatically "wraps" any word that would cross the established margins, to the next line. Thus, unlike text entry with a standard typewriter, the operator need not end each line of text by pressing return.

Word processors can change margins to create "hanging indents" or varied margins on a single page.

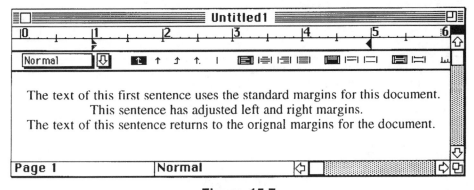

Figure 15.7

Adjusting Left and Right Margins

Justification

Justification provides for text to be placed in one of three positions on a line: flush with the left margin leaving a "ragged" right margin; this is called *left justification* and is the form of most printed text; *right justification* aligns text along the right margin, leaving a "ragged" left margin; and *center formatting* places the text on each line equal distances from the left and right margins. A fourth form of justification, called *block justification,* inserts additional spaces between words on a line to ensure that a printed character appears in the first and last position on the line, making both left and right margins even. The various forms of justification are illustrated on the next page in Figure 15.8.

Word processors can change justification styles at any time.

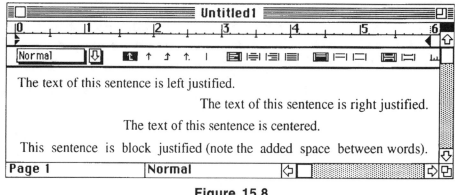

Figure 15.8

The Four Types of Text Justification

Line Spacing

Word processors and printers can handle many spacing formats.

Line spacing sets the amount of space (or "leading") between lines of text. The user can apply a certain spacing to an entire document or to portions of documents. The most common options, shown in Figure 15.9, are single and double spacing. Laser printers offer many options for line spacing in units called *points*, which today's word processors use to create text and spacing in many increments.

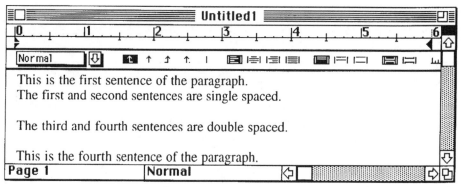

Figure 15.9

Examples of Line Spacing (Leading)

Character Modification

Text can be formatted as regular, bold, or italic.

Word processors also enable users to modify the appearance of text characters. One such modification of appearance is to alter the text's font. A *font* is a family of characters that share distinguishing features, such as shape, size, line thickness, serifs, and so on. A second way to modify text characters is to modify the type style. Most fonts are available as regular ("Roman"), italic, and bold type styles. In addition, most word processors allow the other stylistic features to be added, such as underlined text, outlined text, and shadowed text. Figure 15.10 shows a variety of fonts and type styles.

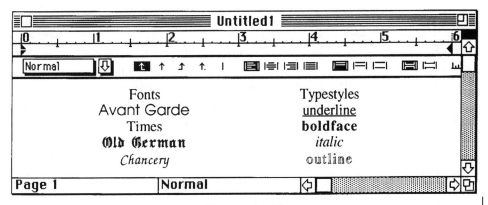

Figure 15.10

Samples of Common Fonts and Type Styles

Pagination

Page breaks determine where one page of text will end and another page will begin. Because the word processing program and the computer monitor text entry, editing, and formatting, while maintaining margins the user specifies, page breaks can be determined automatically.

If the automatically calculated page break is unsatisfactory (for example, it leaves a single line of text at the top of a page or the first line of a paragraph at the bottom of a page), the user generally has an option to insert a mandatory page break, sometimes called a "hard" page break. Documents containing hard page breaks should be examined carefully after any alterations, the software cannot automatically adjust "around" hard page breaks.

Hard page breaks prevent unsightly remnants at the top or bottom of a page.

Headers and Footers

Headers and *Footers* are text that is entered once, which subsequently appears at the top (header) or bottom (footer) of every page when the document is printed, as shown in Figure 15.11. Additional options may allow the header or footer to be centered, left or right justified, or to alternate between left and right margins when printed on facing pages. Word processors commonly enable users to print different headers or footers on left- and right-hand pages and to omit them on the document's first page.

Headers or footers can carry information such as a document's title or author, its date and time created, and successive page numbers—inserted automatically.

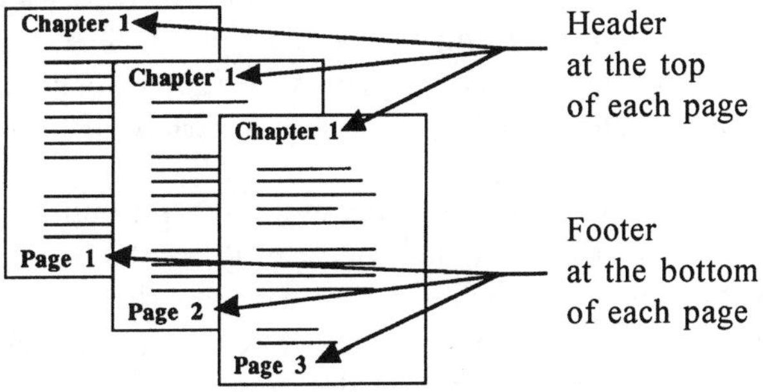

Chapter 1 — Header at the top of each page

Page 1, Page 2, Page 3 — Footer at the bottom of each page

Figure 15.11

Repeating Headers and Footers

EMBEDDED COMMANDS VS WYSIWYG

As shown in Figure 15.12, there are two common methods for implementing formatting commands. The older method, which is still used in popular word processing programs, such as *WordStar,* uses embedded commands. These are special characters that are entered directly into the text. Frequently they must appear in certain positions on the line or on a separate line. Programs give the user the option of displaying or hiding these commands on the screen. When the document is printed, these embedded commands are executed and are not printed. With the WYSIWYG method, the user identifies the text to be formatted, issues the appropriate command, and sees the results displayed on the screen. This is known as "what-you-see-is-what-you-get" (WYSIWYG) formatting, common in software, such as *Word for Windows* and most Macintosh word processors.

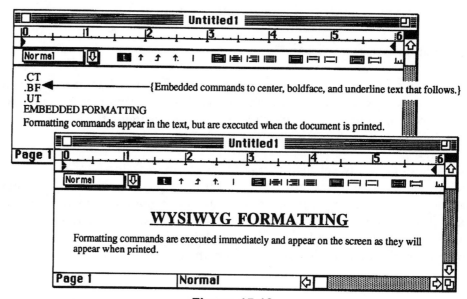

Figure 15.12

Example of Embedded Formatting (Above) and
WYSIWYG Formatting (Below)

DESKTOP PUBLISHING OR WORD PROCESSING?

Sophisticated word processors blur the distinction of word processors and desktop publishing packages.

The majority of current word processors enable users to integrate text and graphics. Word processing programs that provide elaborate formatting capabilities and the integration of graphics generally support basic desktop publishing. Desktop publishing packages provide many unique features that create sophisticated page layouts combining text and graphics. The primary function of desktop publishing software is to create an original document ("camera-ready copy") that can be duplicated using any of a variety of processes.

Today, both word processing software and desktop publishing software are incorporating features that originally were only available in one or the other. As new capabilities are added, the line between the two applications blurs. Although it is beyond the scope of this work to elaborate the distinctions between current word processing and desktop publishing packages, educators should be aware that at the time of publication, desktop publishing packages offered superior features for the manipulation of both graphics and text, especially the manipulation of text on nonsequential pages.

Word processing has spawned a host of features closely related to text entry, editing, and formatting. Sometimes these features are included within the word processing program itself. Two of the most prevalent features of word processing programs are spell checking and mail merge. Additional features include such options as style or grammar checkers and a built-in thesaurus.

OTHER WORD PROCESSING FEATURES

Spell Checking

Spelling checkers compare all the words in a document to a predetermined list of words contained in a file known as a dictionary. Any word that does not match the contents of the dictionary is flagged as a possible misspelling. Some word processors simply mark the words and allow the user to select among flagged terms for corrections. More extensive word processors offer the user alternatives from which to select, then process the corrections.

Most spelling checkers permit the user to create supplemental dictionaries containing specialized terminology that may not appear in the standard dictionary. Many programs permit the user to make additions to the existing dictionary.

Mail Merge

Mail merge capabilities are most useful when the user wants to generate multiple copies of a single document, each copy of which contains unique data. The traditional form letter is the best example of this capability.

The user creates the command document, containing the text that will be identical on all copies. Special commands and symbols are embedded in the document indicating what variable data should be inserted and where it should be inserted. A second document (the data document) containing only the variable data is created. This document may be created using the word processing program, but many word processors can receive data that is transported from other programs such as database managers and spreadsheets.

The *data document* usually has a specific format dictated by the word processor. When the user enters the merge command, the computer begins printing the command document. As the program encounters the embedded commands, it obtains data from the data document and continues printing. The command document will continue to print new copies of itself, each containing new data, until the last data in the data document has been used.

Generally, additional programs, which work in conjunction with the word processor, must be purchased in order to add the following capabilities:

Style or Grammar Checkers

Style checking programs or built in features that review style consistency or grammatical errors analyze such characteristics as the average sentence length in a document, the number of short simple sentences, the variety of sentence structures, and the readability level of the document. In addition, grammar, usage, and punctuation checking options examine texts for writing problems such as subject/verb agreement, proper tense, redundancy, opening and closing quotation marks and parentheses, and final punctuation before initial capital letters.

Many word processors offer these features as menu selections, but their ease of use and thoroughness varies widely among software packages.

Thesaurus

These features or separate programs work much like spelling checkers. The user selects a word and activates the thesaurus. The thesaurus program displays options contained in its data files on the screen and enables the user to select one of or reject all of the suggestions.

INTEGRATED SOFTWARE AND OBJECT LINKING AND EMBEDDING

Integrated Software

As word processors and other application packages have developed, capabilities that were once only available with one package now appear in other software as well. For example, word processing functions now appear in desktop publishing software, spreadsheet functions are included in word processors, and database functions are featured in spreadsheet software. Another expression of this movement to increased capabilities of each software category is the concept of integrated software. Programs such as Great Works, Microsoft Works, and Claris Works combine the separate applications of word processors, spreadsheets, databases, graphics, and communications into a single framework.

Software that is designed this way maintains a common structure that users find appealing. Originally, these integrated packages tended to have fewer functions than their "nonintegrated" alternatives; however, because of continued development and increased capacity of today's microcomputers, the integrated packages are offering comparable features.

Object Linking and Embedding (OLE)

Software producers have also designed a third way to facilitate the interaction of multiple application packages. The concept, known as object linking and embedding (OLE), uses distinct objects. Objects are any pieces of information (from word processors, spreadsheet cells, graphics files, and so forth) created in an application that supports OLE. An object can be copied from a source file created using one application and either linked (left separate on disk with a marker that causes the file to be inserted during display or printing) or embedded (actually duplicated) in the destination file by "pasting" it. The duplicated object retains a connection either to the application in which the object was created or to the source document.

When users embed an object from one application into a file created with a second application, connections to the original file are severed. However, the object retains a connection to the application used to create it. Applications that support OLE enable the user to make changes to an object directly. The user selects the embedded object in the destination document. The application used to create the object is reopened, enabling the user to make modifications without switching from one application to another. Editing an embedded object does not affect the original source document. If a graphic object embedded in a word processing file is modified, the original graphic is not changed—only the embedded graphic is altered. Figure 15.13 illustrates the result of modifying an embedded object.

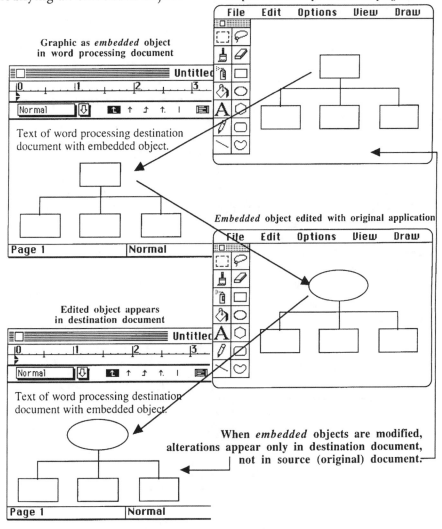

Figure 15.13

Result of Modifying an Embedded Object

When users link an object from one application to a second application, connections to the original file are maintained. When a linked object is modified, both the linked object and the original source file reflect the change. In reality, the destination file contains only a reference to the object in the source file. Because objects can be linked to more than one destination file, linking objects provides a way to modify text or graphics just once that must be identically updated in several different locations. Figure 15.14 illustrates the result of modifying a linked object.

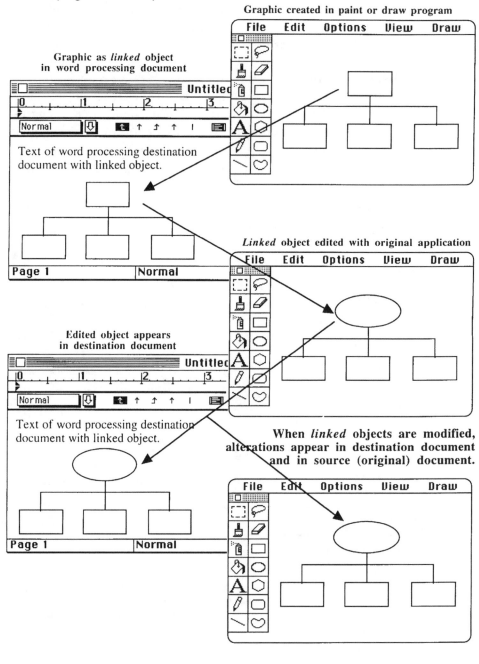

Figure 15.14

Result of Modifying a Linked Object

Personal Productivity Uses

Many educators have found that word processing alone is an adequate justification for teachers to learn to use computers. Teachers can use word processors to create any document that traditionally may have been produced on a typewriter: handouts, worksheets, reports, tests, letters to parents, lecture notes, lesson plans, and on and on. Because these documents can be stored on a hard disk or diskette, they can easily be retrieved and updated or altered. Various forms of the same document can easily be created without reentering text.

Instructional Uses

Once a student has learned the basic operations of a word processing system, the tool becomes available for dealing with subject matter. Teachers can create content-oriented activities, like those listed here, that students complete using a word processor.

Fill-in-the-blank activities: The teacher enters a brief paragraph containing missing words, which may be vocabulary words, spelling words, parts of speech, and so forth. When a student loads the document in a word processor, he or she fills in the blanks according to the assignment given: entering adjectives and adverbs to create a descriptive paragraph; entering appropriate vocabulary words; duplicating the paragraph and completing the second copy with synonyms or antonyms. Upon completion, the student prints a copy and/or saves the document on a diskette. After additional instruction and evaluation, the student returns to previous work, evaluates, and modifies the file

Completion activities: The teacher may enter several "story starters" in a file and allow the students to complete the story of their choice. Students may even collaborate on a story; each student is given a topic or sentence to get the story started, after a number of minutes, the story is saved, regardless of condition, and the diskette is passed to the next student or the next student rotates to the computer and continues the story. The process is repeated until all members of the class have contributed to the story.

Revision activities: The teacher prepares a document according to the skill to be practiced; all punctuation is omitted or punctuation errors are included, all capitalization is omitted, the sentences in a paragraph are out of order, and so forth. The student uses the word processor to correct the errors and saves the corrected version. After additional instruction and evaluation, the student returns to the document to make further correction or to print a final copy for submission.

Prewriting activities: Many teachers have found word processors useful for getting students prepared for formal composition through such activities as freewriting, prompted writing, and outlining. Freewriting encourages the student to use the word processor to enter—quickly and without concern for spelling, quality, or usefulness—any thoughts or ideas that come to mind. When the freewriting period is completed, students review their ideas and thoughts

WORD PROCESSOR USES

Word processors help students store freewriting, promoted writing, and outlines for later refinement.

and select a topic for composition activities. Prompted writing requires the instructor to prepare a list of questions or a template (a file that can be loaded from the diskette that sets up the form for the completed document). Students load the question file or template and enter their responses. These documents are then used to create drafts of complete compositions.

The ability to move, insert, and delete text makes the processes of outlining, reorganizing ideas, and converting an outline to a fully scripted composition an extremely fruitful activity. Some word processors can expand and shrink outline to help students create the shell for papers and reports.

Finding activities to complete on a word processor is not difficult. Virtually anything that a student would write or type probably can be and probably should be adapted to word processing.

SUGGESTED ACTIVITIES

1. Read about and report on instructional uses of word processors in a subject area and grade level of your choice.

2. Use a word processor to create and print a 10-item quiz on a topic of your choice. Use the word processor's text moving capabilities to create and print a second version of the same test.

3. Plan a student activity, in a subject area and at a grade level of your choice, that involves the use of word processors. List the word processing skills students need to know in order to complete the activity.

4. Learn to use the mail merge capabilities of a word processor. Create a command document and a data document that combine to create unique documents for at least five different individuals.

5. Obtain product literature about leading word processing and desktop publishing software. Discuss which systems are best suited for various instructional uses that involve documents, such as term papers, worksheets, school newspapers, and letters to parents. Analyze which uses could justify the additional cost and system requirements of a desktop publishing package.

Chapter 16

SPREADSHEETS

PURPOSES

▶ To identify the basic features of electronic spreadsheets
▶ To describe teacher use of spreadsheet software as a personal productivity tool and as an instructional device

Whereas word processors exploit the computer's capacity to easily store and quickly modify text, electronic spreadsheets exploit the computer's capacity to rapidly calculate and recalculate numerical data. Spreadsheet programs such as Lotus 1-2-3 and Microsoft Excel look very similar to their paper ancestor, the ledger page.

Structure of a Spreadsheet

The software creates a grid of rows and columns that is displayed on the screen. In most spreadsheets the columns are labeled with alphabetical characters and the rows are labeled numerically. The intersection of each row and column is called a *cell*. Each cell is referenced by its coordinates, a combination of the alphabetical column label and the numerical row label; for example, the cell located at the intersection of column "B" and row "5" is called cell "B5."

Spreadsheets can store the contents of thousands of cells. It is not possible to display all of a spreadsheet's cells on the monitor at a single time. Whatever portion of the spreadsheet that is displayed on the monitor is called a *window*. The cells that hold the data for a particular application, the "filled" portion of the spreadsheet, is called the *worksheet*. Most spreadsheets today enable users to select cells by clicking them with the mouse. Additional movement on the spreadsheet can be accomplished on a cell-by-cell basis by using the cursor control keys (up, down, left, and right arrows) or by menu commands that use the cell coordinates. Moving over a large spreadsheet on a cell-by-cell basis would be a key-pressing nightmare, so all spreadsheets provide some type of Goto command. When the Goto command is activated, the computer prompts the user to enter the desired coordinate. After the coordinate is entered and the user indicates that the coordinate is complete, the program instantaneously moves the windows of the spreadsheet to display the desired cell.

TYPES OF SPREADSHEET DATA

Each cell of a spreadsheet may contain one of three types of data:

- ▶ labels
- ▶ numbers
- ▶ formulas

Some data include special characters that must be entered in front of the data, so that the program can interpret the data properly. These special characters are called *data prefixes*.

Labels

Labels show headings and numbers that are not entries to be calculated.

Labels are generally text entries; they are column and row headings, or descriptive information that does not require calculation. The data prefix for text entries often is the double quotation mark ("). Most spreadsheets will default (use a previously established format) to label settings for all entries, unless another data prefix is used or the entry begins with a number. If the user wishes to enter the year 1994 as a textual column heading, not as a number entry, the label prefix character (") would be required ("1994). Figure 16.1 shows a sample prefix being entered.

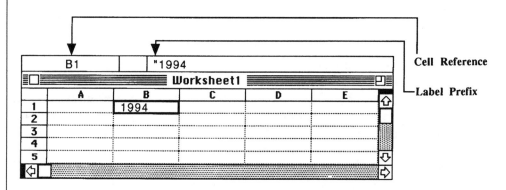

Figure 16.1

Using a Label Prefix to Enter a Heading

Numbers

Entering numbers is straightforward unless the user wants to select special features.

Numbers are the second type of data that can be entered into spreadsheet cells. Numbers are entered using the 10 digit keys. Because the spreadsheet was designed to facilitate the manipulation of numbers, no data prefix is required for numerical entries, except for dates, currency, and any other specialized uses for numerals. Numerical data can be manipulated with all of the mathematical operations such as addition, subtraction, multiplication, division, square root, and many statistical operations such as mean and standard deviation. Figure 16.2 shows a numerical entry.

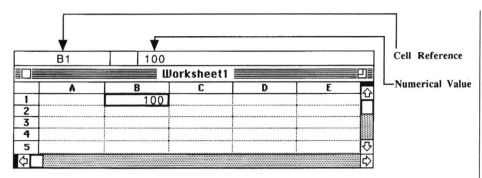

Figure 16.2

Entering a Number in a Cell

Formulas

Formulas are the third type of data used in spreadsheets. Formulas use cell coordinates and mathematical symbols, called *arithmetic operators*, to describe operations that the spreadsheet should perform. Spreadsheets also use symbols called *logical operators* to represent logical constructions in formulas. Logical constructions return a true or false value depending on whether both conditions in a construction are true (and), whether either condition is true (or), and whether the condition is not a specified value (not). This ability to describe both mathematical and logical operations, regardless of data entered is probably the single most powerful aspect of electronic spreadsheets. The data prefix for a formula is usually some arithmetic operator, such as + or = .

Formulas are stored equations that work on cell values.

Entering a formula is as easy as entering text or numbers (see Figure 16.3). If a user has entered the number 5 in cell A1 and the number 10 in cell B1, and wanted to add the two numbers together, a formula, entered in any empty cell would look something like this: =A1+B1 (the formula prefix followed by the first cell coordinate, the arithmetic operator to indicate addition, followed by the second cell coordinate). If the formula were entered in cell C1, the monitor would display the result of the calculation, 15 (the contents of cell A1 plus the contents of cell B1). The formula is not displayed on the grid, only the result. The formula is displayed on a line above or below the window, as shown in the figure.

USING FORMULAS

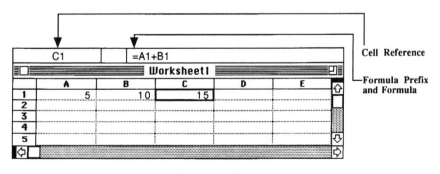

Figure 16.3

Storing a Formula in Cell C1

Writing formulas in terms of cell coordinates is what gives spreadsheets their "power." Cells containing a formula constantly monitor any cell coordinates contained in the formula.

Automatic Recalculation

When the contents of those cells are altered, the formula automatically recalculates the formula and displays the new result. In the previous example, if the user changed the contents of cell A1 to 50, the formula in cell C1 would automatically recalculate 50 plus 10 and display the new sum of 60.

Users can turn off the recalculation feature to speed execution in large worksheets.

In small worksheets, with few entries and few formulas, the automatic recalculation, which happens after each entry, doesn't slow the data entry process. However, in large worksheets containing many entries and many formulas or in small worksheets containing complex formulas, the automatic recalculation after each entry may be intolerable. Therefore, spreadsheets allow the user to turn off the automatic recalculation feature. The operator may then use a command to recalculate the worksheet after data entry is complete or at any point in the process.

Functions

Many mathematical operations on a spreadsheet are common regardless of the application. To capitalize on these common operations, most spreadsheets include special predefined formulas called *functions*. Some common functions are: SUM, totals all the values in a specified list of cells; COUNT, tallies the number of cells containing data in a specified list of cells; AVERAGE, averages the values in a list of specified cells; MINIMUM, identifies the smallest value in a list of cells; MAXIMUM, identifies the largest value in a list of cells. Most spreadsheets have elaborate financial functions that calculate common financial figures such as net present value, periodic payment, future value, the rate of return.

Functions simplify the entry of elaborate formulas. If a user wants to average a row of numeric entries contained in cells A1 through A10, the formula could be written like this:

$$=(A1+A2+A3+A4+A5+A6+A7+A8+A9+A10)/10$$

(the formula prefix followed by each cell coordinate and the appropriate arithmetic operator followed by the division symbol and the number of cells).

Because averaging is a common operation, spreadsheets include an averaging function. Using the AVERAGE function, the formula just shown could be simplified to

$$@AVERAGE (A1...A10).$$

This function would add the contents of all cells from A1 to A10 and divide by the number of cells. Functions usually have a special function prefix, such as the (@) symbol, followed by the name of the function or an abbreviation for the function (AVG), followed by the cell coordinates on which the function should operate. The function does not require that each cell be referenced as in a formula. Instead, the function permits the use of a range reference.

A Range of Cells

A consecutive group of cells in either a row or column or a combination of rows and columns in a block of cells is called a range of cells. Spreadsheets enable users to address a range of cells by indicating the beginning and ending cells only. In the function example, the range of cells to be averaged is indicated by the range reference A1...A10. The function inspects the contents of all cells between and including the reference cells. If a cell is blank (contains no entry) it generally is not included in the function's calculations. Consequently, a blank cell in the range of cells for the average function example would not affect the calculated average; on the other hand, a cell containing a zero would affect the calculated average.

The nature of data and formulas on a spreadsheet is very repetitive. As a result, special commands within the spreadsheet program facilitate the duplication of formulas. Think about the average teacher who has five classes or subjects during the day. If that teacher were to use a spreadsheet to keep a test average and a homework average for each of 25 students in each class, 250 formulas would have to be entered on the spreadsheet. The potential for error is enormous! Although duplicating formulas is an easy process that would eliminate the burden of typing 250 formulas, the teacher would have to understand the difference between absolute and relative cell references.

Relative References

Generally, in the copying process the user identifies the cell to be copied (the *source range*) and the cells into which copies will be placed (the *target range*). Most spreadsheets prompt the user to indicate whether to use relative or absolute references (some systems default to relative references). If relative references are specified, when the formula is copied, only the arithmetic operators and structure of the formula are copied exactly, cell references are changed relative to where the formula is copied. Figure 16.4 shows how formulas would look after a copying procedure using relative references has been completed. As the formula from cell CI was copied to cells C2 through C5, the cell references in the original formula, A1 and B1, were adjusted relative to the row in which the copy was created, that is A2 and B2, A3 and B3, A4 and B4, A5 and B5. If the same formula were copied without relative references, exact copies of the original formula A1+BI would appear in cells C2 through C5.

COPYING OR REPLICATING FORMULAS

Relative references copy the structure and operators of a formula, and automatically change cell references.

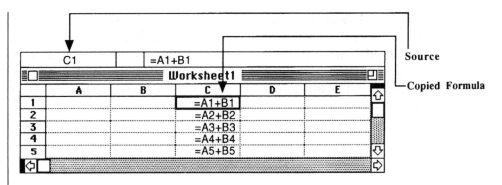

Figure 16.4

Spreadsheet Formula Using Relative Cell References

Absolute References

Absolute references enable a formula to refer to a specific cell regardless of where the formula is moved.

On occasion, a number of formulas must reference a single cell that is not duplicated. This would inhibit the duplicating process, if spreadsheet designers had not planned for absolute references. Usually, absolute references are indicated by typing special characters into a formula. These special characters indicate to the program that if the formula is copied, the designated references should remain exactly as entered, they should not be adjusted; therefore, they are "absolute." The common form for indicating absolute references is to insert dollar signs into the cell coordinates (+A1+B1). If this example were replicated down a column of cells, only the A1 reference would be changed to A2, A3, A4, and so forth, the B1 reference would remain the same in all of the formulas.

FORMATTING SPREADSHEET DATA

As with a word processor, one of the functions of a spreadsheet program is to format the data for printing. Appropriate formatting makes the final printed copy easier to read and understand. Spreadsheet formatting can be established on a cell-by-cell basis, on a row or column basis, on a range basis, or on a global basis (affects all cells in the worksheet). The most common spreadsheet formatting features allow for the following activities, which are illustrated in Figure 16.5.

- *Text formatting*—cell contents are displayed and printed in boldface, italic, underlined, various fonts, and so forth.
- *Justification*—cell contents are aligned on the left, right, or center of the cell. Numerical entries are usually aligned on the right, unless they are entered as labels, which are aligned on the left.
- *Decimal place precision*—numeric entries display and print the specified number of characters following a decimal point.
- *Column width*—all cells in the column are set to display the designated number of characters. Column widths are usually established slightly larger than the largest probable entry.
- *Special characters*—designated cells display contents and special characters such as dollar signs, percent signs, minus signs, parentheses, and commas.

	A	B	C	D	E
1	Text		Justification		Numbers
2	**BOLD**		Left		99.9
3	*ITALIC*		Right		64%
4	FONTS		Centered		$1,000.00
5					

Figure 16.5

Spreadsheet Displaying Various Format Options

ADVANCED FEATURES OF SPREADSHEETS

Charts

Because numerical data is frequently converted to a graphic of some kind, most spreadsheets have chart creation capabilities. Data in the spreadsheet and the type of chart desired are selected by the user; then the computer automatically generates the appropriate graphic. Depending on the particular software used, many other enhancements such as additional text, legends, color, and arrows may be added to the chart. Figure 16.6 shows two different charts generated using the same spreadsheet data.

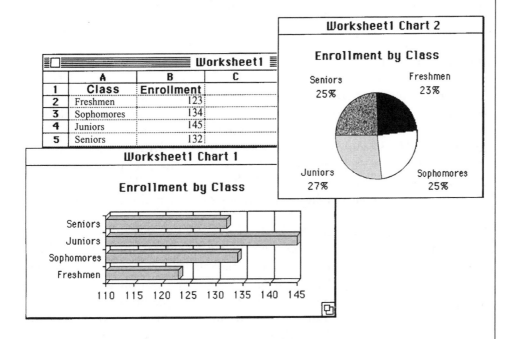

Figure 16.6

Bar and Pie Charts Created Using Spreadsheet Data

Importing/Exporting and Linking Data

Most spreadsheets can store data in multiple forms and transfer data from (import) or to (export) other programs such as word processors and database managers. Charts created in spreadsheets can also be exported to word processors and desktop publishing packages.

Spreadsheets can also share data between worksheets through interactive links. Data and/or formulas in one worksheet can reference data and/or formulas in another worksheet. If the referenced values in one worksheet are altered, the next time the worksheet containing the links is opened, the linked data and/or formulas are automatically updated. Many of the newer spreadsheet packages support object linking and embedding as described in Chapter 15.

SPREADSHEET USES

Personal Productivity Uses

The most obvious use a teacher has for an electronic spreadsheet is in calculating grades. Carefully designed, a spreadsheet can become a very powerful electronic gradebook. Many teachers have used spreadsheets to keep financial records for school organizations and activities, to prepare and maintain budgets, to calculate sports statistics, and to maintain classroom records of attendance and lab equipment. Although spreadsheets are quite adept at making complex calculations, the grid structure lends itself to the rapid creation of charts and tables which may contain no numbers at all. Many teachers use their spreadsheet to create seating charts and word lists for students.

Instructional Uses

Like other application tools, once the basic skills are mastered, students are ready to use spreadsheets with discipline-specific content. Naturally, math activities lend themselves readily to the number crunching capabilities of the spreadsheet. Word problems offer particularly good activities for adaptation to the spreadsheet. Teachers can create the basic template and allow students to experiment with the variables. Activities of this nature allow the student to concentrate on problem-solving strategies instead of lengthy calculations.

Spreadsheets are ideal for constructing models and manipulating variables.

But spreadsheet programs can be used equally well in other curriculum areas. Data from virtually any kind of experiment can be entered into a spreadsheet, if only for organizational purposes. Once students learn to interpret data, they can attempt to construct theoretical models of their experiment. By manipulating the variables, they may predict the outcomes of additional or continued experimentation. Students can collect and enter weather data from the daily newspaper. Data can then be analyzed to determine weekly or monthly averages. When students learn more complex spreadsheet skills, they can sort and organize data and then draw conclusions about what conditions affect precipitation, growth measurements, temperature, and so forth.

Social studies students can enter comparison data (population, crime rate, annual income, cost of housing, and so forth) on a number of localities. The data can be used to identify and analyze relationships among characteristics: Does annual income go up or down with population? How are cost of living and crime rate related? Students studying economics can plan personal budgets or compare the terms of advertised bank and credit union loans. Some foreign language teachers have used spreadsheets to allow students to plan vacations to the countries in which the language being studied is spoken. These plans must include figures for calculating currency exchange rates.

The key to successfully integrating spreadsheets into the curriculum is for teachers to become microcomputer users. When teachers learn to use an application they find helpful, they are more likely to introduce their students to that same tool.

SUGGESTED ACTIVITIES

1. Read about and report on instructional uses of spreadsheet programs in a subject area and at a grade level of your choice.

2. Create an electronic gradebook with the characteristics and format provided by your instructor. Use at least one function and be sure to learn to replicate formulas. Change the format of cells where appropriate.

3. Plan a student activity, in a subject area and at a grade level of your choice, that involves the use of spreadsheets. List the spreadsheet skills students need to know in order to complete the planned activity.

4. Create two charts using a single set of data entered in a spreadsheet.

Chapter 17

DATABASE MANAGERS

PURPOSES

- ▶ To identify the basic features of database management software
- ▶ To describe teacher use of database management software as a personal productivity tool and as an instructional device

INTRODUCTION

The third type of application discussed in this book is a database manager. Database mangers exploit the computer's capacity to rapidly sort and organize large amounts of data. A *database* is an organized collection of data; the computer programs that access and manipulate the data are called *database managers*. Frequently, the terms for the program and the data are used interchangeably.

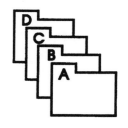

Most educators are familiar with database concepts, though they may not relate them to computer use. Teachers maintain a variety of data for each student: grades, objectives mastered, personality inventories, personal data, and so on. All of this data may be placed in a file folder bearing the student's name. All of the student folders are placed in a filing cabinet, usually in alphabetical order by the students' last names, for later reference. To identify all of the students with a similar characteristic, the teacher must manually inspect each folder, a time consuming and tedious process that becomes more complicated if the teacher wants to check for multiple characteristics. Database application programs were designed to complete these kinds of activities.

STRUCTURE AND FUNCTIONS

Database managers organize data on three levels:

- ▶ field
- ▶ record
- ▶ file

Fields collect data for each entity that is stored in a record. The collection of records is a file.

Each piece of data that is to be collected is assigned a field name. For example, a simple student directory database might contain three fields: a last name field, a first name field, and a telephone number field. All of the fields related to a single entity are called a *record*. One record would contain all of the fields for an individual student. All records have the same number of fields, but each record contains unique information. Finally, all of the student records that have the same format are organized into a single file.

Database software allows users to accomplish their complex organizational tasks through three primary functions. Depending on the software selected, these functions may be separate programs, or they may all be integrated into a single program with many options. Generally, all database programs provide for these three functions:

▶ file design
▶ data manipulation
▶ report generation

FILE DESIGN

File design is the first step in creating a database. The user must decide what types of data will be entered, the order in which it will be entered, and the form in which data must be entered. The file design portion of database programs generally allows users to create field names, specify the length of fields, and indicate the type of data that should be entered (alphabetical or numerical).

Preplanning by the user will facilitate file design. Knowing what the desired outcome should be will help determine what data should be entered and how it should be entered. For example, if a database will be used solely to generate an alphabetical listing by students' last names, a single field for the name is adequate and the name can be entered in the common last-name-comma-first-name format; however, if the database may also be used to generate form letters or progress reports that do not use the last-name-comma-first-name format, two fields should be created, one for the first name and one for the last name.

Some database management software allows the user to specify additional design characteristics. Some fields can be designed to have the computer automatically enter data such as the date or a sequential identification number. Some fields can be designed to require user entry or to automatically enter the same data on every record. Fields may be designed to calculate the result of a formula using data entered in other fields on the same record.

Sophisticated features help database designers to control users entries and ensure accurate data.

More complex database software may allow the user to design fields that will ensure that only unique values are entered; no two records could have the same student identification number. For example, fields may be designed to lookup data, using an interactive link, in an entirely different file based on data entered in a particular field in the current record. Some database programs support object embedding and linking as described earlier.

In essence, during the file design stage, a database designer creates an electronic form that will be displayed during later functions. Data is not entered during this stage, only the characteristics of the data are specified.

DATA MANIPULATION

Data manipulation includes five primary activities:

▶ adding
▶ changing
▶ removing

▶ searching/selecting
▶ sorting

Depending on the database program, these activities may be initiated by issuing a specific command or by selecting the activity from a menu.

Adding Data

Users usually begin to add data in records once the file design is completed. During data entry, the electronic form created during file design is displayed on the screen, as shown in Figure 17.1. The user enters the desired data. Usually, pressing the Tab key moves the cursor from one field to the next, facilitating data entry. Generally, fields can be skipped if no data is available. When data entry for the displayed record is complete, the user can indicate that the program should save the data and display a new blank record for continued data entry, or the program should save the data and stop data entry. Subsequently, all programs provide a command for adding new records.

Database records hold all the information in the fields for one entity and can be manipulated to compare data for some or all entities.

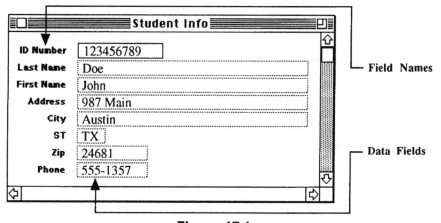

Figure 17.1

Sample Display of Data Entry for a Record

Changing Data

Handling changes to data is one of the strengths of computerized databases. Maintaining current and correct data is essential to getting valid information from a database. To make changes to field contents, users can move through the database on a record-by-record basis or use the database's search capabilities, which will be covered later.

Once the appropriate record is located and displayed on the monitor, the user moves the cursor to the field containing the data to be modified and enters the new data. When the data modifications are complete, the user tells the database manager to save the changes; frequently the computer program will ask for verification before modifying existing data.

Updates can be individual or global.

Some database managers provide commands that enable the user to automatically modify all records that contain identical information in a specified field, generally known as a *global update*.

Removing Data

Users can delete field contents or entire records in much the same way that users change data. The appropriate record is located, the command is given, the program verifies that removal is desired, the user indicates yes or no, and the action is completed. Generally, the removal process is performed on entire records; if only the data in specified fields is to be removed, the change data process is used. Figure 17.2 illustrates a dialog box confirming data removal. Some database managers also enable users to specify groups of records for simultaneous deletion, such as all records with a certain area code or last name beginning with specified characters.

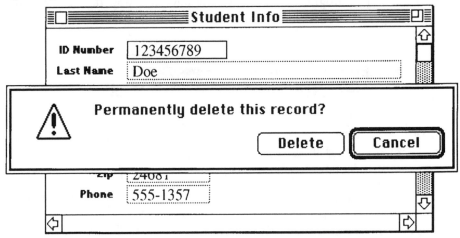

Figure 17.2

Dialog box that prompts user to confirm a record deletion.

Searching and Selecting Data

Searching data is probably the most valuable activity performed by database software. Usually, when the user enters a search command, a blank data entry screen is displayed (other programs may list all of the field names on a record) and the user is asked to indicate which field should be searched and what the field should contain.

Database managers not only display records that match the search criteria, but also can store the subset in a separate file.

The operator types data to be matched, called the *search* or *selection criteria*, in the appropriate field. The computer then uses the criteria to search all of the records in a file, displaying each record that matches the criteria as it is located, or extracting the subset of records for further manipulation. The user indicates that the search should stop or continue searching for other matches.

The primary strength of this activity is that most database programs accept multiple search criteria. The user can specify data in any number of fields, and a matching record must contain all of the data specified in the search criteria, see Figure 17.3. In this manner, computerized databases can quickly accomplish complex time-consuming searches that would be virtually impossible to complete manually.

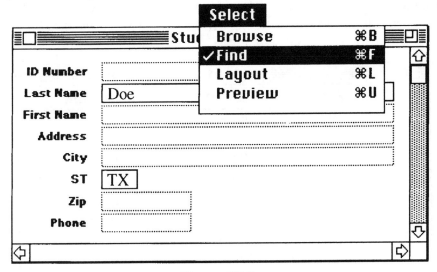

Figure 17.3

Selecting Records with Multiple Search Criteria

Sorting Data

Sorting data primarily affects the organization of records in a file. Most non-computerized databases are limited to a single organizational scheme; the names in a directory are organized by last name, the words in a dictionary are in alphabetical order, the equipment on an inventory may be listed by serial number, and so forth. Because computerized databases can use both the internal memory of the computer and the storage capacity of a disk drive, they can quickly and easily reorganize the way a database displays or prints records on a temporary or permanent basis.

Some databases limit searching and sorting to fields identified as key fields.

The sorting process is similar to searching. The database program prompts the user to indicate which field or fields of data should be used to organize the database. The user must also indicate how data within each field should be organized; generally two choices are available, ascending order (A to Z or 0 to 9) and descending order (Z to A or 9 to 0).

When more than one field is used for sorting, the order in which the sorting is completed is critical. The most important organizational criteria should be sorted first. Each subsequent sort will be completed within the arrangement created by previous sorts. The listings can be in ascending or descending order.

Careful planning of the sorting sequence can produce informative arrangements of the database; for example, if a database file containing the fields GENDER and AGE is first sorted in descending order (9 to 0) by the field AGE and then sorted in ascending order (A to Z) by the field GENDER, the resulting database would display the oldest females of the same age first, followed by the oldest males of the same age, followed by younger females of the same age, followed by younger males of the same age, followed by the youngest females of the same age, followed by the youngest males of the same age (see Figure 17.4).

Student Info		
Age	**Gender**	**First Name**
20	Female	Mary
20	Female	Jane
20	Male	Bob
20	Male	Jim
19	Female	Sally
19	Male	Chuck
18	Female	Alice
18	Male	Tom
18	Male	Steve

Figure 17.4

Results of a Multiple Criteria Sort (Age and Gender)

REPORT GENERATION

Data from a single database can create many reports if a user alters the search and sorting criteria.

Report generation is the primary activity of database users. This feature of the software is responsible for the format that will be used to display the contents of the database when it is printed (programs will display reports on the monitor as well). Columnar reports are the basic format for most database output.

To print a report, the user selects the field(s) that should be included in a report and the order in which fields should be printed. Using the field names for column headings, the first field selected is printed in the leftmost column, and all other selected fields are printed in columns to the right in the order of selection.

Good database software enables the user to employ the search and sort capabilities to create reports that contain only selected records. Frequently these report formats are saved as templates on the hard disk or diskette with the database so that they can be used repeatedly. This does not prevent the user from creating new unique reports as different needs surface.

Formatting features help users create professional looking reports.

Some database packages provide additional functions that can be executed when a report is generated. Numeric figures on individual records can be displayed and totaled in a report. If subcategories are created using the sort function, subtotals for each group may be displayed. The database may simply count the number of records that appear in the report and print that number on the report. Additional print formatting such as boldface, underline, headers and footers, and a variety of fonts are available.

The most popular database programs support many of the advanced features described elsewhere in this book. Database programs can import data from and export data to both word processors and spreadsheets. This capability can be crucial for completing mail merge documents in a word processor or for incorporating data in a spreadsheet for use in a chart. Some database programs include charting capabilities. Among the most recent advances for database programs is the ability to include graphic images. The graphic images may be a field of data, such as scanned photographs, diagrams, and the like; or the images may be incorporated into the layout of the output as displayed on the monitor or as printed. New database programs also support object linking and embedding (OLE).

ADDITIONAL DATABASE FEATURES

Personal Productivity Uses

The key criteria for these applications is the frequency with which the data must be searched and/or reorganized. Many educators use a database to maintain student profiles including personal and academic data. These profiles change frequently and can be searched and sorted so that teachers can group students with similar profile characteristics for specific activities. Another popular database application is to create a "question bank" for the creation of tests. Test items can be identified according to objective, text chapter, difficulty, and so forth. Then a teacher can search and/or sort questions that could be included on an upcoming test. Inventories of classroom equipment or activities and special materials that support specific learning objectives have also been entered on computerized databases.

DATABASE MANAGER USES

Instructional Uses

Database activities in the subject areas generally fall into two categories: database creation and database inquiry.

Database creation: These activities have to do with students determining the types of data to be collected on a given topic, selecting field names and characteristics, designing the record format, and collecting and entering data. Databases can be created on virtually any topic. In language arts students can create databases of irregular verbs and their conjugation, examples of figures of speech or colloquial expressions and their meanings, character analyses and plot summaries, and their own combination dictionary and thesaurus. Some students have even used database programs to replace traditional index cards for gathering sources to complete research papers. In the humanities databases have been created to organize historical dates and personalities. Styles of art, architecture, and music have been entered into databases. Experimental data and records in almost every field of science have been easily adapted to computerized databases.

Database inquiry: Activities that require the student to use data previously entered in a database to answer questions, draw conclusions and test hypotheses, are popular uses of databases. Students may use databases they have created or they may use databases created by the teacher. Some of the more popular education-oriented database programs available commercially include complete database files on such items as the fifty states, the U.S. presidents, animals, and dinosaurs. These files tap the student's capacity to use the database's search, sort, and print routines. Teachers create questions that can be answered by the correct manipulation of the data. Students prepare a search and sort strategy for the computer. After viewing the results, students may continue with other questions or refine the strategy. When the student is confident that the question is answered correctly, reports can be generated to verify and validate responses.

SUGGESTED ACTIVITIES

1. Read about and report on instructional uses of database programs in a subject area and at a grade level of your choice.

2. Create a database for use as a personal productivity tool (such as student information, resources and activities, or an annotated bibliography). Be sure to include at least 5 fields for at least 10 records. Print two reports that show unique arrangements of the data in the database.

3. Create a database containing at least 20 records. Write 10 questions that can be answered by using the database. Be sure to include questions that would require students to search and sort the database correctly. List the skills students would have to know in order to use the database software.

4. Identify examples of printed databases with which you are familiar (such as a telephone directory). What might computerized versions of these databases do that their paper versions can not do? Discuss the advantages and disadvantages of using computerized databases rather than traditional printed forms.

5. Add a graphic data field to the database created in activity 3.

Chapter 18

GRAPHICS APPLICATIONS

PURPOSES

► To identify characteristics of basic types of computer graphics programs
► To identify the differences between paint and draw programs
► To distinguish the characteristics of different types of computer printers in graphics production
► To know some of the devices that can be interfaced with computers to create graphics materials

INTRODUCTION

Computer graphics are used for many types of production, including desktop publishing, video production, multimedia presentations, and others. Terminology describing different forms of computer graphics can be somewhat confusing because of all the variations of illustrations available. Additional information on computer graphics is provided in Chapters 21 and 22, which describe some specific uses.

USE OF COMPUTER GRAPHICS

Graphics programs generally create visuals for two basic types of uses:

► graphics that will be incorporated into other applications' data files that may be used for computer presentations
► other types of materials, including print and nonprint media forms that are produced by a variety of peripheral equipment

PRODUCTION OF COMPUTER GRAPHICS

Users create computer graphics through one of two general methods. Images can be generated using graphics software, with which the user creates every element of a design from the beginning. They can also be created by importing all types of visual information from several different sources of interfaced technologies, such as compact disc-read only memory (CD-ROM) players, digital imaging cameras, or flatbed scanners. When appropriate input equipment and software are available, the capabilities of importing graphic materials into computer applications for design purposes are virtually limitless. Several good graphics packages import visual information so it can be altered in almost any way imaginable.

The basic forms of graphics software are painting and drawing programs, with a third, adjunct type called presentation graphics that has become popular with business people and teachers who create graphs and charts. Some graphics applications combine all three types of programs. The combined packages are usually more versatile, because the designer can use them to take advantage of

Painting programs include templates of geometric shapes and many paint effects to build and manipulate graphics; drawing programs accept free-hand drawings entered with a mouse, light pen, stylus, or joystick.

Paint programs use a building-block approach to create abstract images, business graphics, or diagrams for reproduction as slides or overhead transparencies.

Images from paint programs are not easy to "break apart" for revision.

the values of drawing, painting, and charting without having to import or export to another application. Still, the stand-alone packages may be capable of doing more sophisticated types of processing, because they concentrate on one approach to creating art. These different applications normally have special manipulation tools embedded in the software commands or desktop tools that help illustrators to rapidly incorporate perfectly drawn shapes and lines within free-hand drawings. Graphics packages also include other types of effects, such as shading, textures, colors, graphing, variations in fonts, and special effects. See Chapter 22 for additional information on graphics terminology.

These basic graphics programs usually require the use of a joy stick, mouse, or other type of peripheral as a controlling device. Graphics tablets have long been used to enter freehand drawings with their ability to interpret the movement of a stylus across a specially designed tablet or pad that is sensitive to movement.

Paint Programs

Paint programs create many types of images, including lettering, but after the lettering, objects, or other designs are created, the images are no longer easy to alter or redesign. The paint design is more of an optical image such as a drawing on a chalkboard. The image basically has to be erased to make changes. Colors of objects may be easily altered, but shape, size, and lettering can only be changed by erasing the image and then completely redoing the design or reworking the area like a paintbrush. Some packages are able to distort the original image in different ways, such as stretching the entire image into a longer shape, but the individually drawn shapes or components within the design are difficult to alter, except for color and texture changes. There are numerous paint programs available for both Macintoshes and PC compatibles. Some common paint programs for the Macintosh platform are Superpaint, MacPaint, and Canvas. Commonly used paint programs for the MS-DOS platform are Paint Show Plus and Corel Draw.

Paint programs allow some movement of images on the screen after they have been produced, but the process is basically like cutting the image out of a sheet of paper with a pair of scissors and pasting it in some other position on the page. Lettering that is typed on the paint screen cannot be revised with a word processor after it has been set into place. Simply changing the cursor position on the page is all that is necessary to position the images. Sophisticated paint programs enable the creator to work with an unlimited number of colors and alter visuals in numerous ways. Some paint packages allow easy import or export of images in PICT or other standard graphics formats.

Draw Programs

Draw programs function in a different manner than do paint programs. Their specific design elements can be altered in a variety of ways at any time the graphic is being used. For example, if labeling fonts, boxes, lines, textures, and other features have been created and stored in a file, the user can reopen the file and size or reposition the specific elements in a design. By placing the cursor on any given element in the design and simply clicking the mouse or pressing a joy stick button, the user can make alterations to the image or any of its parts.

The size, shape, position, and texture of any element can be changed by using a variety of software's drawing tools or by rearranging items with the input device. Drawing programs work well for making shapes and freeform images.

Drawing programs are better suited for creating freeform pieces of art or irregular shapes.

Presentation Programs

Several software presentation packages actually help a teacher or student prepare and organize a presentation. The programs format a presentation outline, set up a storyboard of small images to be used, and prepare full-sized slide or transparency masters to be reproduced in that medium. Presentation programs can be displayed on the computer itself, printed out as hardcopy handouts, or done as a combination of the two.

Presentation packages are popular for creating computer slide shows to use with an LCD panel and overhead projector for large group presentations, and some of them can actually produce animated motion color presentations. One example of this type of software is the Aldus Persuasion program.

Presentation packages enable users to manage computerized slide shows or animation sequences.

The intended use of a graphic is important when educators make decisions about its type and quality. Users should know in advance whether the graphic will be transferred to some other computer application or to some completely different medium. These factors may determine the effectiveness of the visual material being produced. For example, color graphics on a computer monitor are high quality and have vivid colors. If those graphic images are transferred to videotape, the colors usually don't look the same on a TV monitor. The stark differences in image clarity and color accuracy between the two can be quite a shock to the designer. If a graphic design is to be printed on a printer to produce a transparency, the type of font and printer being used and various other factors will affect the final visual product.

A common concern with graphic production is the quality of the printer or plotter used to create hardcopies. The availability of fonts and image quality are affected by the type of printer used. Chapter 22 provides more information about lettering and font styles, along with different file formats.

COMMON CONCERNS

Printer Quality

Many schools still use dot matrix printers with their computers. Some of these machines are reasonably fast and can produce near letter quality print, but they are not as desirable for producing high-quality graphics. PostScript laser

Dot matrix printers suffice for word processing, databases, and spreadsheets, but laser printers are often preferred for printing high-resolution graphics.

Many laser printers in schools print 300 dpi; higher-end systems print at least 600 dpi.

Ink jet printers offer a compromise—lower cost than lasers and higher quality than dot matrix.

A technology to watch is development of lower-cost color laser printers.

printers are usually the preferred type of printers for achieving high-quality printed materials. Dot matrix printers use a series of small pins to strike a ribbon to print. The pins do not create a solid print image, so their images do not look as sharp and clear as one might desire. They are, however, less expensive than most laser printers and are adequate for correspondence and various types of word processing, database, and spreadsheet applications. The printers that are capable of producing near letter quality images do an adequate job for typing correspondence and making it look like a personally typed letter rather than a form letter.

The number of dots per inch (dpi) a printer provides also affects the quality of printing. Some systems only produce 72 dpi; others, such as newer laser printers, produce 600 or more. Laser printers that are approaching school budget levels are those capable of printing 600 dpi—very good quality for desktop publishing school projects or term papers. Most schools lack sufficient funding to afford any quality above the 600 dpi printers.

Of the three basic types of printers used most frequently in schools, the dot matrix remains the most common, partially because of its lower cost and operating prices (printer ribbons cost far less than laser cartridges). The ink jet printer is also popular, because it provides an image that is closer to laser quality at a lower cost. Some of the ink jet models also produce fairly good color copies; they mix different inks to yield a rainbow of possibilities. Greater care must be taken in keeping the jets clean on these printers. If the ink jets get clogged with dried ink, they produce an inferior quality image. Some models have built-in cleaning systems to minimize this problem. Such machines are considered by many to be superior to dot matrix printers for graphics applications other than word processing.

Color printing on school computers has not been a primary concern of most teachers and students. Most printing work has been for word processing, database, and spreadsheet output, for which black ink printing has been satisfactory. Many dot matrix and ink jet printers can produce color copy if users simply insert a color ribbon or color ink wells, but the demand hasn't been that high. If interest in color graphics continues to grow, there will probably be greater demand for color printers.

As of this writing, color ink jet printers are capable of producing fairly good-quality, multicolored transparencies at a price that is within some schools' budget range. Color laser printers are much more expensive, and most K-12 schools have not been able to justify the cost. There are more costly wax or thermal types of color printers on the market that are well beyond the price range of most schools at the current time.

Font Selection

In the area of word processing, the number and types of fonts are usually of interest to the producer. Fonts refer to the general characteristics of different types of lettering and accompanying characters. Certain fonts are better for basic word processing to type a report or letter; others are better for labeling graphic images for other media. Unique or custom-generated fonts are usually reserved for special projects, such as using the Old English typeface for calligraphy-like lettering of names on certificates. A large selection of fonts is desired to provide several combinations to accommodate specific needs with relative ease.

The current status of computer technology is somewhat complicated when it comes to fonts and printing capabilities of various systems. Computers, printers, and applications allow multiple fonts to be created in a variety of ways. It should be noted that, in the past, Macintosh platform fonts had to be loaded into the computer's operating system before they could be created. However, just having certain fonts loaded onto the computer did not guarantee that the font would print on a printer in the same manner as seen on the monitor. Many printers also needed to have fonts loaded into their operating system. If the printer didn't have a particular font loaded that the computer was using and the printer was not a PostScript printer, the characters would not necessarily look the same when they were printed out. This is especially true for nonalphanumeric characters such as § or [3] .

IBM platform computers basically control their fonts through the application programs. This could also be complicated, because different applications might have different fonts. There is a new generation of software on the market, such as the Super ATM (Adobe Type Manager) for the Macintosh, that will permit the printer to match any font required. Both MS-DOS with Windows and Apple Macintosh platforms should soon be able to print any desired fonts using this type of software. Soon educators will not need to be concerned about complicated configurations for creating certain fonts.

Various image-capturing devices are being used to input visual data into computers. Video cameras with special video boards, still-image digital cameras like Canon's Zap Shot, and flattop or handheld scanners are some of the devices being used. They can capture images and enter them into a computer's memory to be manipulated by programs that save data in various types of file formats to be used in various ways. Just as was the case with printers, image quality produced by these devices can be partially determined by the resolution quality of the capturing device. Higher-resolution scanners or video cameras are more expensive but provide a much sharper image. Chapter 21 provides additional information on file formats that are used to store or transfer images from one application to another.

Many of the special input devices produce optical information that can be treated with a paint program. The sophistication of the software makes a difference in the amount of alterations users can perform on the images.

FONTS
CHICAGO
GENEVA
VENICE
LONDON

The printer driver for an application and a specific printer must know which fonts are available before the fonts can be used; printers emulate fonts that are unavailable.

IMAGE-CAPTURING DEVICES

Scanners

Although many scanners read-in text characters as graphics that are not editable by word processors, some optical character recognition (OCR) scanners can reproduce textual material so it can be revised by word processing. In fact, some software can now convert optically scanned images of print into recognizable fonts and allow the text material to be altered in a word processing mode.

CD-ROM Devices

Currently several CD-ROM players on the market provide an unlimited supply of visual images that can be incorporated into graphics. They contain maps, full-color pictures, clip art, cartoons, and numerous other images that are available for graphics production in educational settings. This medium may become one of the most valuable resources for reproducible graphics, because of the enormous collection of materials that is available.

Digitizing Cameras

The Cannon Zap Shot is a special electronic camera that can capture up to 50 electronically digitized images on a small diskette. The images can then be immediately downloaded to the computer to be saved in graphics files. The diskette can then be reused to store more photographs. The instant image access of the digital camera is a significant improvement over photographic film in terms of turnaround time for manipulation in desktop publishing systems for projects such as school papers. Several school systems are acquiring this technology to improve their desktop publishing capabilities. The camera isn't an extremely high-resolution imaging system, but with the right type of software and printer, the print quality is quite satisfactory for school papers and projects. It can be used to produce flyers, election campaign materials, school newspapers or newsletters, and any other type of pictorial copy work that is needed.

Video Digitizing Boards

These special circuit boards are inserted into a computer to allow it to grab visual images from any source of video, including videotape, laser discs, live camera shots, and CD-ROM images. They are relatively expensive for many schools to acquire, but they are beginning to gain recognition and popularity. Chapter 21 provides more information about video boards.

Palmtops

One of the more recent developments is Apple's Newton technology, which (as well as an array of other palmtop computers) can actually convert handwriting into a text mode on the computer for word processing. This device permits someone to write notes in longhand and then use the machine's resident software to store the characters as text that can be edited by a word processor.

COMPUTER GRAPHICS FOR VIDEO

Producing computer graphics for video production can be either simple or complicated, depending on the degree of sophistication of the hardware and software used. For example, the Apple IIE and software program VCR Companion is relatively simple to use but creates rather simple, low-quality graphics. The Amiga, Macintosh, or PC compatible systems may be more complicated but create higher-quality images.

There are distinct differences between computer and motion video technology. Video recording systems use analog information and computers work with digital information. In most cases, some form of interface device is required to allow these two different formats to exchange electronic signals that can be recorded, interpreted, revised, and played back on either system. It is similar to using a telephone modem with a computer on a bulletin board or LAN. The device must convert analog telephone messages to digital information that can be read on a computer monitor and visa versa. If high-quality visual results are desired through video and computer interfacing, there must be a way for the two data forms to be converted for compatibility. Several computer interface boards, such as Targa or Nuvista, are capable of resolving these interface problems.

Video recorders are analog; computers are digital.

Most systems require a special board or device to convert the two types of data back and forth. In addition to the way data is stored, pictures formed on TV screens and video projectors are electronically created in a different way than on a computer monitor. Regular TV produces an image that meets the National Television System Committee (NTSC) standards. NTSC (or interlaced) screens make a picture by scanning the screen differently than do computer (noninterlaced) monitors. The complicated technical explanation needed to describe the differences between these two technologies is not important here. It is more practical to identify concerns that may result from these technical differences.

Generally speaking, paint and draw programs include a what-you-see-is-what you-get (WYSIWYG) feature for creating graphics on a computer screen and transferring them to video. This is because the graphics are large enough images to create a fairly good resolution image on a TV. On the other hand, when basic nongraphic applications are run on a computer and their output transferred to regular video screens, the picture quality is less desirable, because the lettering and images are usually made of small, thin lines that do not appear as sharp on the television screen.

Computers offer more than twice the resolution of common television screens.

Aside from software differences and scanning differences of monitors, one additional item may affect visual quality between computer and TV monitors. Most TV sets display approximately 300 lines of resolution per screen, whereas computers often display 640 or more. If there are more lines of resolution on a screen, the image will have sharper definition. What all this means is that playing a computer graphic on a regular TV set or video projector will probably yield a picture that is not as sharp as the computer monitor image.

Some newer display devices can enhance the sharpness of graphic images.

The bottom line is that TV monitors and video projectors may be used to play computer graphics programs with some degree of image quality, but word processing and database applications' output will not look good on a regular TV monitor or video projector unless there is some way of converting the scan lines. Viewing of those types of programs should be done on an LCD projector, multiscan monitor, or a noninterlaced scan monitor to provide a sharper definition image. It would be wise for instructors to read more extensively about these technological differences before determining which system to buy for a school. Note: High-definition television (HDTV) may provide the answer to some of these image problems in the near future.

Some LCD projection panels on the market can display good-quality text from computer programs as well as playing full-motion, true color video programs. These panels may help eliminate the need for a separate TV and LCD panel to play different types of image output for viewing by a large group. Past technology required a large television or video projector to show analog video images, such as laser disc recording, while requiring an additional LCD panel or expensive multiscan monitor to show computer applications screens simultaneously. The new, active matrix, many-color LCD projection panels are capable of playing both types of signals with reasonable quality. Thus, active matrix panels eliminate the need for two different projection devices.

Some practical considerations for better-quality video graphics are as follows:

▶ Use bolder, block style lettering when possible.
▶ Avoid the use of standard-sized word processor text, because it is too thin and will shimmer on a television screen.
▶ Use shadowed letters to make them stand out better against the background.
▶ Do not use white lettering for titles. If white is desired, use a gray-scaled lettering that appears to be white on the television screen. White lettering tends to shimmer on the television screen.
▶ Three-dimensional letters often look better than do "flat" characters in video images.

SUGGESTED ACTIVITIES

1. Load a paint program, draw program, presentation graphics package, and a combination program into a computer and work with the basic tool kits to see what they can do and what differences exist among the programs.

2. Use a computer that is interfaced with a scanner to scan an image and load it into a software package for manipulation.

3. Work with a basic word processing program and look at all of the different types of fonts and variations that are available.

4. Print a single file on different types of printers to compare the quality of print.

5. Use a computer that is interfaced with a digitizing camera, video system, or CD-ROM player to input some visual material for alterations.

Chapter 19

NETWORKING AND TELECOMMUNICATIONS

PURPOSES

- ▶ To identify the characteristics of all computer networks
- ▶ To identify various types of computer networks
- ▶ To describe the instructional applications of computer networks

The proliferation of computers in the educational environment has given rise to many significant issues. One of the most formidable is the need for isolated computers to communicate with other computers. Networking, which in its most basic form means connecting computers, has two primary purposes: better communications and lower costs. Networking provides the means for exchanging data among computer systems, and networking enables users to share high-cost resources, such as laser printers, bulk storage devices, and backup systems.

All computer networks share common characteristics. The first characteristic is that the devices (computers and peripherals) must be connected; a communications channel must be established. Second, the devices must be capable of transmitting and receiving signals over some communications channel. Although some computer manufacturers have designed networking capabilities into their computers, the vast majority of networks are created by purchasing additional hardware and software.

Network Hardware

Network hardware may include switch boxes that exist outside the computers, expansion cards and network interface cards (NICs) that are installed within computers, or modems (either internal or external). The various types of communications cables, such as telephone or twisted-pair cable, copper coaxial cable, or fiber optic cable, are considered part of the network hardware. In some network configurations, an additional computer (for the central storage system, called the file server or host) must be dedicated to the management of the network. Although the need for and the advantages of networked computers may be evident, the cost associated with purchasing additional hardware to establish a network is a critical consideration.

TYPES OF NETWORKS

Network Software

After the physical network is in place, the logical operation of the network is controlled by network software. Generally, all computers connected to a network must have some type of communications software installed. The centralized computer acting as the network controller has file server or host software installed. File server software recognizes other computers connected to the network and controls the network communications between and among all the networked resources. Computers on the network without control responsibilities are generally referred to as network clients. Each client computer has some additional communications software installed that allows for interactions with the host computer or file server.

The sophistication of a network and the type of activity conducted via a network generally determines what additional hardware and software must be purchased.

Network to Share a Peripheral Among Computers

A shared-peripheral configuration requires a multiposition switch box to connect all the computers to the peripheral.

The most basic form of computer networks (though most computer professionals would not consider it a network) that many educators may encounter is a configuration that connects several computers to a single peripheral, such as a printer (see Figure 19.1). The only additional hardware required for this type of network would be a multiposition switch box and perhaps more cabling. Each position on the switch would represent one of the connected computers. Each of the computers would be connected to the switch via a cable. In this example, each computer would have a printer cable connected from the computer to an input connector on the switch box. A single printer would be connected to the output of the switch box.

Each computer user would turn the switch box indicator to that computer's letter to access the peripheral.

Because computers and printers are generally designed to communicate directly, no additional software would be needed. In order to use the networked resources, the user would have to manually set the switch in the appropriate position. This type of network has limited applications and works only with devices, such as printers and external modems, that can be directly connected to a computer's input/output ports.

Network to Share Files Using a File Server

When the inexpensive method of sharing data by exchanging diskettes (known as a "sneakernet") is no longer satisfactory, a more sophisticated network is required. Such a file-sharing network is created by linking computers to a centralized computer dedicated to managing the network and housing files centrally. This type is commonly referred to as a local area network (LAN). The centralized computer controlling the network acts as the host or file server. The other computers are said to be network clients. Such a configuration is diagrammed in Figure 19.2 (bottom, following page).

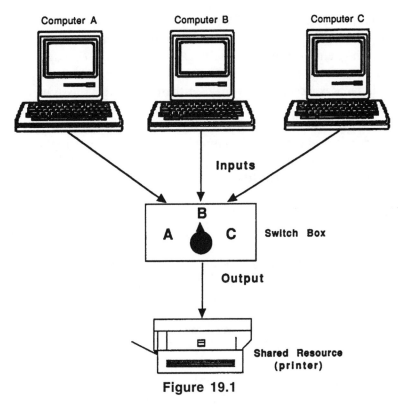

Figure 19.1

Networking to Share a Peripheral

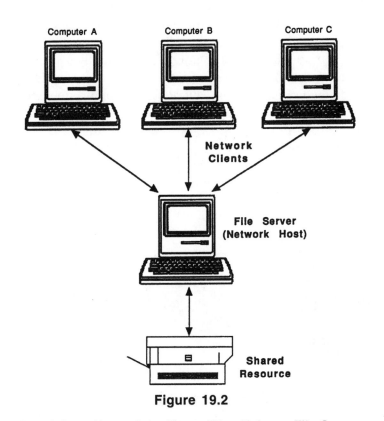

Figure 19.2

Local Area Network to Share Files Using a File Server

LANs offer the advantages of shared data as well as shared devices.

It is beyond the scope of this work to describe the various topologies (physical layouts in which computers are connected to one another, such as daisy chain, star, token ring, and bus) of these networks; however, the educator should recognize that networks of this type offer some advantages. Certainly, high-cost peripherals such as laser printers may be shared through this type of network as well as by a switch box. However, the file server computer can monitor network activity, provide centralized storage of data many users must access, and connect users who are too distant to share devices by using a switch box. LANs compile and record both individual and group data; this function is at the heart of many integrated learning systems.

This type of network can facilitate the sharing of data and communications between client computers. Some third-party networking solutions also offer the advantage of allowing computers (such as PCs and Macs) produced by a variety of manufacturers to share the same network. An easily overlooked advantage is a centralized means of data backup LANs provide for the network's administrator (manager of network activities and facilities).

Most LANs are confined to a rather limited geographic area, such as a single room or building. Networks that cover a larger geographic area, such as the network for an entire school district, are considered WANs (wide area networks). A new term is being used to describe networks that are distributed among a variety of locations: MANs, or multiple area networks.

TELECOM-MUNICATIONS SYSTEMS

On occasion, an educator wishes to take advantage of computer resources beyond those connected via the LAN. Many of these resources are available through telecommunications. Telecommunications is the transmission and reception of data via an electronic form (telephone line, satellite transmission, radio or TV broadcast, and others). Optical fiber is rapidly becoming the most popular means of establishing the communications channel. The dominant form of telecommunications among educators is computer-to-computer communications via telephone systems, as shown in Figure 19.3.

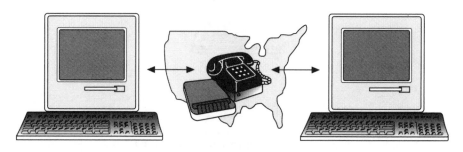

Figure 19.3

Network to Access Remote Data from a Distant Host

Network to Link a Computer to a Remote Host

Communicating with another computer requires both computers to include modems that are connected to telephone or other communications lines; this provides the connection and the communications channel. Control for sending and receiving data is provided by telecommunications software. A modem (an abbreviation for modulator/demodulator) is the hardware device that converts the digital signal used by the computer to analog signals used by the telephone system. The process of converting the digital signal of the sending computer to the analog signal for telephone transmission is known as modulation. The process of converting the analog signal to the digital signal for the receiving computer is known as demodulation. Figure 19.4 shows the telecommunications process. Modems generally vary in cost according to how quickly they can convert and transmit their signals.

A remote host is a computer not hard-wired to the educator's system; connecting the two requires modems.

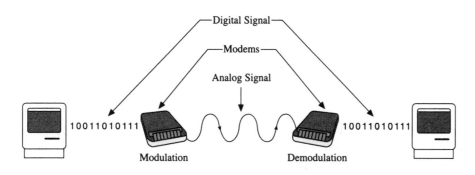

Figure 19.4

Signal Modulation and Demodulation Using Modems

The amount of data transmitted by a modem in one second is called the baud rate. The baud rate of a modem is critical for two reasons:

▶ Both the sending and receiving modem must communicate at the same baud rate.
▶ If telecommunications require a long-distance connection, the faster a modem completes the transmission, the lower the cost.

Currently, the most popular baud rate for modems is 2400 baud. Newer technologies are permitting significantly faster baud rates, and some consumer-type modems transmit at 9600 baud or more.

Once the computers are connected to the modems and the modems to the phone line, telecommunications software is used to establish and control the communications between the two systems. Generally a series of parameters, or settings that can vary, must be specified. These parameters are discussed in detail in the communications software and modem manuals. The primary concern is for both systems to use the same parameter settings.

For two modems to communicate, their parameters must match.

REMOTE RESOURCES

Knowing who or what to call is as important as knowing how to call. Most educators use telecommunications to perform two tasks: communicate directly with another individual or gather information.

Electronic Bulletin Boards

Students and educators have set up numerous bulletin boards devoted to information sharing and innovations in special interest areas.

One method for doing both tasks is to use an electronic bulletin board. Once a computer is connected to a telecommunications channel via modem and communications software is installed, all that the user requires to connect to a bulletin board are its telephone number and (for restricted-access bulletin boards) an account number or password. A teacher or student can use the communications hardware and software to dial the number and connect. Once connected, an individual may need to enter an account number or password; then all posted messages are available, or the user can post a message to be read by others. Bulletin boards generally develop around a particular interest of the bulletin board administrator. Some schools have established electronic bulletin boards to provide parents with information about school events or closings.

Information Utilities

Information utilities such as CompuServe and Prodigy offer specialty bulletin boards, shopping services, and on-line publications such as newspapers or encyclopedias.

Another method for communicating with others and obtaining information is the use of an information utility—a computer facility that users access by applying for a subscription or paying a fee. When the user pays the fee, he or she is given a password and procedures for connecting to the service. Information utilities generally have broad resources. When the user connects, via modem and telephone line, a menu of options appears. The user selects the desired activity and has immediate access to the most up-to-date information in the field served by the utility. Many utilities also contain transaction services, which allow the user to complete financial transactions such as purchasing goods, making hotel and plane reservations, or paying bills.

Electronic Mail

One feature of networked computers, which some information services provide, is electronic mail (E-mail), which allows users to send private messages to other users via their computer. The electronic mail transmissions reside in an area of the host computer that can only be accessed by the designated receiver. When the person to whom the mail was sent connects to the network or information utility, a message indicating that mail has been received is displayed. The recipient may read and discard the message or save the mail for later reference. If necessary, the user can send a reply.

INTERNET links a variety of academic computer users.

Beyond the local level, networks may be connected to other networks at the state, regional, national, and international level. One such network of networks is called INTERNET. This is primarily a network of research organizations such as colleges and universities, government agencies, and commercial developers. Through this network, computer and information resources are made available to any individual who can legitimately gain access through the home institution's computer system. Some of the resources available include on-line catalogs at a variety of institutional libraries, special on-line conferences related to myriad topics, archived program files, and even on-line journals.

Many teachers are finding valuable resources through information utilities, bulletin boards, and networked resources.

Networked computers have provided many opportunities for educators and students. Networked computers have been used to deliver instruction, provide testing experiences, provide a collaborative work environment, facilitate communication, and expand the impact of expensive resources.

When individual computers and/or networked computers use any of the vast array of communications channels now available, new horizons of opportunity are accessed.

Many state educational agencies are providing bulletin board services that list materials and speakers on a variety of subjects related to public school education. Some teacher organizations have created services that connect subject area specialists with classroom teachers for assistance in preparing instructional activities. Educators themselves have used telecommunications to open the classroom to a variety of resources. On-line conferences have been held with experts in virtually every field. Electronic penpals have exchanged messages in foreign languages. Creative writing activities have been transmitted between schools in different regions of the country and the world. Software packages enable students in a variety of locations to interact with simulations via telecommunications. Electronic research is being conducted in many educational institutions. Students are no longer limited to the resources contained in their own school library. Major news and information services are available via the computer and telecommunications.

INSTRUCTIONAL USES OF TELE-COMMUNICA-TIONS AND NETWORKS

Educational bulletin boards help educators share resources and research; students share messages and experiences.

SUGGESTED ACTIVITIES

1. Read about and report on instructional uses of networks and/or telecommunications.

2. Visit at least two sites at which different kinds of computer networks are established. Identify the type of network installed. What advantages are provided by each? What are the limitations of each network? Summarize your findings.

3. Dial in to an information utility such as CompuServe or Prodigy. Write a brief summary of your experience.

4. The U.S. Department of Education Office of Educational Research and Improvement (OERI) maintains a free bulletin board system. Set your modem to 8 bits, no parity, 1 stop bit, and dial (800) 222-4922. Write a brief summary of your experiences using telecommunications and computers for educational purposes.

Chapter 20

SOFTWARE SELECTION AND UTILIZATION

PURPOSES

- ▶ To identify inappropriate "de facto" guidelines that affect software selection
- ▶ To recommend appropriate selection and evaluation guidelines for application and instructional software

INTRODUCTION

In September 1988, the U.S. Congressional Office for Technology Assessment (OTA), released a report on the current use of technology in American public education: *Power On! New Tools for Teaching and Learning.* One of the issues covered in the report was the selection and evaluation of instructional software. After consulting 36 public, private, and governmental software evaluation agencies; school teachers; software publishers; university professors; and private consultants; the OTA listed 185 characteristics considered in evaluating educational software.

These characteristics do not include subject-specific and population-specific characteristics, which some participants felt would be necessary for a thorough review. It would be impossible for each teacher to apply all 185 characteristics to each piece of software considered, but it is important for educators to make selections based on appropriate criteria.

"DE FACTO" GUIDELINES

In almost every instance where educators must choose from among alternatives, certain practices which facilitate the selection process are developed. Over time, these practices become so ingrained that they are often applied without real thought. The validity of such practices is at least questionable; however, in the area of microcomputer software selection, certain inappropriate practices have almost attained the level of selection standards or criteria.

Educators should avoid common software purchasing mistakes to obtain appropriate, useful programs.

Although few would agree that these practices should be used as primary purchasing guidelines, through repetitive practice, they have become "de facto" guidelines. Teachers involved in the software selection process should be aware of these de facto guidelines and should make every effort to avoid the thoughtless repetition of practices such as those listed here:

- ▶ Purchase the least expensive package available. Although expense is certainly a consideration, many inexpensive programs have been abandoned because they were too limited, they failed to meet student and teacher expectations, and they could not be modified to meet curriculum modifications. As in other areas, quality generally costs.

▶ Purchase programs that are copyable. The issue of illegal software duplication has already been addressed, but it is worth another warning. Educators should not practice the illegal duplication of software nor should they tolerate the use of illegally duplicated software. Unfortunately, some educators select programs that are not copy-protected with the sole intent of making multiple copies, generally violating the software license agreement and copyright law.

▶ Purchase whatever is available and use it. This is particularly true where selections are limited. Many teachers and students have lost interest in using computers because their initial experiences using low-quality software were negative. Don't let zeal for the technology overshadow instructional value.

▶ Purchase programs without preview or review. Educators are introduced to software packages through a variety of sources: publisher catalogs, brochures, and advertisements; educational conferences and inservice meetings; other teachers; and so on. Generally, a demonstration of a complex package is inadequate; teachers need extended periods of time for hands-on experimentation with a program.

▶ Purchase programs before determining instructional goals and applications. It is much better to purchase software that can be modified to fit the determined curriculum than to purchase software that will determine the curriculum.

The general guidelines for selection presented earlier in this book (Chapter 3) also apply to microcomputer software, but some additional guidelines specifically for microcomputer software are suggested here.

TECHNICAL QUALITY GUIDELINES

Technical considerations deal with how well the program operates. If the program is difficult to operate, the instructional content may never receive the student's full attention. Guidelines for the technical quality of a program revolve around four major areas: usability, reliability, display quality, and documentation usefulness.

Usability

How easy is the program to use? What skills are required of the student and/or teacher? Is keyboard entry minimized where appropriate? Is on-line help available? Are commands concise and consistent? How much teacher supervision is required? Is printing easy and simple to accomplish with a variety of popular printers?

Reliability

Is the program "crashproof?" Does the program include few important errors? Are peripherals included with the package durable, easy to install, and tamper resistant? Are peripherals returned by the package difficult to acquire or inappropriately expensive? Is adequate warranty and technical support available for both hardware and software?

Audio and Video Displays

Are audio and video used effectively and appropriately for the intended audience? Are text displays grammatically accurate, well formatted, and displayed without delay? Can the audio be adjusted (turned down or off)? Are graphics clear on a variety of monitors (including monochrome monitors or LCD screens)? Is the organization of screen displays logical and consistent?

Documentation

Are printed directions clear, easy to use, and accurate? Are illustrations and diagrams that assist the user provided? Are on-screen prompts available and clear? Can the program be used without reference to printed documentation?

Assuming that the technical quality is satisfactory, attention must be given to the subject matter presented. Instructional characteristics determine the learning outcomes that are achieved by using the computer software. Guidelines for the instructional quality of a program revolve around three major areas: organization, content, and educational strategy.

INSTRUCTIONAL QUALITY GUIDELINES

Organization

Is the purpose of the program clearly stated? Are program activities sequenced logically? Are the diskette and support materials appropriately packaged for student use? Are appropriate teacher and student instructions available? Are suggestions for instructional activities included? Are student record files maintained on diskette or on the hard disk?

Content

Is content accurate, up-to-date, and free of bias or stereotyping? Is content appropriate for audience? Is the breadth of the content appropriate and can it support the school curriculum? Does the content lend itself to computerized presentation? Can the teacher modify the content? Has the content been field tested and are the results available? Are instructional objectives clearly stated and evaluated?

Instructional Strategy

Is the strategy appropriate for intended audience and content? Does the program provide for branching based on student response? Can the student or teacher alter the general program flow? Is feedback for correct and incorrect responses appropriate? Does the instructional strategy make appropriate use of computer capabilities? Does the program maintain student interest and motivation? Are graphics and audio used for instruction? Is the level of difficulty automatically adjusted according to student response?

Utilization guides help teachers to select software according to professional criteria.

Selection and utilization imply criteria and standards. Teachers are generally guided by written criteria or checklists that attempt to integrate national and local professional opinions and standards. A number of organizations have developed extensive indepth evaluation guides for instructional software. A sample evaluation instrument, based on criteria established by the Computer Technology Program of the Northwest Regional Educational Laboratory in Portland, Oregon, appears at the end of this chapter.

ADDITIONAL GUIDELINES

If students are to use application software to manipulate subject matter, the primary consideration is ease of use. The tool must not be so difficult to use that it distracts the user's attention from the subject matter. The teacher must determine the relative importance of each feature. In order to determine the relative importance of each feature, the teacher must have some idea of the activities that will be completed with the software tool. The following should be considered for all application packages:

▶ Is the package compatible with available hardware?
▶ What amount of memory is required?
▶ What number of disk drives or hard disk capacity is required?
▶ Are student copies/versions available?
▶ Are there tutorials students can use?
▶ What are the quality and cost of additional manuals?

SUGGESTED ACTIVITIES

1. Use an instructional software program. Evaluate the program using the form provided at the end of this chapter, a form you have located in professional literature, or a form provided by your instructor.

2. Interview a practicing teacher who uses instructional software. How was the software selected? What criteria were used? Obtain a copy of the evaluation form, if possible. Were any of the de facto guidelines a part of the selection decision?

3. Gather information on at least two different packages in the same application area (two word processors, two spreadsheets, and so on). Compare the characteristics listed for both packages to the list of characteristics presented in this chapter. Can you draw some conclusions about features and cost? Can you think of applications that might be inhibited or enhanced as a result of the features available?

Microcomputer Software Evaluation Guide

Program Title_____ Copyright Date _____

Medium: 5.25" diskette_____ 3.5" diskette_____ CD-ROM_____

System requirements (brand, model, memory, disk space) _____

Distributor/Producer _____

Address_____ Phone _____

Cost: $____purchase $___ rental $___ backup copy $___ lab pack $___site
(multiple copies) license

Program Description
Subject area/Specific topic_____

Grade/Ability Level_____

Program use(s)

___ Simulation   ___ Testing   ___Multimedia Development

___ Drill and Practice ___ Classroom management   ___Other

___ Instructional game ___ Remediation

___ Tutorial   ___ Enrichment

___ Problem Solving   ___ Utility

___ Application_____ ___ Authoring/Presentation

Documentation available: Circle all that are available in the computer program (P) or in the supplementary materials (S).

P S Suggested grade/ability levels	P S Teacher's information
P S Instructional objectives	P S Resource/reference information
P S Prerequisite skills or activities	P S Student instructions
P S Sample program output	P S Student worksheet
P S Program operating instructions	P S Vocabulary list(s)
P S Pretest	P S Relationship to standard textbooks
P S Posttest	P S Follow-up Activities

Brief description (include objectives and special strengths and weaknesses)

_____

_____

_____

_____

	Excellent **(E)**	Good **(G)**	Fair **(F)**	Poor **(P)**

Technical Quality	*E*	*G*	*F*	*P*
The documentation is comprehensive and effective	_____	_____	_____	_____
Information displays are effective	_____	_____	_____	_____
Users can easily and independently operate the program	_____	_____	_____	_____
Teachers can easily employ the courseware	_____	_____	_____	_____
Program appropriately uses relevant computer capabilities	_____	_____	_____	_____
The program is reliable and free from system errors	_____	_____	_____	_____

Instructional Quality				
Content is accurate	_____	_____	_____	_____
Content has educational value	_____	_____	_____	_____
Content is free of racial, ethnic, sexual, and other stereotypes	_____	_____	_____	_____
The purpose of the courseware is well-defined	_____	_____	_____	_____
Presentation of content is clear and logical	_____	_____	_____	_____
Level of difficulty is appropriate for the target audience	_____	_____	_____	_____
Graphics/color/sound used for appropriate reasons	_____	_____	_____	_____
The courseware is motivational	_____	_____	_____	_____
The courseware stimulates student creativity	_____	_____	_____	_____
Feedback on student responses is effectively employed	_____	_____	_____	_____
Learner controls rate and sequence of presentation and review	_____	_____	_____	_____
Instruction is integrated with previous student experience	_____	_____	_____	_____

Overall Evaluation

_____ Excellent program. Recommend without hesitation.

_____ Good program. Consider purchase.

_____ Fair. Might want to wait for something better.

_____ Not useful. Do not recommend purchase.

Evaluated by:_____ **Date** _____

Criteria listed above are based on recommendations developed by the Northwest Regional Educational Laboratory in Portland, Oregon.

Chapter 21

MULTIMEDIA

PURPOSES

▶ To identify a working definition for *multimedia*
▶ To identify the two basic forms of multimedia delivery
▶ To identify technologies used in the production of multimedia
▶ To list the basic components of and describe the function of a digitizing system

The field of instructional media and technology has been involved with the concept of "multimedia" since Comenus created the first picture book, *Orbis Sensualium Pictus* (The Visible World Pictured) for instruction in 1657. As discussed earlier in this text, research has indicated that the learning process is enhanced when instruction is delivered in a variety of forms. These various forms address the learning styles of a diverse classroom population and ensure that the desired message is effectively and efficiently communicated. Many of the newest technological advances have had a dramatic impact on the concept of multimedia instruction.

Currently, multimedia instruction is a trendy concept. Many use the term to refer to any technology that incorporates more than one communication channel. For the purposes of this chapter, multimedia means user-controlled computer delivery of a variety of media forms, including text, still graphics, moving images, and sound. In the field of education there are two popular forms of multimedia delivery: computer-controlled systems and authoring/presentation systems.

Computer-Controlled Multimedia Delivery

Many of the newer technology forms are capable of being interfaced with a computer, so the computer and appropriate application software can control the other devices. Some of the devices are able to import and export visual and auditory data with the computer. In some cases the computer just controls the interfaced external devices.

The first form of multimedia delivery is based on one of the characteristics of technology highlighted in Chapter 13, the centripetal nature of centralized control; computer technology offers such control over other electronically controlled devices. This concept is at the heart of first generation multimedia. This form, shown in Figure 21.1, is characterized by the variety of devices connected to the computer.

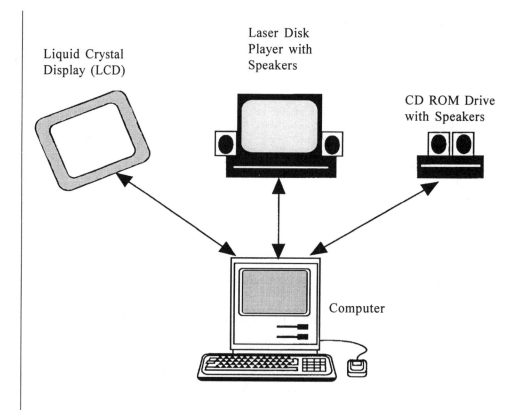

Liquid Crystal
Display (LCD)

Laser Disk
Player with
Speakers

CD ROM Drive
with Speakers

Computer

Figure 21.1

Sample Computer-Controlled Multimedia Configuration

Multimedia provides computer control over devices for presentations.

In many instances, it will become commonplace to have a laser disc player, with accompanying monitor and speakers, a CD-ROM drive, with accompanying speakers, and a liquid crystal display (LCD) device connected with a single computer to deliver a presentation before a large group. What is important to note is that the *computer* controls these separate devices. Usually, the presenter establishes some preprogrammed sequence of events using an authoring system or a multimedia development package. During the presentation, the instructor would activate each sequence and the computer would send the instructions to each of the connected devices.

Authoring and Presentation Systems

Many software packages called "authoring" programs provide teachers and students with a user friendly method of creating presentations and/or lessons. These packages take advantage of computer interaction capabilities in addition to using driver software for controlling external audio and video devices. Hypercard on the Macintosh platform has been a leader in this process; however, newer packages include Video Voyager, Personal Presenter, Laser Works, and Podium. LinkWay Live from IBM has also been given considerable attention for putting together computer-controlled multimedia presentations.

Although this form of multimedia offers great potential, many individuals find the process of connecting all of the devices overwhelming. Because much of the equipment that can be controlled by a computer is new—and, at times, expensive—it is impossible to obtain in many classrooms. Even when the technology is available, time for mastering it is limited. Initial development of a short presentation could take hours. Many teachers, experienced in providing a variety of media experiences sequentially, have little frame of reference for developing simultaneously delivered media experiences. Computer-controlled multimedia has a long way to go to reach its full potential, due to financial limitations and teacher knowledge, but it has initiated a very crucial development—the "interface" concept.

Computer-controlled presentations are not common because of cost and lack of teacher experience with the technology.

The most important concept of computer-controlled multimedia delivery is the fact that the computer can control a wide variety of electronic devices. In order for a computer to control an external device, the computer must be physically connected to the device. Generally, this is accomplished through one of the communications ports of the computer; many devices connect to unused modem or printer ports (occasionally, an additional communications port may need to be installed).

INTERFACED TECHNOLOGIES

Once two devices are physically connected, a common communications scheme must be adopted. Usually this process requires some type of software to be installed on the computer; at that point, the computer can take over operation of the external devices, much like a remote control. Establishing both the physical connection and the logical communication is called interfacing.

Interfacing is done on both the physical and the logical levels.

Virtual Reality

One of the newest advancements in computer-controlled sensory stimulations is the virtual reality movement. It is being used in entertainment, industry, and many other fields. Virtual reality actually places the learner in a computer-simulated environment that interacts with the learner's movements and responses. It provides computer-animated visual and sound stimuli and responds to the learner's actions to provide more of a realistic experience.

The area of virtual reality is basically an interfacing issue. Computers have long been able to produce elaborate graphic images. Originally based on the same concepts as computer-assisted design (CAD), computers are now creating detailed three-dimensional images, a process called rendering. Because these images are created by the computer, it can also be used to manipulate them. The technology currently under development is related to how humans control these images. The flight simulator is a virtual reality concept. Using realistic controls, humans interact with visual, auditory, and in some cases tactile information provided by a computer. Virtual reality requires a sophisticated computer system containing an enormous amount of memory and a wide array of multisensory input/output devices. Virtual reality technology is gaining considerable attention in industrial, medical, and military training circles, but it has also made significant strides in the world of entertainment. The commercial movie industry has already created some films with virtual reality sequences.

The applications of virtual reality in education are as yet untapped.

As the cost of computing power declines, virtual reality may provide many educational opportunities. In the near future, driver education courses may be offered on virtual reality simulators.

Although the ability to interface technologies is important and is leading to exciting developments, another revolution is occurring. The digital revolution is changing the form of multimedia delivery.

Digital Multimedia Delivery

The second generation of multimedia is characterized by a single concept—digitization. Digitization is the process of converting some other electronic signal, usually analog, to digital. Telephones, videotape, and audio tape originally transmitted signals in a wave pattern (analog). Computers use digital signals; they can be processed faster and are less subject to distortion. So, while some industries worked on creating new hardware and new software so that computers could control more and more external devices, other industries worked on developing new hardware and software that would convert analog signals to digital signals.

Digitization has followed a logical progression, creating new media along the way.

Modems, which convert analog telephone signals to digital computer signals, were probably the first such device. Modems were soon followed by digital audio recording (such as for DAT cassettes), which led to the development of compact discs, which has led to digital video recording, which has led to digital multimedia delivery. The primary advantage of digital multimedia is that all the media can be delivered by a single device: the computer. Because the computer specializes in handling digital data, if textual, aural, and visual data can be converted into digital data, the computer can deliver all of it without any external devices (see Figure 21.2).

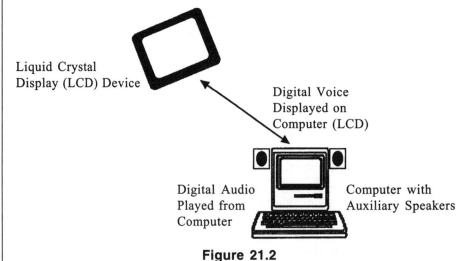

Liquid Crystal
Display (LCD) Device

Digital Voice
Displayed on
Computer (LCD)

Digital Audio
Played from
Computer

Computer with
Auxiliary Speakers

Figure 21.2

Sample Digital Multimedia Configuration

PRODUCING MULTIMEDIA

Most of the current developments in multimedia products fall in the area of digital multimedia. An educator interested in producing digital multimedia should become familiar with a wide range of technologies designed to enhance multimedia development. It is important to remember that the technologies and processes in this discussion share a common element: digital creation for digital reproduction on a computer.

Digital Graphics

Since the creation of graphics applications that paint and draw images, computers have been used to create visuals; however, until recently, these images were always identifiable as computer-generated images. They lacked the quality and realism of photographs and other forms of visual reproduction. To overcome that drawback, two devices have been developed—the digital scanner and the still video camera.

Scanners come in a wide variety of forms and capabilities: handheld, flatbed, black and white, color, 300 dots per inch (dpi), 600 dpi, and more. The purpose of most scanners is to convert existing images to a digital format that can then be altered electronically for inclusion in a variety of applications.

Scanners digitize existing images.

The concept of *still video* is based on recording visual images electronically, hence the reference to video. Perhaps still electronic visual would be a better term to use, but video cameras are actually one type of image-capturing device available for such activities, so the term is somewhat appropriate. The value of capturing electronic images instantly and being able to alter them electronically opens up a whole new mode of photographic concepts that were unavailable during the era of film and its processing. As the term recognizes, these images also lack one characteristic that is traditionally considered a strength of video: motion. There are newer adaptations, such as Apple's Spigot board and Quicktime software that facilitates motion reproduction.

Still video cameras capture images and store them on disk for transmission to a digitizer.

All digitizing systems contain three primary components, as illustrated in Figure 21.3:

▶ capture device
▶ digitizing device
▶ output device

Depending on the computer platform and types of interfaced equipment, a microcomputer serves in one or more of these various roles.

The most common image-capturing device for visual images is an ordinary video camera. Technological advances continue to improve the quality of the images that even inexpensive video cameras can record. One of the drawbacks of using traditional video cameras is that they are designed to capture motion. Usually, a triggering device of some type is incorporated into the system to freeze the moving video image. Some manufacturers have created "electronic lens-shutter" or "still video" cameras that are designed to work like traditional

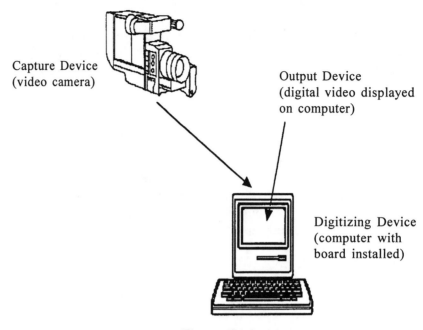

Figure 21.3

Sample Basic Video Digitizing System

35mm cameras. When the shutter is released, the image is captured electronically and stored on a magnetic disk (much like a floppy diskette).

The digitizer converts the signals for use on a computer.

Images captured by the video camera are transmitted to a digitizer, which may be an external component or an expansion card that has been installed inside a microcomputer. The digitizer converts the video camera signals, which a computer cannot use, to digital signals, which a computer can use. Still video cameras, as mentioned earlier, accomplish both tasks—capturing and digitizing—simultaneously.

Eventually, the user must be able to view and possibly alter the image that has been captured. Generally, the digitizing component produces a signal that can be viewed on the computer monitor. In microcomputer-based systems, the image may be viewed or incorporated into a variety of application packages, some of which will permit the user to modify and manipulate the image. Frequently, the output device may be a printer, which would produce a hardcopy of the captured image, or it may be a videotape recorder that can record the computer-altered image on tape.

Digital Video

Digital video images can be displayed directly on computer monitors but consume a lot of hard disk space.

The concept of digital video expands the concept of digital graphics to include motion and, in some cases, sound. This process takes live or traditionally recorded video, converts the images to digital form, and stores the data on the computer's hard disk. These digital images can then be incorporated into a wide variety of applications. Digital video can be displayed directly on the computer monitor; no additional video monitor is needed. The primary disadvantage of digital video is the amount of memory required to store the video and audio information in digital form. The computer's processing capability is also a consideration. The computer and its operating system must be capable of transmitting large amounts of data rapidly to provide high-quality sound and motion. The industry is currently working toward greater memory capabilities, such as optical drives and WORM (write once, read many) drives or compression systems that squeeze more information into less space.

Digital video has the same basic components as still video; however, the capture device and the digitizing device must be capable of handling a moving image. One of the systems that has been given considerable attention for this type of production is the Video Spigot board from SuperMac (digitizer) and Apple's QuickTime (digital video control software).

Other digital effects such as animation can be used to add motion to text or still images. Traditionally, animation would have to be created on a frame-by-frame basis; advances in software make it possible to create three-dimensional objects that move in a variety of ways on the computer screen.

Digital Audio

With greater attention being given to the quality of sound production, many teachers and students are learning about computer programs that can create and record sophisticated digital audio. Once digitized, the audio data can be manipulated by the computer; special effects such as an echo can be added electronically, and digital sound effects and multitrack recordings can be mixed on the computer. Some audio software enables up to 64 audio tracks to be produced and can record and play back CD-quality sound.

Digital audio systems use computers to create special effects and mix multiple tracks.

Musical instrument digital interface (MIDI) devices can also be used to record and produce digital sounds that can be manipulated by the computer. The MacRecorder Sound System from Macromedia is a good example.

The use of a multiple forms of media has been proven educationally sound. Recent developments in technology have provided a wealth of options for multimedia (which is the user-controlled computer delivery of a variety of media forms, including text, still graphics, moving images, and sound). One basic form of multimedia—computer-controlled multimedia delivery—emphasizes the interfacing of external devices controlled by the computer. The other basic form—digital multimedia delivery—emphasizes the conversion of all signals to a digital form that can be delivered by a single device, the computer. The basic elements of a digitizing system are a capturing device, a digitizing device, and an output device. These devices are helping teachers and students produce a wide variety of instructional materials.

SUMMARY

SUGGESTED ACTIVITIES

1. Read and report on the current uses of multimedia instruction.

2. Create a brief presentation using the computer-controlled multimedia delivery method as described in this chapter.

3. Create a brief presentation using the digital multimedia delivery method as described in this chapter.

4. Interface an external device (CD-ROM player, laser disc player, scanner, VCR, and so on) with a computer. Note what hardware and software were necessary to accomplish the task.

5. Use a scanner, audio digitizer, and/or video digitizer to capture appropriate computer data. Use application software to modify the digitized data.

6. View a videotape or a movie about virtual reality. Observe the ways in which the interface between the computer and the user is created. If possible, visit a virtual reality center.

Recommended Readings

Bennett, Randy E. *Planning and Evaluating Computer Education Programs.* Ohio: Merrill Publishing Co., 1987.

Ambron, Sueann, and Kristina Hooper, ed. *Learning with Interactive Multimedia: Developing and Using Multimedia Tools in Education.* Raymond, WA, 1990.

Bitter, Gary G., Ruth A. Camuse, and Vicki L. Durbin. *Using a Microcomputer in the Classroom.* 3rd ed. New Jersey: Prentice Hall, 1993.

Bröderbund Software, 17 Paul Drive, San Rafael, CA ɣ4903-2101. (800) 521-6263.

Brownell, Gregg. *Computers and Teaching.* Minnesota: West Publishing Co., 1987.

Burstein, Jerome S. *Computers and Information Systems,* New York: CBS College Publishing, 1986.

Cannings, Terence R. and Stephen W. Brown. *The Information Age Classroom: Using the Computer as a Tool.* California: Franklin, Beedle & Associates Publishers, 1986.

Capron, H. L. *COMPUTERS: Tools for an Information Age.* California: Benjamin Cummings Publishing Co., 1987.

Clayton, Dean and Ok D. Park. *Apple-Works: Integrated Applications for Microcomputers.* Ohio: South-Western Publishing Co., 1987.

Coburn, Peter, Peter Kelman, Nancy Roberts, Thomas F. F. Snyder, Daniel H. Watt, and Cheryl Weiner. *Practical Guide to Computers in Education.* U.S.: Addison-Wesley Publishing Co., 1985.

Coilis, Betty. *Computers. Curriculum, and Whole-Class Instruction: Issues and Ideas.* California: Wadsworth Publishing, 1988.

Day, John. *Microcomputers in Business: Spreadsheet, Word Processing, and Database Management Systems.* Illinois and England: Scott, Foresman, and Co., 1986.

Echternacht, Lonnie J., Mark Ehlert, and Mary Henrikson. *Introduction to Microcomputer Applications in Education.* Iowa: Kendall/Hunt Publishing Co., 1988.

Eckhardt, Robert. *The Fully Powered Mac.* New York: Brady, 1988.

Hallenbeck, Mark J. and Donald F. Boetel. *Teacher Friendly: A BASIC Programming Course Just for Classroom Teachers.* California: David S. Lake Publishers, 1985.

Klemin, V. Wayne and Ken Harsha. *PC Applications: Comprehensive Problems and Review.* U.S.: McGraw-Hill Book Co., 1989.

Lewis, Raymond J. *Meeting Learners' Needs through Telecommunications.* Washington, D.C.: American Association for Higher Education, 1983.

Lockard, James, Peter D. Abrams, and Wesley A. Many, *Microcomputers for Education.* Boston, Mass: Little, Brown and Co., 1987.

Macromedia, 13665 Eureaka Rd., South Gate, MI 48195. (800) 288-4797.

Maddux, Cleborne D., D. LaMont Johnson, and Jerry W. Willis. *Educational Computing: Learning with Tomorrow's Technologies.* Boston: Allyn and Bacon, 1992.

Mandell, Steven L. *Working with Application Software/Apple II (2.lB Version).* California and New York: West Publishing Co., 1986.

Merrill, Paul F., Marvin N. Tolman, Larry Christensen, Kathy Hammons, Bret R. Vincent, and Peter L. Reynolds. *Computers in Education.* New Jersey: Prentice Hall, 1986.

Nickles, Herbert L. and George H. Culp. *The Practical Apple: A Guide for Educators.* California: Brooks/Cole Publishing Co., 1988.

Parker, Charles S. *Understanding Computers and Data Processing: Today and Tomorrow.* New York: CBS College Publishing, 1987.

Silver, Gerald A. and Myrna L. Silver. *Computers and Information Processing.* New York: Harper and Row Publishers, 1986.

SuperMac Technology. P.O. Box 60069, Sunnyvale, CA 94088. (408) 245-2202.

Taylor, R.P. ed. *The Computer in the School.* New York: Teachers College Press, 1980.

Troutman, Andria P., James A. White, and Frank D. Breit. *The Micro Goes to School: Instructional Applications of Microcomputer Technology.* California: Brooks/Cole Publishing Co., 1988.

Turner, Sandra and Michael Land. *TOOLS for Schools: Applications Software for the Classroom.* California: Wadsworth Publishing Co., 1988.

U.S. Congress, Office of Technology Assessment (OTA). *POWER ON! New Tools for Teaching and Learning.* Washington, D.C.: Government Printing Office, 1988.

Van Horn, Royal. *Advanced Technology in Education: An Introduction to Videodiscs, Robotics, Optical Memory, Peripherals, New Software Tools, and High-Tech Staff Development.* Pacific Grove, Calif.: Brooks/Cole Publishing Company, 1991.

Vockell, Edward and Eileen Schwartz. *The Computer in the Classroom.* Cailfornia: Mitchell Publishing Co., 1988.

White, Charles S. and Guy Hubbard. *Computers and Education.* New York: Macmillan Publishing Co., 1988.

Willis, Jerry W. *Educational Computing: A Guide to Practical Applications.* Arizona: Gorsuch Scarisbrick, Publishers, 1987.

GLOSSARY

ASCII: American Standard Code for Information Interchange; the most common bit combination coding scheme for microcomputers.

Backup: A duplicate copy of program or data files prepared in case the original files are damaged or lost.

BASIC: Beginners All-Purpose Symbolic Instruction Code; a popular programming language for beginning programers.

Baud Rate: The speed at which a modem converts and transmits bits, or items of information.

Binary: The base-two numbering system; a condition or situation having only two possibilities.

Binary Digit: In binary notation, either of the digits 0 and 1; the smallest unit understood by the computer.

BIT: Binary digit; the smallest unit of computer data, represented by the value of 0 or 1.

Booting: The process of loading the operating system into the microcomputer memory (see also cold boot and warm boot).

Bug: A mistake in a computer program or a malfunction in a computer hardware component.

Byte: A group of adjacent binary digits operated on by the computer as a unit. The most common sizes contain 8 or 16 binary digits or bits. One byte translates into one typed character.

CAI: Computer-assisted instruction; the process of teaching by use of computers. A system of individualized instruction using a computer program as the teaching medium. Common modes include drill and practice, tutorial, and instructional game formats.

Cartridge Drive: A magnetic storage device that uses removable hard disk cartridges.

CD-ROM: Compact disc-read only memory; an optical bulk storage device that cannot be altered.

Chip: A small piece of silicon containing electrical paths (circuits).

CMI: Computer-managed instruction; the computer directs the instructional process by lessening clerical and managerial loads.

Cold Boot: Starting a computer when the power has been off.

Command: An order to the computer to execute a task, either immediate or deferred.

Compiler: A computer program used to translate high-level language programs into machine-language programs that can then be executed by the computer.

Computer: An electronic device used to process data at a very high rate of speed.

CPU: Central processing unit; that part of a computer system containing the control unit, arithmetic/logic unit, and internal storage. The CPU directs the flow of information in the computer and does the actual computing.

CRT: Cathode ray tube; an electronic vacuum tube with a screen for visual display of output information in graphical or alphanumeric form.

Cursor: A patch of light on the display that indicates where the user is in the text and where the next input will be inserted.

Debugging: The process of detecting, locating, and removing all mistakes in a computer program or malfunctions in the computer system hardware.

Digitizing Board (Card): A circuit board, generally installed inside the computer, that converts analog signals, such as audio and video transmissions, to digital signals.

Digitizing Camera: A camera capable of recording visual images in a digital format.

Disk Drive: The hardware that permits reading from or writing on a disk or diskette.

Diskette: A form of low-cost storage for microcomputers. This is a flexible disk coated with oxide to store information in a magnetic form. Also referred to as a floppy disk, because it is thin and flexible. Usually measures 5.25" in diameter (see also microfloppy).

Display: The information on the screen.

Documentation: A set of written instructions that explain how to use the computer hardware or software. Documentation should include installation and operating instructions, troubleshooting guidelines, and system requirements.

DOS: Disk operating system; the program(s) that instruct the computer's CPU to transfer information to and from the disk.

Dot Matrix Printer: A common, lower-cost printing device; creates an image by placing dots in patterns on the paper.

Editing: A process to revise, delete, and add data or information to an existing program or data file.

Electronic Bulletin Board: A service offered by a computer operator that enables individuals to access a central computer file to read and post public messages.

Electronic Mail (E-Mail): A service that can be provided to networked computers that enables individual users to send and receive private messages. Generally, E-mail messages are held in memory until a user signs onto the network, is notified of received mail, reads it, and either discards or saves the message.

File: An organized collection of related data stored on an auxiliary storage device. A file can consist of a program, an equation, a form letter, a set of database records, a document, and so on.

Floppy Diskette: The lowest-cost magnetic bulk storage device, generally produced in the 5.25" or 3.5" (microfloppy) format. Data is read from and written to the magnetic surface of the disk. Floppy diskettes have limited storage capacity.

Flowchart: A graphical representation used by a programmer to display the logical steps needed to write instructions to solve a problem on the computer.

Formatting: The process of preparing the surface of a blank diskette so that data may be stored and retrieved from the diskette (see also initializing).

Hardcopy: A printed copy of computer output (printed reports, lists, documents).

Hardware: The physical equipment in a computer system—mechanical, electrical, or magnetic devices, such as the printer, monitor, or disk drive.

I/O: Input/output; a term usually used to represent the process of entering and storing data; also refers to hardware used during this process.

Initializing: The process of preparing a blank diskette so that data may be stored and retrieved from the new diskette (see also formatting).

Ink Jet Printer: A printing device that creates an image by spraying small ink dots on paper.

Input: The process of entering data from an external medium or device into a computer's internal storage unit or memory.

Input Device: A device used to transmit data into a CPU, for example, a keyboard, a mouse, a disk drive, a touch-sensitive screen, or an optical scanning device.

Interface: The process of creating the physical and operational connections between two or more electronic devices. Computers can be interfaced with a wide range of electronic devices.

Internal Memory: The type of storage that is addressable and controlled by the CPU, also called primary, immediate access, or main storage.

K: Kilobyte; the unit of measurement that represents about 1,000 units of storage (bytes). Therefore, 16K would represent about 16,000 bytes of memory.

LAN: Local area network; generally, a group of connected computers all located within a fairly limited distance.

Language: A limited list of words and symbols with specific meanings and the syntax rules that govern their use. Used to write instructions for execution by the computer.

Laser Printer: High-quality output device that uses a laser beam to create printed images on paper.

Load: A command or process used to retrieve data or programs from an auxiliary storage medium into the computer.

Machine Language: The basic language of the computer, with all instructions in binary notation.

Mail Merge: A feature of most word processing programs that allows the combination of unique data (such as addresses or names) and standard document text to create multiple documents with identical form and content except for the unique data.

Memory: A computer's storage facility and/or capacity; memory can be random access (RAM) or read only (ROM).

Memory Expansion: The process of increasing the total internal memory of a computer, generally accomplished by adding additional memory chips.

Menu: A video display of tasks or options that the software can be ordered to perform. The task is chosen by moving the cursor to the appropriate command or by typing a letter or number.

Microfloppy: A low-cost storage medium for microcomputers consisting of a flexible diskette coated with oxide to store information in a magnetic form. Measures 3.5 inches in diameter (see also diskette).

Microprocessor: The CPU of a microcomputer that is implemented in a single integrated circuit that performs all data manipulation, programs, and decision-making logic and arithmetic/logic functions.

Microsecond: One-millionth of a second.

Millisecond: One-thousandth of a second.

Mouse: Among the most popular input devices for microcomputers; converts physical movement into digital signals that the computer can interpret.

Nanosecond: One-billionth of a second.

Network: The physical connection, communication channel, and logical operation of computers connected to other computers.

Off-Line: Peripheral units that operate independently of the CPU or devices not under the control of the CPU; also indicates the user is not communicating directly with the computer.

On-Line: Peripheral devices operating under the direct control of the CPU; also indicates the user is ready to communicate with the computer.

Operating System: Software that controls the execution of computer programs and performs housekeeping tasks of the system.

Optical Scanner: A device used to translate printed characters or marks into machine language.

Output: The process of transferring data from a computer's internal storage unit to auxiliary storage or an output device.

Output Unit: A device capable of recording data coming from a computer's internal storage unit, for instance a speaker, a printer, a monitor, or a magnetic disk.

Pascal: A programming language generally used for structured programming.

Peripheral: Accessory parts of a computer system not considered essential in the operation. Modems and printers are examples of peripherals.

Picosecond: One-trillionth of a second.

Plotter Printer: An output unit that graphs data.

Printer: An output unit that provides a hardcopy version of data for the user. There are many types of printers available, such as thermal, ink-jet, laser, daisy wheel, and dot matrix.

Program: The instructions, written in a computer language, that are to be executed by the computer.

Prompt: A symbol or question given to the user about what to do next.

RAM: Random access memory; volatile electronic memory; a temporary location for computer data that can be addressed rapidly.

ROM: Read only memory; permanently programmed memory that cannot be changed by the user.

Run: A command used in many computer languages instructing the computer to execute a program.

Save: A command used with some computer languages when a program is to be placed on an auxiliary storage device.

Scanner: One of any of a number of devices (handheld and flatbed) that converts visual information to digital images to be manipulated by a computer program. With appropriate software, scanners can accept images of characters for direct conversion to text for use in a word processing program, eliminating the need to reenter the text.

Simulation: The process of representing a physical system and its functions by a mathematical model or a computer program.

Software: The programs and data written to control the operations of a computer system or for the purpose of solving a problem.

Tape Drive: The hardware that permits reading from or writing on magnetic tape.

Terminal: Any of a varied number of keyboard devices used to input data into a computer system.

Time Sharing: A process used with large computer systems to serve many users at the same time.

Tutorial: A computer program used for instructional purposes; the computer serves as tutor.

User Friendly: Refers to a program or computer that is easy to operate.

Virus: A computer program that attaches itself to other programs without being detected with the goal of deleting data or corrupting program files. Most viruses cause only minor irritations to users, but some are known to destroy files and cause computer system failures.

WAN: Wide area network; generally, a group of connected computers that are separated by some distance.

Warm Boot: Restarting a computer without turning the power off and back on; generally accomplished by pressing a multikey combination.

WORM: Write once, read many; an approach used in optical storage devices (WORM drives) that allows for initial creation of data that becomes read only after creation.

Part IV

Materials Preparation and Production

Graphics Design Principles and Techniques

Overhead Transparencies

Lamination and Mounting Processes

Introduction

This part of the text describes the design and production of instructional materials that can enhance the quality of teaching and learning. Numerous media are available for teachers to use, and some of the more commonly used techniques for creating media—dry mounting, laminating, and transparency production—are described. In addition, several new multimedia forms are revolutionizing the way teachers and students produce presentation materials. Part IV also discusses some of those production techniques to provide an awareness of the types of production skills that will be needed for future media projects.

Advancements in production systems are providing today's classroom teachers with unique and easier ways to produce professional-looking materials. As the newer technologies become available to schools, teachers must be prepared to take advantage of these more efficient and effective production methods.

Teachers should be able to choose the most practical ways to create instructional materials tailored to a wide range of student abilities and learning styles. Teachers must make critical choices regarding the instructional value of the materials and weigh them against time spent in production and cost. If the instructional value of visual materials seems insignificant, teachers should initiate better planning and instructional design.

Teachers who are skilled in the development of visual communications materials should be able to demonstrate these skills to their students. Students can then be shown how to communicate more effectively and how to develop their own materials for class presentations and projects by modeling after the teacher.

Graphics skills such as lettering and composition are important in producing any visual media—displays, projected media, and handouts. Technical quality and aesthetic appearance of visual media are important. Information about refining these skills appears in Chapter 22, which should provide a general understanding of how to create effective visuals. The information in Chapter 22 serves as the foundation for designing all visual materials. Building on this base, Chapter 23 describes techniques for designing overhead transparencies, and Chapter 24 is a hands-on presentation of creating dry mounted and laminated instructional aids.

Careful study of the information and suggested activities in Part IV will provide necessary competencies for creating some of the basic classroom aids employing media that many teachers use. Once the basic production techniques have been mastered, there will be greater stimulus for creativity in designing the materials.

Even though Part IV does not repeat earlier advisories about copyright laws and illegal duplication of materials, instructors and students should pay serious attention to those references in earlier discussions, because they also apply to manipulation of existing copyrighted materials to create transparencies or laminated handouts. Additional information may be found in Appendix A of the text.

Chapter 22

GRAPHICS DESIGN PRINCIPLES AND TECHNIQUES

PURPOSES

- ▶ To realize the importance of design principles in producing visual materials
- ▶ To understand basic design principles for creating aesthetically pleasing visual images
- ▶ To understand and use appropriate design elements to enhance the effectiveness of visual materials
- ▶ To create graphics to fit different media formats
- ▶ To create appropriate graphs to simplify and enhance presentations of numerical data
- ▶ To understand the basic guidelines for labeling instructional materials
- ▶ To identify methods and procedures for producing lettering and graphic designs
- ▶ To understand the advantages of enlarging and reducing visuals and equipment that can be used to do so

INTRODUCTION

Graphic forms of communication are becoming more important within our global society in helping us cross language and other barriers to communication. We live in a visual world in which most of our students easily relate to movies, television, magazine advertisements, cartoons, posters, and other visual forms. Occasionally, visual symbols can still be confusing to certain cultural groups, so educators should be aware of this potential when producing graphics. For example, various types of designs or pictures are often used on restroom doors to distinguish the men's from the women's. These unique symbols can sometimes be a bit difficult to interpret and may cause considerable embarrassment.

In educational settings, teachers commonly use a variety of visual media—bulletin boards, displays, slides, filmstrips, transparencies, videotapes, and printed handouts. Teachers who produce these materials should be aware of design principles. Visual elements that attract attention and hold the interest of the viewer usually communicate more effectively. A well-designed visual can enhance the learner's understanding of the instructional material. Its effectiveness can be measured by the way the learner continues to recall the visual and remember the information.

The effectiveness of visuals is measured by the degree of learner recall of its content.

Computerized and other electronic systems for creating graphics are rapidly replacing many of the older, less efficient means of production. Computer technology is revolutionizing graphics production, because software can create numerous variations in lettering size and style and redesign shapes with a simple keystroke or mouse click. Sophisticated computer systems have expanded classroom teachers' and students' graphics capabilities through media production and desktop publishing packages.

The same typographic guidelines apply to manually or computer-generated visuals.

No matter what means are used for producing graphics materials, there are some basic guidelines for type that should be considered in the process of production. Lettering techniques are as important to creating effective visuals as are the basic design elements. Research has proven that type styles can impact the effectiveness of communications, because they affect the text's readability. A portion of this chapter is devoted specifically to typography for that reason.

Teachers should have a good grasp of proper graphics techniques for the development of visual displays, and they should pass those skills on to their students so they too may become better communicators.

Design principles comprise balance, emphasis, simplicity, and unity.

When developing communications materials, teachers and students should ensure that their message is attractive, interesting, explicit, and effective. Principles of design are the rules by which graphic elements are assembled into visual form. The design principles of balance, emphasis, simplicity, and unity may be applied to producing all types of visual communication materials.

DESIGN PRINCIPLES

Balance

Balance is a form of equilibrium within a composition that is used to provide coherence for all the other elements.

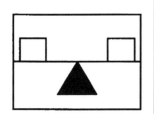

There are two kinds of balance: formal and informal. *Formal balance* can be visualized by imagining an axis running through the center of a visual, showing that one half of the design will be the mirror reflection of the other half. Formal balance is used when an expression of stability, passivity, dignity, and seriousness is desired. With a little more effort, the designer can achieve *informal balance,* as shown in Figure 22.1, which is usually more interesting to the viewer. Informal balance provides a balanced appearance without the symmetrical or mirrored image.

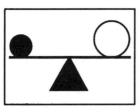
A brightly colored small shape balances a dull, large shape.

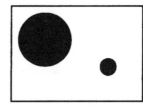
A small shape placed low balances a larger one placed higher.

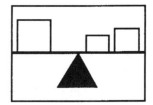
Two or more small shapes balance a larger one.

Figure 22.1

Examples of Informal Balance

Emphasis

In a successful graphic design, the viewer should never have difficulty in identifying the main theme. A visual normally presents a single idea, but there may be a need to emphasize some of its aspects more than others.

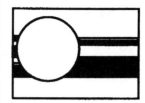

The main elements of design are line, texture, color, shape, and space. All of these elements, in addition to those of contrast and size, can be used to direct attention to a certain portion of a visual.

The use of pointing arrows and other images or shapes can direct the viewer through a visual. Our society is accustomed to reading from left to right and top to bottom, so the general rule is to follow that flow of information in a visual design unless exceptions are meaningful. If an illustrator were preparing materials for the Chinese culture, the layout would be the opposite, because the direction for reading follows that layout.

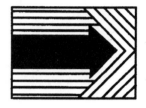

Simplicity

Only a few elements should be presented in a single visual. It is better to plan a series of simple visuals with areas of emphasis than to crowd too much information into one visual, thereby making it difficult for the viewer to identify key elements. For example, speakers often try to provide too much information on overhead transparencies. A simple design with brief statements or key points will enhance the effectiveness of a transparency. Transparencies containing a full page of text information are too cluttered; the viewer cannot read or distinguish key points if the information is too "solid."

Limit text messages to 20 words for projected visuals, and use a single line rather than multiple lines for titles. Place captions for a graphic inside the image area when possible, and try to avoid placing words close to the edges of a visual page.

Unity

The elements of a visual design should provide for continuity of thought and ideas. The pieces in the visual must fit together so its overall effect is one of unity or harmony.

Various techniques can provide unity in a visual, such as overlapping images over a common background, using a border around objects to keep them optically contained, or using repetition of a shape or color.

VISUAL ELEMENTS OF DESIGN

The main visual elements that contribute to the success of the four design principles are lines, shapes, color and contrast, texture, and space and size.

Lines

Lines can attract attention by directing the eye to a specific object or area in addition to holding the visual design together. Different types of lines, as shown in Figure 22.2, can create a variety of effects such as motion, instability, or calmness.

 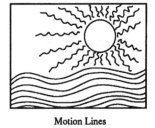 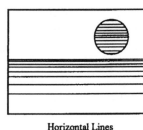

Diagonal Lines   Motion Lines   Horizontal Lines

Figure 22.2
The Effects of Lines

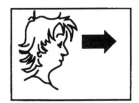

The direction in which an object faces guides the eye from one element of the visual to another. For example, photographers and video camera operators usually attempt to have the subject facing into the visual field rather than facing out. In graphic composition, the main points of emphasis should be concentrated in the body of the visual and not too close to its edge.

Shapes

Shapes can be used to attract attention or represent universal images recognized across cultures so as to provide clearer communications. The automobile industry offers good examples of using universally accepted shapes and symbols as labels for dashboard controls.

Shapes might be geometric, symbolic, or abstract representations of familiar objects. For example, to represent the concept of a human female or male, the designer could use several representative shapes, depending on the effect desired.

Color and Contrast

Color enhances most visuals, because it directs attention or helps to clarify, as well as adding viewing enjoyment to a visual. Occasionally, using black and white helps to simplify the visual concept. However, research indicates that the appropriate use of color makes a visual more attractive to the viewer. Harmonious colors in a design unify its appearance. Contrasting colors can be used to highlight or emphasize a portion of the design. Brighter or darker images that contrast with the background will also draw greater attention to parts of a visual.

Texture

Representations of texture in a visual are usually repetitious patterns created by variations in lines or dots. They may take on a characteristic of cloth or other material forms. Texture can provide emphasis to certain parts of a visual as well as contribute to the overall unity. In addition to creating textures or patterns by drawing with pen, pencil, or brush strokes, several commercial products such as adhesive sheets of texture and pattern materials are available for graphics production. When school budgets are limited for purchasing commercial products, items such as discarded wallpaper pattern books may serve as sources for textured materials. If a graphic is produced using a computer drawing program, numerous textures and patterns are available within graphics packages.

Space and Size

Space can be either negative or positive. The unused or open portions of a design are referred to as *negative space*. The use of negative space is as important as the placement of positive space in a design and should be considered part of a total composition. Open space prevents the visual from looking too crowded or complicated. The contrast of positive and negative space can be attractive and can enhance a visual or help to convey emphasis.

The size of the spaces and images can also attract attention to certain elements of a visual. Larger images usually gain greater attention from the viewer, if all other visual elements are equal.

Teachers should incorporate the principles and elements of design in producing graphic materials. The overall effectiveness of a visual, as shown in Figure 22.3, is determined by appropriate use of these principles and elements.

Good Design

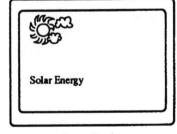
Poor Design

Figure 22.3

Art That Does and Does Not Incorporate Elements of Design

VISUAL COMPOSITION

Horizontal Versus Vertical Format

Most projected visuals use a horizontal format more than a vertical format, because of the shape of screens used for viewing. Common types of screens, as shown in Figure 22.4, are wider than they are tall. If a graphic is produced in a vertical format to be displayed on a horizontal-format television screen, some visual composition problems might weaken the visual's impact. Most photographers use their 35mm cameras in a horizontal position, so that the width of the photographed image is larger than the height. Consequently, it is usually more appropriate to use horizontal formats for preparing graphics for visual media.

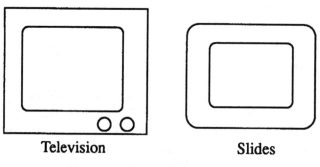

Television   Slides

Figure 22.4

Television Screens Are Less Horizontally Oriented Than Slides

In addition to the horizontal characteristics of various media, projection screens are normally opened to expose a horizontally shaped projection surface. For overhead transparencies, a horizontal format often accommodates the exposed screen shape better. Images on vertically designed transparencies may not fit on the screen or may be too high or too low for all of the viewing audience to see. Occasionally, it may still be desirable to create a vertical format transparency to get the needed effect.

Reproduced and duplicated materials are often prepared to fit the vertical format of a standard 8-½" ´ 11" sheet of paper. Some photocopy machines can copy material in both horizontal and vertical formats, and the instructor may have a choice of producing a visual in either format. In addition, many photocopy machines enlarge or reduce the size of visuals, so graphics can be resized to fit a desired format.

Ratio

In addition to considering horizontal and vertical formats of various media forms, the ratio of height to width of visuals, such as those shown in Figure 22.5, is also important. For example, most video and computer graphics are designed on monitors that produce images in a 3:4 ratio.

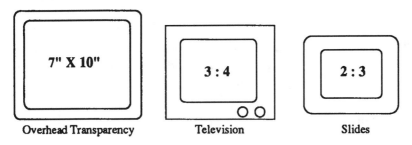

Figure 22.5

Common Height-to-Width Ratios of Projected Visuals

Slides from a 35mm camera used in the horizontal position produce visual compositions with a ratio of 2:3, and transparencies require an approximate 7:10 ratio. The designer should produce graphics in appropriate ratio and format to fit the specific, final medium. If a graphic is designed via a computer to be transferred to another medium, the final product should determine the appropriate ratio to be used and not the screen on the computer. As computers gain more prominence in graphics production, greater attention must be given to visuals that are created electronically on a computer's horizontal, 3:4 ratio screen. Creating transparency originals with a 7:10 horizontal ratio with a printer that prints on an 8.5:11 vertical ratio from a computer screen that is on a 3:4 horizontal ratio may require some adjustments in alignment and/or spacing.

Illustrators should plan a visual to match its final medium's format, not the computer screen's.

Graphics techniques can improve an instructor's ability to communicate numerical information efficiently and effectively. Circle (pie), bar, line, and picture graphs can create professional looking visuals that present data in a simple and clear manner. Each of these four types of graphs have certain advantages, depending on the type of data being described or the way the data is to be compared. Instructors should use graphs whenever possible to simplify or clarify their presentation of quantitative data.

GRAPHING TECHNIQUES

Circle Graphs

The *circle graph* or *pie chart* is often used to show portions or percentages easily as they relate to a whole. A pie chart is useful for comparing proportions of factors for a single item whose components are being divided.

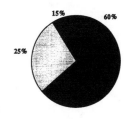

Bar Graphs

A *bar graph* can show grouped data for comparisons on some common measure that can be easily understood by the viewer. It is a good means of showing relative performance of one or more items for one or more factors.

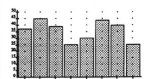

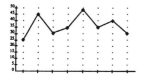

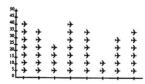

Nongraphics programs also create graphs and charts, and users can experiment with which type of graphic best presents the data.

BASIC LETTERING GUIDELINES

Line Graphs

The *line graph* may provide an overview of data by showing continual trends from one stage to the next rather than periodic data as shown in bar graphs.

Picture Graphs

The *picture graph* is a variation on the bar graph that uses a variety of shapes or representative images to attract the attention of the audience and depict the items being represented in the data.

Many computer programs, graphics, and other types of applications on the market can easily help teachers or students create most types of graphs. For example, some spreadsheet programs can actually take numerical data from a series of columns or rows on a page and convert the numerical data into a graphic form. The speed and ease of producing graphs from raw numerical data makes the job of creating such graphics less time consuming and more practical for teachers. Also, drawing programs enable teachers and students to compare the suitability of various types of graphs by physically manipulating output using different drawing tools.

The use of basic elements of design can affect legibility and visibility of text and labels on a visual. Legibility of type is determined primarily by the typeface (font) and spacing used, and visibility is mainly controlled by the size and style (contrast) between the letters and the background.

Size

Characters for visual displays such as bulletin boards, magnetic boards, and posters should be at least ¼" high for each eight feet of distance the viewer is from the visual. For example, an exhibit to be viewed from a distance of 24 feet should have lettering at least ¾" high.

Lettering for materials to be projected on a screen, such as overhead transparencies or slides, should be clearly visible to the viewer in the last row of the audience. Some presenters use transparencies with lettering too small for the audience to read, and the success of their presentation is diminished. As a general rule, lettering for projection should be a minimum of $^1/_{25}$ the physical height of the actual visual. For example, letters for a transparency designed on a horizontal format should be approximately ¼" high, or $^1/_{25}$ of 7". These are generally recommended sizes that can sometimes be altered due to variations in lighting conditions, size of screen being used, distance of the projector from the screen, type of projection lens being used, and boldness of the characters.

Type Style

As was mentioned in the discussions of graphics design, the contrast of the characters with their background in value and/or hue can affect the visibility of the type. Bright or dark images work quite well on high-contrast backgrounds. Combinations of complementary colors make the labeling stand out from the background. *Italic* type styles highlight words and make them stand out from the normal style but are sometimes hard to read on projected materials. **Bold** type styles provide better contrast.

Figure 22.6

Comparing Readability of Sans Serif Type with Ornate Serif Style

As shown in Figure 22.6, the simplest type style is generally the most desirable for clarity. Bold and blocky (*sans serif*, or without endstroke) styles are usually preferred over fancy, ornamental (*serif*) styles. Fancy styles of serif lettering such as Old English should normally be reserved for special uses and display lettering, and be avoided in the preparation of common instructional materials and body text.

The slant, darkness, and capitalization of characters should match their usage.

Using all capital letters is fine for titles, short statements, tables, and short captions. However, for entire sentences or phrases of more than six words, lowercase letters should be used; longer headings are more readable with upper- and lowercase capitalization. Also, simpler serif typefaces, such as Times Roman, are more readable than the blocky sans serif fonts for longer expanses of lettering.

Spacing

Both horizontal and vertical spacing affects the legibility of type.

The amount of space between letters in a word should be equal, as illustrated in Figure 22.7, and spacing should normally be done by visual appearance rather than using ruled measurement or software's default measurement.

Readability of characters depends on the horizontal and vertical spacing used between characters.

Spacing between words should be approximately 1 to 1.5 times the average letter width, with 2 to 3 letter widths between sentences, especially for sentences that will be read from a distance (science fair exhibits, posters, or transparencies, for example). Desktop publishing has established some new rules for preparing documents that may be submitted to editors or publishers. There is no necessity for extra spacing after punctuation as is taught in typing classes, because the publishing people or typesetters have to remove them (published

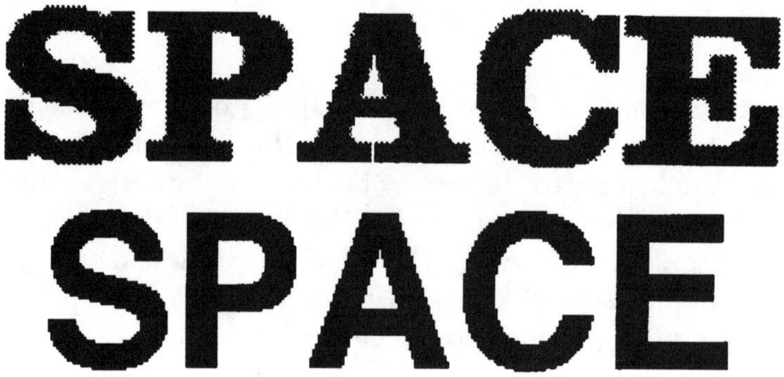

SPACE
SPACE

Figure 22.7

Words That Use Default Letterspacing (Top) Should Be Corrected to
Show Equal Visual Space Between Letters (Bottom)

texts use single spacing after periods and so forth). Teachers and students who
are preparing reports and other documents for classroom use may still need to
use the older rules of typing, but they should adopt professional publishing
rules for material that will be typeset.

Vertical spacing between lines is also called *leading,* which rhymes with *bed-ding.* As shown in Figure 22.8, vertical spacing should be slightly shorter than
the capital letters and slightly taller than the lowercase letters in the text. If
only capital or lowercase letters are used, the space should be approximately
the same size as the letters used.

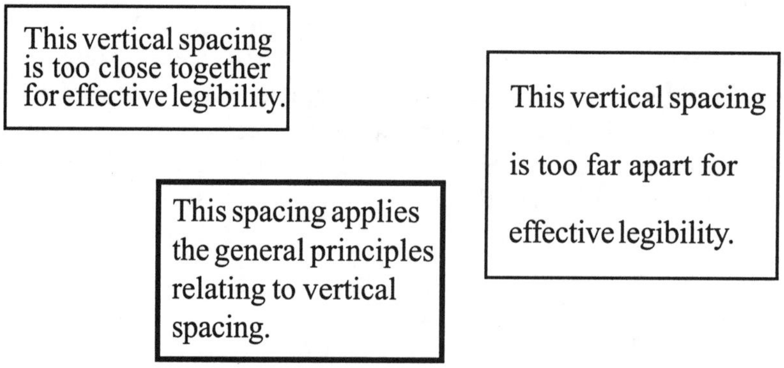

This vertical spacing
is too close together
for effective legibility.

This vertical spacing

is too far apart for

effective legibility.

This spacing applies
the general principles
relating to vertical
spacing.

Figure 22.8

Examples of Good and Bad Line Spacing

Many of the instruments people use to create type characters may have a stan-dard or *default* method of spacing, such as with a typewriter or a computer
word processing package, but computer desktop publishing and paint and draw
software programs enable the creator to make those judgments and alter spac-ing visually. Therefore, it is wise to know some of the general rules of spacing.

**LETTERING
METHODS**

Many teachers and students, especially at the elementary level, still use basic
types of lettering materials, such as stencils, templates, and adhesive backed
letters, because these tools offer larger type sizes and manipulative characteris-

tics. These items remain popular for specific needs such as producing bulletin board displays or other special display materials. School supply stores or graphics supply shops usually carry a large variety of these materials for lettering various visual displays. Although there are many lettering techniques and devices available for producing visuals, some of them are gradually being replaced by computer technology.

The introduction of computer graphics software along with libraries of CD-ROM clip art and low-cost computer peripherals have provided an almost unlimited selection of type capabilities. Optical scanners and high-quality laser printers enable many teachers and students to create graphics and lettering more efficiently and effectively than ever before. Therefore it's important for teachers to have a good knowledge of computer-based techniques for producing graphics.

Display labeling, like drawing, is gradually becoming computer-based.

Printing Terminology on Computers

Considering the vast amounts and types of computer hardware and software configurations available, it's understandable that confusion occurs in determining what graphics capabilities each system has. Numerous alternatives may be derived by changing any of the computer, software, and printer combinations. Teachers should have some knowledge about these variations to make proper decisions for graphics that they and their students want to design.

To start, teachers should learn the differences among word processing, database, spreadsheet, and paint and draw programs. Once instructors grasp the significance of these general differences, the teachers are prepared to understand how the techniques indicated by the following terms affect graphics output.

Learning the kinds of media obtainable by using standard types of software is a start in gaining technical expertise.

The following types of files and forms of visual output are commonly associated with graphics production. Some are associated with text or font output, some are associated with paint or optical image output, and others may involve both. It would certainly be wise to investigate these terms in greater detail, as future decisions for purchasing equipment and software are planned.

Bitmapped — A version of font styles that is created by a pattern of dots. If bitmapped fonts are being used, the image created on the computer screen may not look exactly like the image printed on a printer. Bitmapped images are usually associated with draw programs, in which each element in the graphic can be altered. Bitmapped images or letters are not considered as smooth or finished-looking as PostScript. The larger the size of bitmapped characters, the more jagged the curved or sloped edges will appear.

Bitmapped
Outlined

EPS — Encapsulated PostScript; files that are capable of printing PostScript-quality images but display as bitmapped images. They can print high-quality images on a good

PostScript printer, but they may require a lot of printer time. They also require a printer with considerable internal memory to store the file or they will tie up the computer while the printer is working.

Fonts
The many unique designs of type characteristics, such as those shown in Figure 22.9. No printer can reproduce all types of fonts. Many fonts print differently than they display on the monitor, because the application tracks what display fonts are available, and the printer tracks what print fonts are available. Some fonts are bitmapped; others are TrueType or outlined. Various configurations of the software, printer driver, and printer accessories determine the quality of output of each type and size of any given font.

Near Letter Quality
A term often associated with dot matrix printers, indicating their best quality output. Characters may look close in quality to ones produced on an electric typewriter. Any lower quality usually means the printing will show the small, individual dots that make up the image.

OCR
Optical character recognition scanners; these scanners can store scanned text as editable characters for word processing rather than a paint image that cannot be altered using a word processing (unless the user converts the image using special translation software such as OptiScan).

Paint
These files usually are bitmapped images and are limited to a specific page size. If the designer is not working on a full-page monitor to see the entire working surface of the image, there may be a composition problem. If the design extends too close to the edge of the working page, there may not be enough space to complete it. The working surface cannot be scrolled beyond the dimensions of an 8" X 10" page to complete an image.

PCX
These files are often transferred from paint programs' files and produce good-quality images. It is sometimes difficult to resize the images without distorting them. They are usually associated with PC software. When the graphic file is imported from a paint program to a desktop publishing application, there might be a dramatic change in image size.

PICT
Basic picture files. These are the object-oriented or bitmapped graphics files that are used in draw and/or

paint programs. You can cut and paste these picture files into any number of graphics applications to create altered images.

PostScript

A programming language developed by Adobe to work with text and graphics; now the term is also applied to types of laser printers. PostScript provides a better-quality printed image in higher-quality printers that are configured for PostScript printing. Postscript capabilities are found mostly in laser printers and not in dot matrix or ink jet printers. Instead of producing a jagged, bitmapped letter, PostScript creates smooth-edged characters by first outlining the edges of each letter and then filling it in solid. PostScript capabilities are desirable for desktop publishing activities.

Size

The size of characters is usually referred to by the measurement called *point size*. In real graphics terms, 72 points=1 inch in height. This equivalence does not always hold true on computers and their visual or printer output. The font's design may affect the point size somewhat. In most bold, sans serif fonts that would be used for video production, 24 and 36 point are good sizes to use. The size used for printed materials depends on the type of graphic needed and how it will be viewed. Remember the dimensions suggested for viewing.

Style

This could refer to whether the lettering is **bold**, *italic*, underlined, shadowed, outlined, or a number of other forms of the same font. Each of these styles are variations of the same font, but highlight it in a different way.

TGA

A file format developed by Truevision. Its images are produced by using digitizing boards to capture video images. These files consume considerable memory space but can recreate extremely high-quality images in full color.

TIFF

The tagged image file format; these files are bitmapped, but their size can be changed as well as their resolution quality without distortion to the ratio of the original design. These images are often associated with scanner output. These files may print faster than EPS files do on a laser printer.

Several other type style characteristics (described earlier in this chapter) should also be considered. There are certain characteristics of lettering that are universal for almost all fonts.

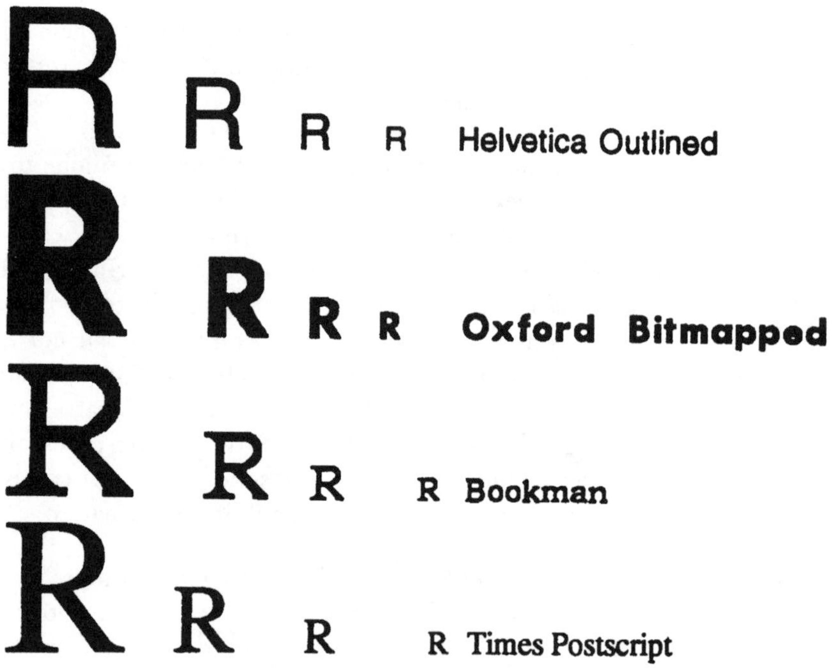

Figure 22.9

Comparing Typefaces and Sizes

The printed images in Figure 22.9 are just a few examples of the variations in typefaces that can occur. The bitmapped images usually don't look as refined as the PostScript or outlined characters for the larger sizes.

ENLARGING AND REDUCING GRAPHICS

Photocopy machines are used to make hardcopy reproductions.

Projection devices are used to trace images.

Instructors are sometimes interested in copying a visual that is not the appropriate size for projection or display. If it proves difficult to resize, they may choose not to use the supporting visual at all or use it in its existing size, which may result in an ineffective presentation. The ability to enlarge or reduce such visuals can be quite helpful in making communications more productive. There are several ways to enlarge or reduce the size of visuals, and the method used depends partially on the final product needed.

Schools are now using photocopy machines, and many of them can reduce and enlarge images. Because of the speed and quality of this process, photocopiers have become quite popular for producing handouts or originals for other production projects. Before using a photocopy machine, the operator should read any instructions attached to the machine regarding its operation. Determine what steps to perform to allow the machine to enlarge or reduce images and what options the machine has for changing image sizes. One common use of the photocopier is to produce transparencies by enlarging small pictures to the appropriate size and producing the copies on acetate sheets.

Most projection equipment, such as overhead, slide, and filmstrip projectors, can be used for enlarging visuals. To enlarge with any projection system, simply insert the visual material into the machine, adjust the projected image to the desired size on the appropriate surface, and trace it.

Opaque projectors are often used for enlarging visuals because they can project two- and three-dimensional opaque objects. They are especially popular with students preparing large banners for promoting athletic events or in doing backdrops for musicals or plays. The projector is often used for creating life-sized murals for walls of a classroom or hallway to help create interest in a topic. It may also be used to decorate for a party or open house.

A newer multimedia technique for classroom presentations is being adopted by many teachers to enlarge images of computer screens. LCD projection panels and an overhead projector with computer graphics programs are enabling teachers and students to create a variety of electronic graphic displays for enlarged projection in the classroom. This newer technology provides for rapid electronic editing of graphics with great ease and versatility. As these newer technologies become more available in classrooms, they are replacing some of the older forms of media such as slides and transparencies for lectures and formal presentations.

LCD projection panels can produce electronic graphic displays for viewing enlarged computer screens.

If an instructor wishes to use a visual that is in a copyrighted publication, copyright laws may allow the production of a single copy of the visual such as a diagram; cartoon; graph; or picture from a book, periodical, or newspaper if it is to be used solely for teaching in a class. You should be familiar with the copyright laws, such as those described in Appendix A, to determine what is appropriate in the reproduction of graphics.

COPYRIGHT LAW

SUGGESTED ACTIVITIES

1. Design an educational visual for your content field to be used in a teaching situation. Write a critique of your visual, explaining how you used general design principles and visual elements to enhance its quality.

2. Find two advertisements and analyze them according to the principles and elements of design. Attach copies of the advertisements to your evaluation statements.

3. Design three visuals that could be used in your content area that fit the format of a transparency, video image, and a 35mm photograph.

4. Select a small visual that has instructional value in your field. Enlarge the visual using the most appropriate of either the opaque or overhead projection methods to make a visual for a display.

5. Find a small image you would like to have enlarged for a transparency original and use a photocopy machine to enlarge it to the appropriate size. Attach the original image to the enlarged copy for comparison.

Chapter 23

OVERHEAD TRANSPARENCIES

PURPOSES

▶ To design aesthetically and technically acceptable overhead transparencies
▶ To produce handmade transparencies
▶ To produce thermal transparencies with a 3-M Secretary (thermofax) machine
▶ To produce photocopy transparencies
▶ To produce computer-generated transparencies
▶ To produce creative revelation techniques for transparencies

INTRODUCTION

Transparencies used on an overhead projector provide a large, clear image and are commonly used to support speeches or lectures by directing the viewers' attention to key points. They help teachers present visual information via outlines, summaries, diagrams, and illustrations in an organized manner. They are usually easy to produce and can be designed to fit specific needs. They can be developed in a series to build concepts and may feature special effects or revelation techniques to enhance the effectiveness of presentations.

There are several good sources of commercially prepared transparencies for teaching, but many teachers prefer to produce their own to fit the specific needs of their classes. For the past several years three of the more common types of teacher-produced transparencies have been handmade, thermal, and photocopied. Even though these transparencies remain popular, the availability of computers and better-quality printers has increased the production of computer-produced transparencies. Each of these techniques has certain advantages. Teachers who have knowledge of all of the production techniques described here should be able to select the most appropriate form for the occasion and be more successful in making presentations.

Once instructors master basic transparency production skills, the instructors' creativity in designing and producing transparencies should be limited only by their imagination.

CREATIVITY IN DESIGN

Teachers should try to be creative as well as practical in planning visuals for instruction. For example, a transparency produced to teach the phases of the moon and their relationship with the earth and sun may be demonstrated in the following manner.

Teachers should always match the presentation style to the content and concepts of the subject.

Use negative space with a masking technique to divide the transparency in half. One half of the transparency should contain a line drawing of the sun and earth with the moon drawn in different positions to represent the moon's phases. The other half of the transparency should be masked off completely, with a round hole cut out of the mask. When projected, the round hole could represent the moon as it appears in the night sky. Small pieces of the cutout circle could then be placed back into the hole to represent the various phases of the moon. The student could then see the alignment of the moon, earth, and sun on the drawing part of the transparency as the students viewed an image representing the moon in a night sky on the other half of the projection. It is important for teachers to think visually to match transparencies to the content and concepts being taught.

PRE-PRODUCTION CONSIDERATIONS

Before producing an overhead transparency, teachers should consider its physical dimensions. Transparency film usually comes in 8½" ´ 11" sheets, but transparency frame apertures are approximately 7½" ´ 9½", so all visual information should be easily contained within the latter dimensions if the transparency is to be mounted on a frame. Some transparency films are heavy enough that no frame is needed for stability, but aesthetically the transparencies are more appealing if they are framed.

Production options available to the instructor depend on the equipment and materials available. If several types of production equipment are available, time, cost, and desired quality will help determine the best form to produce.

Transparencies should incorporate the basic elements of good design.

Follow the rules of graphics design to make visuals more effective. The basic elements of design mentioned in Chapter 21, such as lettering size, should be considered in designing transparencies. Consider the amount of information to be included in a visual. Remember the basic rule about keeping visuals simple. Too much information in one visual may cause it to appear too cluttered and overwhelm the viewer.

Revelation techniques are tailor-made for use with transparencies.

Special revelation techniques, such as progressive disclosure, should be considered in the initial planning of transparencies. Methods used for disclosing information to students will contribute to the effectiveness of a presentation by controlling such factors as focus of attention and rate of communication.

DISCLOSURE TECHNIQUES (REVELATION)

Three basic techniques are used for progressive disclosure of visual information on transparencies, and each can have several variations. Creative planning can be helpful in obtaining a good match between the disclosure style and the transparency's content.

Overlays

The technique of using overlays involves attaching additional sheets of transparency film to the base cell of the transparency by hinging them to the top of the frame. It allows the presenter to disclose certain aspects of the visual in the desired order and at the appropriate time. Multiple overlays may be attached to the same edge of a frame to add sequential information to a presentation, or they may be hinged to different edges of the frame to show comparative information.

Cover Sheets

As was mentioned in Chapter 8, cover sheets enable the instructor to disclose information one piece at a time in a linear design. They may simply be a sheet of paper placed on top of a transparency. However, the use of special guides attached to the transparency frame are recommended, because they hold the cover sheet sturdily in place to make the disclosure of information smoother and more manageable.

Masks

Masks are usually hinged to a transparency frame in the same basic manner as overlays. It is better to use durable material such as oak tag board, like that used for file folders, to produce the masks. Common sheets of paper or construction paper are not sturdy enough to make good masks.

There are numerous types of transparencies on the market. Some of the more common ones are discussed here.

TYPES OF TRANSPARENCIES

Photocopies

The only difference between producing transparencies and paper copies on a photocopier is that special transparency film must be placed in the machine's paper tray instead of copy paper. Usually, photocopier transparency film has one treated edge that is opaque. The treated edge facilitates proper passage of the transparency film through the copier; therefore, the treated edge is fed into the copier first.

Photocopy machines are rapidly gaining popularity because they can produce transparencies as quickly as a thermofax machine, but they have the added advantage over thermal transparencies of being able to reproduce images that are not carbon based.

Photocopier-made transparencies are becoming more popular than ones made with a thermofax.

Most images can be used to produce transparencies on a photocopier; exceptions include some light-colored images. The machine scans the visual and places an electrical charge that matches the image on the transparency film. A carbon-based black powder called toner is then affixed to the film by heat and pressure to form a permanent transparency.

Color photo copiers are about to become a common source for full-color transparencies.

Many companies now sell special transparency film for photocopy machines. Most schools have regular photocopy machines that can produce black line or gray tone transparencies on clear or colored film. Color photocopiers are still too expensive for most schools to own, but multicolored transparencies may become more commonplace as color copiers become more affordable.

Smart instructors resist the temptation to overload a transparency.

One common mistake is often made by people producing transparencies via this method. They ignore the basic rules of good design and often use an original with print that is too small or too crowded to meet acceptable visual standards. Normally, the original contains entirely too much information and makes the visual appear too busy.

Most copiers in schools are capable only of producing black image transparencies. Colored adhesive film and marking pens can be used to add color to these images.

Many photocopiers can enlarge or reduce images from other sources to the appropriate size for a transparency production. As always, teachers should observe copyright laws in reproducing illustrations from books and other copyrighted sources.

Computer-Generated

Computer-produced transparencies are gaining in popularity as the required hardware and software becomes widely available in schools. One of the major advantages of computer-printed transparencies is the enormous flexibility computers offer for creating graphics: different types and sizes of fonts, special effects capabilities, and features for creating custom fonts.

Computers can easily merge labels with clip art and scanned images.

In addition to creating visuals with graphics programs, graphics and images can be taken from commercial diskettes or CD-ROMs that contain clip art and lettering templates. Some teachers are even using devices such as scanners or digital cameras to capture images and transfer them to graphics files to be printed. It is possible to photograph students with a digital camera and place their pictures in graphics files to be printed on a transparency in just a few minutes. These new computer technologies make it possible to reproduce virtually any type of image as transparencies. Some relatively inexpensive color ink jet printers are now capable of producing full-color transparencies and are within a reasonable price range for most schools' budgets. Color laser printers are still a bit too expensive for this level of use.

Some people attempt to use common plastic sheets in computer printers, but special transparency film is available and recommended to be used for the different types of printers to avoid melting plastic onto laser drums.

Many schools still use dot matrix printers that were purchased several years ago or are more affordable than are ink jet or laser printers today. As is the case with regular printing, dot matrix copies are not as sharp as ink jet or laser printers' copies, especially for transparencies. Some of the variations in quality may also be attributed to the type of software and hardware being used. The quality of a printed image is magnified when a transparency is projected on a screen. The printing pattern and density affect the quality of the image. Laser printers are usually preferable, because they normally provide good-quality PostScript images that appear to be more dense, have better resolution, and contain smoother edges.

Some dot matrix, ink jet, and laser printers can produce multicolored transparencies. They can be produced from computer-generated graphics the same way paper copies are produced. Because many computers and graphics programs are capable of producing colored images, multicolored transparencies are also possible to produce. These high-quality graphics can result in professional-looking transparencies if the means is at hand for printing them in color.

One major advantage of computer printer transparency production over photocopier and thermal transparency production is the ability to create complex graphics designs and convert them to multicolored transparencies with relative ease.

Recall from Chapter 22's discussion of design principles that computer printers normally feed paper or transparency film in a vertical position, and unless the computer or software allows for rotation of the image for printing, the visual information will always print in a vertical format and need to fit into a vertical transparency format.

If the computer cannot print directly onto transparency film, the teacher can still print a paper copy of computer-generated graphics and make a photocopy or thermal transparency from it.

Handmade

Handmade (direct process) transparencies require no special machine for production. They can be produced simply by attaching materials to a sheet of clear plastic or by writing on the film with special marking pencils or pens. Some overhead projectors have rolls of clear film attached to the machine for hand-produced visuals.

There are permanent and water-soluble markers made especially to write on transparencies. Some instructors use water-soluble markers on the film in a fashion similar to using a chalkboard, by erasing completed work to reuse the film. A soft damp cloth works well for removing the water-soluble ink. Other teachers use permanent markers on film and keep the transparencies for later reuse. If they make a mistake or wish to change or remove the permanent ink, lighter fluid may be applied to remove the markings.

Teachers can use water-soluble or permanent markers to make transparencies.

Handmade transparencies are inexpensive compared with other transparency forms, so they are popular with institutions that have limited materials budgets.

Cleared x-ray film and other clear or color-toned pieces of plastic can be used to make handmade transparencies. However, the instructor should be aware that some forms of plastic do not accept ink from transparency marking pens very well.

Transparent or opaque objects can be attached to transparencies for various effects.

Various materials may be attached to handmade transparencies, such as special transparent adhesive film for highlighting or other transparent items that will project. In addition, opaque objects like cut-out paper hands for a clock could be used.

Not all overhead projection materials must be produced on sheets of film. There are several commercially produced items such as LED calculators and various transparent measuring devices that are now available to project with an overhead.

Some models of liquid crystal display calculators are designed so they are transparent, and the working parts don't show. The number and function keys appear on the calculators with the calculator's window. This way the teacher can let the whole class observe the use of the calculator manipulating data as its window contents are projected on an overhead projector. Transparent rulers and other measuring devices may also be used over transparencies.

Thermal

Thermal transparencies are heat sensitive.

Thermal transparency production provides a rapid means of reproducing a visual on film in a permanent form. The transparency film used is sometimes referred to as infrared film. The film is heat sensitive and will turn dark or change color wherever there is a heat concentration on it. Because of this sensitivity to heat, take care to never leave thermal film in an extremely hot place such as a car window during the summer or it may turn dark and be permanently ruined.

The film is used on a thermofax (3M-Secretary) machine that is usually found in most schools. There are several types of thermal film available that provide different visual effects. There are black line on clear, color image, black line on colored background, and negative image types of film. The films are also available in different thicknesses or weight.

Thermal transparencies are permanent and may not be erased or reused. They must be exposed to a carbon original and heated to create the image on the film.

Carbon Originals

To produce a technically acceptable thermal transparency, a high carbon content original must be used. The original should not contain unwanted marks or blemishes. The visual information should be placed on a full sheet of clean paper. Following are some examples of good carbon-based materials:

- ▶ photocopies from photocopy machines
- ▶ soft leaded pencils (softer than #2)
- ▶ India ink and most black drawing inks
- ▶ black printer's ink (such as used on newspapers)
- ▶ special ballpoint pens with reproducible ink
- ▶ carbon typewriter ribbons
- ▶ the black Vis-a-Vis transparency marking pen
- ▶ heat resistant dry transfer materials

Items to be avoided are these:

- ▶ most ballpoint pens
- ▶ most felt tip pens
- ▶ hard leaded pencils (#2 or harder)
- ▶ colored printing inks
- ▶ spirit duplicated materials
- ▶ sheets typed on typewriters
- ▶ sheets produced on a dot matrix computer printer

Remember that carbon-based materials are usually black, but not all black materials are carbon based.

If an unwanted blemish is on the original visual, using correction fluid to cover the blemish will not totally solve the problem. Thermal transparency film is sensitive to heat, and when exposed to an original with blemishes covered by correction fluid, it will still react to the hidden carbon material and burn the unwanted image into the film. To eliminate the blemish, correction fluid may first be used to cover the blemish and then a new photocopy of the corrected original should be made.

The paper suitable for preparing an original should be typing paper or one of similar weight. The thin sheets of separation paper used for storing transparencies or thinner tracing paper may cause production problems and should be avoided when making originals. Originals must be pliable enough to go through the thermofax without jamming, because this could ruin the visual and the belt in the thermofax. Full sheets of paper should be used for making originals, or a backing sheet or transparency carrier should be used to protect smaller originals.

Originals should be prepared on paper that is neither to thin nor too thick.

Supplies needed for thermal transparencies include

- ▶ carbon original from which the overhead transparency is to be copied
- ▶ thermal transparency film
- ▶ thermal copy machine

Thermal Transparencies Procedures

1. Select or create the carbon original desired for preparation of a thermal transparency.

2. Select the type of transparency film to be used.

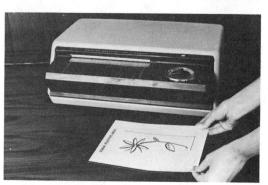

3. Place the film over the paper original. If the film has a notched corner (such as black-line-on-clear film), the notch must be placed in either the upper right or the lower left position of the original. This will ensure that the treated side of the film is turned right-side-up. Center the film over the material to be copied. If there is any printing on the back of the original, place a blank sheet of paper beneath it. This will prevent carbon from adhering to the belt of the machine and causing unwanted spots on future transparencies. Note that some types of thermal film do not have a notched corner, and directions from the film box should be followed. Directions for using donor film is included in following information.

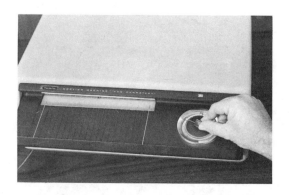

4. Set the exposure dial on the thermofax machine to the recommended setting. The setting for printing transparencies should be posted on the machine, because it may vary from one machine to another. If the setting is not posted, set the dial at approximately a 10 o'clock position and run a test copy to determine whether a speed adjustment is required for better contrast.

5. If the machine has an Power switch, place it in the "on" position. If it does not have such a switch, the machine will turn on automatically when the material is inserted into the machine. Feed the materials into the machine until the rollers grasp them. Never insert materials containing staples or paper clips into the machine. Never run thick materials, folded sheets of paper, or heavy cardboard material through the machine, or they may jam and ruin the materials along with the expensive plastic belt in the machine.

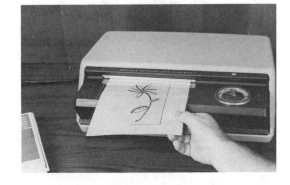

6. In a matter of seconds the master and transparency will emerge from the bottom slot at the front of the machine. Catch the materials as they roll out of the machine, but do not pull them out.

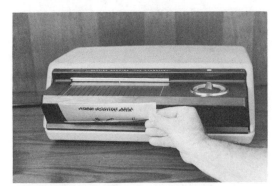

7. Separate the film from the paper master. The film should be an accurate duplicate of the image printed on the original. If the transparency is not printed satisfactorily, relate the problem to one of the following conditions.

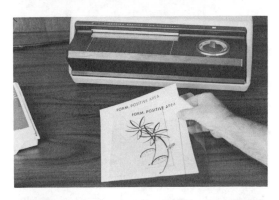

a. If the image is printed too lightly (some lines faded out or not dark enough), turn the exposure dial to a darker (counterclockwise) setting and print another copy.

It is virtually impossible to reuse the same piece of film to make it darker, because exact image alignment is difficult to accomplish.

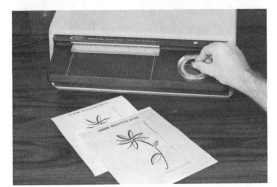

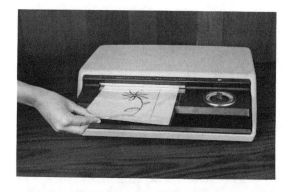

b. If the printed image is too dark (lines and letters are running together), turn the exposure dial to a lighter (clockwise) setting and print another copy.

8. If the transparency sheet came out blank, check for the following problems.

a. Was the notched corner of the film in the upper right or lower left corner of the original? If the notched corner was oriented improperly, correct the alignment and reprint. Misalignment of chemically coated donor film sheets may also result in no image. Ensure that donor film sheets' chemically treated sides are properly aligned.

b. Was the transparency film placed on top of the paper original? If the film is placed under rather than over the paper original, a blank transparency will result. Place the film on top of the original and expose again.

c. Was the original made with a reproducible carbon material? Originals with no carbon base will result in a blank transparency. One way to correct this problem without having to completely remake the original is to copy the material on a photocopier that produces carbon copies, then use the photo copy as an original for the thermofax. Otherwise, simply make a photocopy transparency.

Donor Film

In addition to black-line-on-clear (notched corner) thermal film, another common thermal film is "donor" film. Donor film produces colored image transparencies to enhance the visual. Each piece of film is capable of producing a single color, and different donor films produce different colors. This film consists of two pieces of material. Just as was done with the black-line (notched corner) film, this film is placed on top of a carbon original and inserted into the thermofax. As shown in Figure 23.1, the heavier transparency film should be on top, and the lightweight intermediate (chemically coated) donor film should be next, with the carbon original on the bottom facing up. The setting on the thermofax machine should be just about the same as for the black-line film, but it may take a slightly different setting.

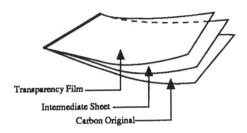

Figure 23.1

Layers of Donor Film

Transparencies may be mounted in frames to provide rigidity and durability, to enhance ease of handling and filing, and to extend the life of the materials. The frame also provides a good place to write notes pertaining to the material presented on the transparency.

Mounting frames are made from lightweight cardboard or plastic and may be purchased readymade or handmade from lightweight poster board. Be sure to work on a flat surface to mount transparencies.

TRANSPARENCY FRAMING

Mounting frames can be purchased or made by hand.

Transparency Framing Procedures

1. If only one piece of film (base cell) is to be attached to the frame, turn the frame over and place the transparency face down on it. Center the visual on the frame. Use short pieces of tape to attach each corner of the film to the frame from the back.

2. Use long tape strips to seal all edges of the film to the frame. Overlap the tape at the corners of the transparency.

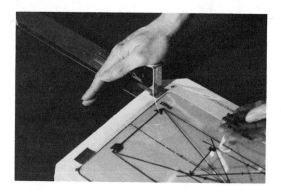

3. Some kinds of information can be best presented when divided into comparative or sequential parts. When overlays are used, the base cell is still mounted on the bottom of the frame, but the overlays are mounted on the top side of the frame. Special hinging tape is best for attaching overlays to a frame. A small tip of the hinge should be attached to one side of the film and then folded over so the other tip is attached to the other side of the film. The protruding part of the hinge should then be stapled to the frame.

Masking or some other type of durable tape could be used to produce temporary hinges, but Mylar hinges are desired for lasting results.

Sequential information overlays may all be hinged to the same edge of the frame. However, comparative information overlays need to be hinged to different edges of the frame so each overlay can be shown independently from the others.

4. Several overlays may be used when needed. Attach each overlay separately, ensuring that they are properly aligned when all sheets are projected. Do not allow any information to overlap that will make the visual confusing or difficult to read. It is not advisable to use more than seven overlays on one transparency.

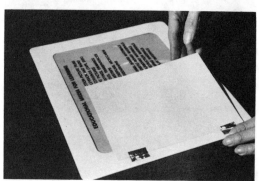

5. Hinged masks may be attached when a revelation technique is desired. Masks can be designed to fit the size and shape necessary to block the view of certain information. Each mask can be opened to expose the desired part of the visual at the appropriate time. Masks should be hinged to the transparency frame in the same manner as overlays.

ADDING COLOR AND TEXTURE TO TRANSPARENCIES

Transparent color can be added to any transparencies after they have been produced. Color can help clarify details or give emphasis to selected content. Transparent color adhesive-backed sheets are available that teachers use to cut out pieces to attach to transparencies. The material can be attached to either side of the transparency. If the instructor intends to write on the visual at any time, it is probably best to attach the adhesive to the bottom side of the transparency. Two or more colors of transparent adhesive film may be overlapped to form different colors.

Permanent and nonpermanent felt tip transparency marking pens may be used to add color to transparencies, but they are not usually as neat for coloring large areas as the colored adhesive.

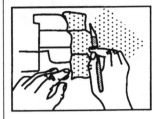

Felt tip marking pens or adhesive-backed sheets can be used to add color to transparencies.

TRANSPARENCY PRODUCTION QUALITY CHECK

Following is a checklist to determine the quality of transparency production.

_____ 1. Is the transparency image clean?

_____ 2. Does it incorporate good use of design elements?

_____ 3. Is color used to enhance communication?

_____ 4. Is there an appropriate use of the overlay technique?

_____ 5. Is there appropriate use of the masking technique?

_____ 6. Are tape hinges attached properly?

_____ 7. Is the size used for lettering large enough?

_____ 8. Is the base cell attached properly?

_____ 9. Is the image contrasted correctly?

SUGGESTED ACTIVITIES

1. Design and produce a direct process (handmade) transparency that could be used in your teaching area.

2. Design a carbon original and produce a thermal transparency from it that could be used in your teaching area.

3. Prepare a transparency using a masked revelation technique.

4. Prepare a transparency using an overlay technique.

5. Select a small visual and have it enlarged on transparency film in a photocopy machine.

6. Use a computer to create a visual with various types of graphics, then print it out on a printer.

7. Compare the quality of transparencies printed on dot matrix, ink jet, and laser computer printers.

Chapter 24

LAMINATION AND MOUNTING PROCESSES

PURPOSES

- ▶ To develop an understanding of processes which are used in mounting instructional materials
- ▶ To develop skills in dry mounting with a dry mount (heat) press and standard dry mount tissue
- ▶ To identify tools and materials that can be used for dry mounting
- ▶ To develop a knowledge of the various processes and devices that are used in laminating instructional materials
- ▶ To have a basic knowledge of the various materials available and necessary for laminating visuals
- ▶ To develop skill in laminating instructional materials with a dry mount press and tacking iron
- ▶ To develop skill in laminating with a roll laminating machine

INTRODUCTION

Educators often find clippings and pictures in newspapers and magazines that are valuable for instructional use. Out-of-date catalogs, brochures and calendars make excellent sources for visual materials. Governmental, commercial and trade organizations offer a large variety of free materials that are useful in presentations and displays. Unfortunately, these materials deteriorate with age or are easily damaged from handling. Mounting materials on durable backing generally extends their life and makes them more visually appealing.

Various materials may be used to mount visuals to durable backing, such as spray glue, rubber cement, double-sided tape, or dry mount tissue. *Dry mounted* materials, when prepared properly, yield the best visual and technical results of any of the processes. Most schools have dry mount presses for such activities, but mounting may even be done at home with an iron.

Lamination involves placing a protective plastic coating over the surface of materials. The plastic coating protects maps, pictures, and other visuals from dirt, moisture, fingerprints and stains. Laminated materials usually show no appreciable wear or soiling.

Materials that have been protected by lamination may also be marked or drawn on with "grease" pencils or water soluble felt pens and markers. This permits marks to be made and then easily removed from materials such as maps, charts, educational games, and self-correction instruments.

Flat objects other than pictorial materials may also be laminated for use in instruction. Specimens such as leaves will hold both shape and color after being sealed under plastic. Students may use lamination to preserve specimens that they have collected and studied.

DRY MOUNTING

Dry mounting is a process by which many different types of thin materials such as pictures, charts, posters, tear sheets, photographs, and newspaper clippings may be attached permanently to backing materials such as tagboard, matte board, cardboard, and masonite. The process makes use of special dry mounting materials that seal the picture to the mounting board. Dry mount materials are clean and easy to handle during production stages, but when heated, they soften and become a sticky bonding material. Unless special dry mounting material designed for later removal is used, the final bond between the visual and backing is permanent.

Equipment Needed

Several devices may be used for dry mounting materials, such as

▶ dry mount press
▶ tacking iron
▶ home iron
▶ thermofax machine

Each of these devices may be used with differing degrees of efficiency or quality. The dry mount press used in conjunction with a tacking iron will provide the best results. There are new vacuum presses on the market that provide even more versatility.

Supplies Needed

In addition to the heating devices, a number of other materials and tools are necessary for quality dry mountings:

▶ dry mount tissue or material
▶ clean butcher, newsprint, or special coated paper
▶ backing material for the mounting
▶ visuals to be mounted on the backing
▶ paper cutter, scissors, and sharp knife or blade
▶ heavy, flat, weighted material such as a sheet of metal or large books

Dry Mount Press Procedures

1. Dry mounting may be done quickly and easily with a dry mounting press or any household hand iron that would provide the heat and pressure needed. If a dry mount press is used, plug the press and tacking iron into an electrical outlet. Set the temperature control on the press at 225° F and turn the tacking iron control to the high setting. Remember to allow a few minutes for the machine to heat. This machine is thermostatically controlled and will remain at the assigned setting once it has heated to 225° F.

2. Place the mounting board and visual material between a folded sheet of clean paper or special "seal release paper." Insert the two items in the mounting press, close the press, and leave for approximately 60 seconds. This will remove moisture and wrinkles from the materials. Remove the materials from the press and let cool.

3. Adhere sheet of dry mounting tissue to the back of the visual. Tack it securely to the visual in the center of the back, using the tip of the tacking iron. The tissue should be exactly the same size as the visual, or a little larger, so it can be trimmed with the visual after it has been tacked in place. If the visual is large and more than one sheet of dry mount tissue is needed, butt the edges together and tack, but do not overlap.

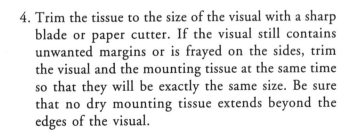

4. Trim the tissue to the size of the visual with a sharp blade or paper cutter. If the visual still contains unwanted margins or is frayed on the sides, trim the visual and the mounting tissue at the same time so that they will be exactly the same size. Be sure that no dry mounting tissue extends beyond the edges of the visual.

Be sure to use a paper cutter properly so the edges are trimmed evenly. Alternatively, you should use a sharp knife or scissors for better results.

5. Place the visual on the mounting board. If you desire a border around the visual (usually recommended), use a ruler to center the picture on the mount. Raise two opposite corners of the visual and tack the mounting tissue to the board. If the board margins around the visual are not the desired size or shape, tack the visual to the board and then trim the excess board. You may choose to measure the board ahead of time and cut it the appropriate size. If you cut the board first, be careful to tack the visual on the board straight.

6. Place the attached visual and mounting in a folded sheet of clean paper or seal release paper. This paper protects the visual from direct contact with the heat elements of the press and protects the stainless steel surface of the press from possible transfer of ink and adhesive. The stainless steel platen should be kept clean or it may ruin work that follows.

7. Insert the materials in the press. Close the press, making sure that it is fully closed, applying maximum pressure to the materials. Leave the materials in the press for 20–30 seconds. Some machines will have a flashing light that blinks every second; others will not.

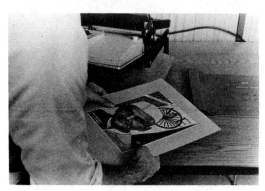

8. Remove the materials and quickly inspect them. If the visual does not appear to be sealed to the backing, place the materials back into the press for another 30–60 seconds.

9. If the visual appears to be securely sealed to the backing, place the materials under a weight and allow 3–5 minutes for cooling. When regular steel weights are used, cooling will require less time than when books or heavy objects are used.

Remove from under the weights and check very carefully to ensure that the entire back of the visual is securely fastened to the mount. Check carefully for bubbles, wrinkles, or areas of nonadhesion.

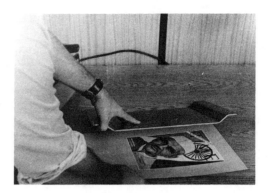

Mounting Problems and Solutions

Bubbles and wrinkles sometimes occur in the mounting process. They are caused by excessive heat or by improper tacking. To correct such flaws, replace materials in the press for 60 seconds or more. If this does not correct the problem, iron the problem area with a clean tacking iron, working out the wrinkle or bubble as much as possible, then replace in the press for another 60 seconds or more. Nonadhesion of large areas of the visual is usually caused by inadequate heat or pressure. Check to ensure that the press has reached the desired heat level. Ensure that the press is closing properly. Replace the materials in the press for approximately 60 seconds.

Prevent nonadhesion by pressing only when the press is hot enough and ensuring the press closes completely.

Professional photographers dry mount their photographs, and they must be careful when they use the resin-coated photographic papers. Wax surfaces and special plastics on photographic prints may melt when exposed to heat. Standard mounting materials such as Seal MT-5 tissue should not be used on photographs for this reason. There are several other dry mounting tissues that can be used.

Tacking Iron Procedures

The basic tacking iron used to tack the materials when doing dry mount press work may also be used by itself, if the material to be dry mounted is small, such as an ID card or name tag.

Just turn the heat up to the high setting and carefully hold the material in place while you tack it. Once it is tacked to the backing, run the tacking iron over the entire surface and seal it totally.

Home Iron Procedures

A home iron can be used for the process, but care must be taken to keep the work flat and covered with a protective piece of clean paper. Rather than throwing away an old steam iron that no longer steams properly, use it for such projects and there will be no worry about getting tissue stuck to the good home iron that is still used on clothes.

An old steam iron is perfect for dry mounting.

Set the iron on the "silk" setting. Be careful to tack the visual to the backing before sealing the entire project. Be careful to keep the materials flat and use just the tip of the iron as a tacking iron to tack down the opposite corners. Then you can finish mounting the entire visual with the iron's surface, just as if you were ironing clothing. One of the main concerns is to get a good flat seal with no wrinkles.

Creativity in Dry Mounting

Visuals can be mounted in a variety of ways, and their use is limited only by the imagination. Greeting cards, place mats, gift wrapping paper, printed commercial paper bags, printed cardboard boxes, candy wrappers, and aluminum foil can be mounted and used as borders, bases, or frames for other visuals.

Materials may be dry mounted in layers to create a collage effect.

A portion of one picture may be cut out and attached to another to create a combined visual effect. Frames or borders such as a double matte can enhance plain visuals and make them more appealing.

Dry Mounting Quality Check

Following is a checklist to determine the quality of the dry mounting:

__1. Are the visuals clean?

__2. Is the visual mounted straight?

__3. Is the backing cut neatly?

__4. Are there any air bubbles?

__5. Are there any wrinkles?

__6. Does the dry mount tissue show?

__7. Is the visual completely adhered?

LAMINATION

Some methods of laminating are considered primary methods for production: others are considered less common. Quality lamination is usually done by heat process with a dry mounting press, tacking iron, or roll laminator. Occasionally a thermofax machine or home iron may be used. The cold lamination process only requires special adhesive film and no special equipment, which means it can be done almost anywhere. Each of these methods of laminating has its advantages in preserving visual materials. A knowledge of all of the processes should provide the instructor with enough versatility to adapt to the local situation.

Film Types

Lamination film is available in a variety of types, including gloss, luster, satin, matte, and textured finishes. In addition, lamination comes in different thicknesses and dimensions for a variety of strengths and uses. The heat-laminating process is usually the most durable, practical and attractive. Laminating film consists of a tough mylar plastic, with one side being coated with heat-sensitive adhesive. When heat and pressure are applied to the plastic, the adhesive softens and adheres tightly to the visual material.

Heat lamination covers materials with mylar adhesive film.

Dry Mount Press

The dry mount press is the most common tool used for heat lamination, and it is the most versatile of all the processes mentioned. Presses are available in a variety of sizes.

Roll Laminator

The roll laminator is a more expensive piece of equipment than some of the other devices used, but it works much faster and has more versatility for laminating than the dry mount press, tacking iron, or home iron. This device is quite popular with many media centers because of its speed and quality. Roll laminators are available in a variety of sizes.

Tacking Iron

If a small item such as an ID card or name tag needs to be laminated, the tacking iron can usually do the job. Take care to keep the material flat and tack it before you attempt to do the whole surface.

Pocket Laminators

There are machines called "pocket laminators" that are sold for laminating small items, and the film is available in the shape of small pockets to insert items to be laminated.

Home Irons

Home irons can also be used for laminating materials. It is wise to use an old iron that is no longer used for clothing, because you could accidentally melt film onto it. The home iron method is useful in emergencies, but be careful to tack the material first and keep it very flat to prevent wrinkling problems.

Roll Lamination

The "roll laminator" laminates both sides of a visual at the same time. Different sizes of roll laminators are available to laminate materials up to 60 inches wide with almost an unlimited length. The roll laminator operates like a conveyor belt, and a major advantage of the system is the speed at which it can finish the process and the excellent quality of the work.

Supplies needed for roll lamination include

- ▶ visual materials to be laminated
- ▶ paper cutter, scissors, or sharp knife
- ▶ roll laminator properly loaded

Roll Lamination Procedures

1. Turn the roll laminator Power switch and/or the heat control on to allow the machine to heat to the proper temperature. Warmup usually takes about 3 to 5 minutes, depending on the model used.

2. Arrange the visuals to be fed into the machine.

3. Press the Start switch.

4. Insert the materials between the rollers and feed them through the machine.

5. Several items may be laminated all in a row, or the machine can be stopped after laminating each item. When the lamination is finished, allow the last laminated visual to run a few inches past the tear bar and press the Stop switch.

6. Tear the film loose from the machine by using the perforated edge (tear bar) on the machine.

7. Trim the materials as desired.

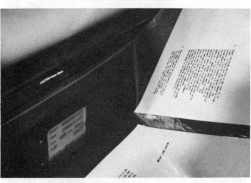

Dry Mount Press Lamination

Supplies Needed for Dry Mount Press Lamination include:

- ▶ visual materials to be laminated
- ▶ lamination film
- ▶ dry mount press
- ▶ tacking Iron
- ▶ masonite board
- ▶ paper cutter, scissors, or sharp blade
- ▶ large sheet of clean paper

Dry Mount Press Lamination Procedures

1. Plug the dry mounting press and tacking iron into an electrical outlet. Set the temperature of the press to 270° Fahrenheit and the tacking iron on high.

2. Insert the masonite board and allow the press to rest in a closed (but not pressured) position. This will enable the masonite to heat with the rest of the press during warmup.

3. Place the instructional materials in the press for about 10 seconds and heat them to drive out the moisture. The materials must be thoroughly dry or the laminating process will seal the moisture in with the materials. It will turn the moisture to steam and damage the surface of the materials or cause air bubbles.

4. After the materials have cooled, measure and cut enough laminating film to cover the entire mounting surface and allow at least one-half inch overlap.

5. On laminating film the dull "treated" side of the film is the adhesive or "sticky" side. Place the dull side against the visual to be laminated. When you use matte finish film, it is more difficult to distinguish the dull side, so you need to be careful. Tack the film lightly on the corners to hold it in place. Be careful to keep the film flat while tacking or it may wrinkle.

If the visual has been mounted on flat, heavyweight board, you can wrap one piece of film around one edge and tack it to both sides. Take care to keep the material flat while you are tacking. If the backing is thick board, it will not allow enough heat to transfer through the board to seal the film on both sides, so each side will need to be heated separately.

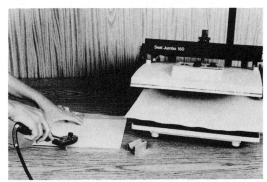

If the visual to be laminated is not dry mounted and remains flimsy (usually when there is information on each side that needs to be seen or special storage is required), each side should be laminated with a separate piece of film to avoid wrinkling problems.

6. Place the visual materials into a protective folder of clean paper and insert it into the dry mounting press.

7. Close the press tightly and leave the materials in the press for 30 seconds. You may simultaneously seal both front and back if desired, as long as the backing is thin enough to allow the heat to pass through it. Otherwise, you will have to turn the visual over to sufficiently heat and seal each side.

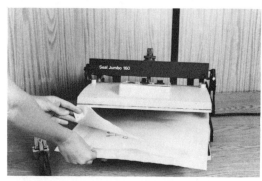

8. Remove the materials from the press and quickly check for wrinkles or bubbles.

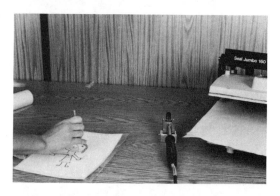

9. If air bubbles are present, punch holes in them with a straight pin or other sharp object. Place the materials back into the dry mounting press for an additional few seconds.

10. If the materials appear to be satisfactorily laminated, quickly place them under flat weights and leave them for 1–3 minutes to cool. This will help keep them from curling badly.

11. Remove the materials from the weights and check to ensure the laminating film is adhered securely and no air bubbles or wrinkles are present. Neatly trim excess lamination film from the edges to make it visually appealing.

In order to preserve valuable materials indefinitely there should be a little overlap of film from each side, (approximately one-eight inch), to seal out moisture and air and prevent deterioration.

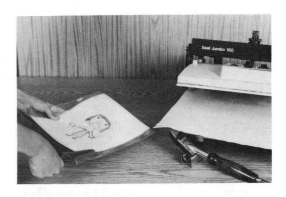

12. Laminated materials are well preserved and should withstand considerable handling from students.

There is often a need to laminate an item that is larger than the dry mount press. In order to do this, tack the laminating film to the material in the normal manner and insert parts of the visual into the press until it is completed. It is best to start in the middle and work toward the corners, as shown in Figure 24.1.

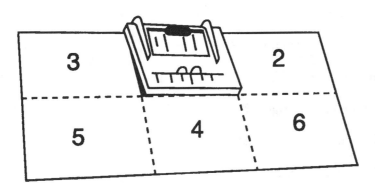

Figure 24.1

Process for Laminating a Large Surface

Masonite board should be used only when the dry mounting press is being used for laminating. The masonite provides the increased pressure necessary for laminating. A higher temperature is necessary for laminating than for dry mounting, and drying (preheating) of materials is more crucial for laminating. It is difficult to dry mount and laminate materials simultaneously because the proper temperature is different for each process.

It is difficult to laminate photographs successfully with standard laminating film. There are special films available for such activities. Regular laminating film requires so much heat that it could damage the surface of photographs.

Use special film to laminate photographs.

Avoid laminating dark colors.

Special effects can be created with heat laminating film such as the "crinkle" effect. Simply cut a piece of film larger than the material to be laminated and wad it up tightly until it is well wrinkled. Flatten the film out and tack it to the visual in the normal manner. Then laminate it as usual. If visual detail is important, do not use the "crinkle" effect.

Black-colored materials such as poster board are difficult to laminate well. The color fades and the film does not always stick well. Try to avoid black and very dark backing material.

Laminating only one side of a visual sometimes causes the visual to curl. Laminate both sides to keep it flat. Besides, laminating only one side leaves the other exposed to the elements and defeats the purpose of preservation.

Fragile objects such as butterflies, leaves, ferns, and other nature items can be laminated. Some of these items can be dry mounted first if desired. These items should be dried before they are laminated.

Lamination Quality Check

Following is a checklist to determine the quality of the lamination:

__1. Are the materials clean?

__2. Are the materials trimmed neatly?

__3. Are there any air bubbles?

__4. Is the film adhered tightly?

__5. Are there any signs of moisture?

__6. Are the materials curling?

1. Laminate a visual and use the "crinkle" method.

2. Select a visual that can be used in your field and use the dry mount press and tacking iron to dry mount it on backing material.

3. Select a small visual and use the tacking iron or a home iron to dry mount it to a piece of material.

4. Dry mount a visual that is composed of more than one piece of material.

5. Select a visual that has been dry mounted and laminate it using the dry mount press method.

6. Select a visual that has information on both sides that is needed and laminate it on a dry mount press.

7. Use one of the other techniques of laminating besides the dry mount press method to laminate a visual.

Recommended Readings

Brown, James W., and Richard B. Lewis. *AV Instructional Technology Manual for Independent Study.* 6th ed. New York: McGraw-Hill, 1983.

Brown, Robert M. *Educational Media: A Competency-Based Approach.* Columbus, Ohio: Charles E. Merrill, 1973.

Bullard, John R., and Calvin E. Mether. *Audiovisual Fundamentals.* 3rd ed. Dubuque, Iowa: Wm C. Brown, 1984.

Curtiss, Deborah. *Introduction to Visual Literacy.* Englewood Cliffs, N. J.: Prentice-Hall, Inc., 1987.

Eastman Kodak Company. *Basic Titling and Animation for Motion Pictures.* 2nd ed. Rochester, NY:

Eastman Kodak Company. *Picture Taking—A Self Teaching Guide.* Rochester, NY:

Eckhardt, Robert. *The Fully Powered Mac.* New York: Brady, 1988.

Fuller, Barry J., Steve Kanaba, and Janyce Brisch-Kanaba, *Single Camera Video Production.* Englewood Cliffs, NJ: Prentice-Hall, Inc., 1982.

Heinich, Robert, Michael Molenda, and James D. Russell. *Media and the New Technologies of Instruction.* 3rd ed. New York: John Wiley & Sons, 1989.

Kemp, Jerrold E., and Deane K. Dayton. *Planning and Producing Instructional Media.* 5th ed. New York: Harper and Row, 1985.

King, Kenneth L., John A. Ludrick, Bruce A. Petty, Gene L. Post, and J. D. Strickland. *A Systematic Approach to Instructional Media Competency.* 5th ed. Dubuque, Iowa: Kendall Hunt, 1977.

Langford, Michael. *Visual Aids and Photography in Education.* New York: Hastings House, 1973.

Laybourne, Kit. *Doing the Media: A Portfolio of Activities. Ideas and Resources.* rev. ed. New York: McGraw Hill, 1978.

Leggat, Robert. *Photography in School.* Hertfordshire, England: Fountain Press, Argus Books Limited, 1975.

Minor, Ed. *Handbook for Preparing Visual Media.* 2nd ed. New York: McGraw Hill, 1978.

Naiman, Arthur, and Nancy E. Dunn. *The Macintosh Bible,* 4th ed. Berkeley, Calif.: Peachpit Press, 1992.

Talab, R. S. *Copyright and Instructional Technologies: A Guide to Fair Use and Permissions Procedures.* 2nd ed. Washington, D.C.: Association for Educational Communications and Technology, 1989.

Turner, Sandra, and Michael Land. *Tools for Schools.* Belmont, Calif.: Wadsworth Publishing Company, 1988.

GLOSSARY

Balance: A term used with graphics regarding a visual's equilibrium.

Bar Graph: A simplified visual representation of quantitative data using bar shapes in graph form.

Carbon Original: A visual consisting of carbon-based material that is required for thermal reproduction processes on the thermofax machine.

Clip Art: Commercially available sources that provide pictures and lettering that can be clipped out and used for graphics design. It comes in print form as well as on computer diskette and CD-ROM.

Computer Graphics: The use of graphics software and techniques for creating various lettering fonts and visual materials with a computer.

Design Principles: The basis for analyzing the quality of a design based on balance, emphasis, simplicity, and unity.

Disclosure Techniques: Methods of using revelation techniques such as masking or overlays on transparencies.

Donor Film: Heat-sensitive film that consists of a chemically coated transparency and a chemically coated, disposable, intermediate sheet of film that creates colored transparencies when used together with a carbon original on a thermofax machine.

Dry Mounting: A process that uses heat-sensitive, adhesive-coated paper to adhere visuals to poster board or other backing materials.

Dry Mount Press: A large heat press used for heating, dry mounting. and laminating visuals.

Fonts: Various lettering types such as Gothic and Old English.

Formal Balance: The type of aesthetically matched appearance that occurs when a graphic design has one-half that is symmetrical with the other half.

Format: The basic horizontal or vertical shape of a visual's dimensions.

Graphics: A combination of special design principles and elements used to create visuals.

Graphing Techniques: Methods using various graphs such as pie, bar, line, and pictorial to provide a simplified visual form for data analysis.

Handmade Transparencies: Transparencies made without the use of machines.

Image Ratio: The ratio of height to width of a visual image.

Informal Balance: The type of aesthetically matched appearance that occurs when a graphic design has the feeling of being balanced, but the two halves of the design are not symmetrical.

Interfacing: To connect a computer with any number of peripheral devices to exchange data, create graphics or sounds, or control the other devices.

Lamination: A process in which materials are sealed in plastic to protect them from deterioration.

LCD Projection Pad: The liquid crystal display pad that is placed on an overhead projector that can project good-resolution computer images onto a projection screen for viewing by a whole class.

Lettering Guides: Special tools, devices, and techniques used to create lettering for graphics production.

Lettering Guidelines: Basic elements of design regarding legibility and visibility of lettering.

Masking: The use of opaque materials to cover certain portions of a transparency for controlled disclosure.

Multimedia: A combination of interfaced devices incorporated with a computer.

Original: A visual that is used to produce other visual materials or masters.

Overlay: Additional sheets of transparency film attached to the top side of a transparency to display comparative or sequential information.

Photocopy: A high-quality reproduction process in which a machine creates an electrostatically charged image on paper and applies a carbon-based toner with heat and pressure to produce duplicate copies.

Photocopy Transparency: A transparency that is produced with a special film on a photocopy machine.

PICT: Associated with pictures or graphics files produced on a computer that are normally used in paint types of programs.

PostScript: A program language used for the production of higher-quality printed images on a computer printer.

Referent Confusion: The communication difficulties or lack of understanding that occurs because of differences in people's cultural or environmental experiences.

Superimposed: To create a graphic over a live video image or some other type of visual image.

TIFF: Bitmapped images that can be altered in size.

Visual Elements: The graphic components that make up the design principles such as line, shape, color, contrast, texture, and space and size.

Visual Composition: The horizontal and vertical arrangement of images.

Appendix A

COPYRIGHT

Since its founding, our nation has recognized the importance of assigning ownership of authored materials, encouraging the development of original works, and stimulating the distribution of these materials. The U.S. Constitution assigned to Congress the power "To promote the Progress of Science and useful Arts, by securing for limited Times to Authors and Inventors the exclusive Right to their respective Writing and Discoveries," (Article 1, Section 8, of the U.S. Constitution). The U.S. Congress has passed a series of copyright laws designed to address this constitutioul mandate.

Most crucial among copyright legislation are the Copyright Acts of 1909 and 1976. Protection is provided through these acts to authors, creators, producers, and publishers of most of the materials used in today's schools. Educators must develop a working familarity of copyright regulations so that appropriate uses are made of educational material, the rights of the owners are regarded, and copyright laws are obeyed.

U.S. copyright legislation grants five exclusive rights to copyright owners:

1. The right to reproduce the work.

2. The right to prepare derivative works.

3. The right to public distribution of the work.

4. The right to publicly perform the work, if literary, musical, dramatic, choreographic, motion picture, or other audiovisual work.

5. The right to publicly display the work, such as photographs, motion pictures, audiovisuals, computer screen displays, and so forth.

The principle of "fair use" addressed by Congress in the 1976 law is of special concern to educators. Under this provision, reproduction of copyrighted materials is permitted for uses such as criticism, comment, news reporting, teaching, scholarship, or research. This principle permits limited copying for classroom use when specified criteria and tests are followed. These have been applied to specific types of educational materials through guidelines from various organizations.

Concern for copyright is especially critical today because of the ease with which materials in most forms may be copied, and consequently the copyright laws breached. Teachers should possess four specific competencies relating to copyright and ownership of materials they desire to use:

1. Know whether the materials are copyrighted, and if so, who owns the copyright. Information at or near the front of the materials will indicate whether the materials are copyrighted. If so, the year of the copyright and the owner will be given.

2. Know what uses a teacher may make of copyrighted materials and the extent of copying and distribution that may be done under existing guidelines.

3. Know how to seek approval from copyright owners to use, copy, or distribute materials in ways not covered by guidelines.

4. Know how to appropriately give credit for all materials used.

GUIDELINES

Copyright guidelines pertaining to the types of materials discussed extensively in this publication are presented here. They should be consulted when a question arises concerning whether specific materials may be copied in a given circumstance.

Books and Periodicals

I. Single Copying for Teachers

A single copy may be made of any of the following by or for a teacher at his or her individual request for his or her scholarly research or use in teaching or preparation to teach a class:

A. A chapter from a book;

B. An article from a periodical or newspaper;

C. A short story, short essay or short poem, whether or not from a collective work;

D. A chart, graph, diagram, drawing, cartoon or picture from a book, periodical, or newspaper.

II. Multiple Copies for Classroom Use

Multiple copies (not to exceed in any event more than one copy per pupil in a course) may be made by or for the teacher giving the course for classroom use or discussion, provided that:

A. The copying meets the tests of brevity and spontaneity as defined below; and

B. The copying meets the cumulative effect test as defined below; and

C. Each copy includes a notice of copyright.

Definitions

Brevity

(i) Poetry: (a) A complete poem if less than 250 words and if printed on not more than two pages; or (b) from a longer poem, an excerpt of not more than 250 words.

(ii) Prose: (a) Either a complete article, story, or essay of less than 2,500 words; or (b) an excerpt from any prose work of not more than 1,000 words or 10 percent of the work, whichever is less, but in any event a minimum of 500 words.

[Each of the numerical limits stated in "i" and "ii" above may be expanded to permit the completion of an unfinished line of a poem or an unfinished prose paragraph.]

(iii) Illustration: One chart, graph, diagram, drawing, cartoon, or picture per book or per periodical issue.

(iv) "Special" works: Certain works in poetry, prose, or in "poetic prose," which often combine language with illustrations and which are intended sometimes for children and at other times for a more general audience, fall short of 2,500 words in their entirety. Paragraph "ii" above notwithstanding such "special works" may not be reproduced in their entirety; however, an excerpt comprising not more than two of the published pages of such special work and containing not more than 10 percent of the words found in the text thereof may be reproduced.

Spontaneity

(i) The copying is at the instance and inspiration of the individual teacher, and

(ii) The inspiration and decision to use the work and the moment of its use for maximum teaching effectiveness are so close in time that it would be unreasonable to expect a timely reply to a request for permission.

Cumulative Effect

(i) The copying of the material is for only one course in the school in which copies are made.

(ii) Not more than one short poem, article, story, essay, or two excerpts may be copied from the same author, nor more than three from the same collective work or periodical volume during one class term.

(iii) There shall not be more than nine instances of such multiple copying for one course during one class term.

[The limitations stated in "ii" and "iii" above shall not apply to current news periodicals and newspapers and current news sections of other periodicals.]

III. Prohibitions as to I and II Above

Notwithstanding any of the above, the following shall be prohibited:

A. Copying shall not be used to create or to replace or substitute for anthologies, compilations, or collective works. Such replacement or substitution may occur whether copies of various works or excerpts therefrom are accumulated or reproduced and used separately.

B. There shall be no copying of or from works intended to be "consumable" in the course of study or of teaching. These include workbooks, exercises, standardized tests, test booklets, answer sheets, and like consumable material.

C. Copying shall not:

(a) substitute for the purchase of books, publishers' reprints, or periodicals;

(b) be directed by higher authority;

(c) be repeated with respect to the same item by the same teacher from term to term.

D. No charge shall be made to the student beyond the actual cost of the photocopying.

Agreed MARCH 19, 1976

Ad Hoc Committee on Copyright Law Revision:

By SHELDON ELLIOTT STEINBACH.

Author-Publisher Group:

Authors League of America: By IRWIN KARP, Counsel.

Association of American Publishers, Inc.: By ALEXANDER C. HOFFMAN, Chairman, Copyright Committee.

AN ICCE POLICY STATEMENT

Suggested Software Use Guidelines

The 1976 U.S. Copyright Act and its 1980 Amendments remain vague in some areas of software use and its application to education. Where the law itself is vague, software licenses tend to be much more specific. It is therefore imperative that educators read the software's copyright page and understand the licensing restrictions printed there. If these uses are not addressed, the following guidelines are recommended.

These guidelines do not have the force of law, but they do represent the collected opinion on fair software use by nonprofit educational agencies from a variety of experts in the software copyright field.

Backup Copy: The Copyright Act is clear in permitting the owner of software a backup copy of the software to be held for use as an archival copy in the event the original disk fails to function. Such backup copies are not to be used on a second computer at the same time the original is in use.

Multiple Loading: The Copyright act is most unclear as it applies to loading the contents of one disk into multiple computers for use at the same time. In the absence of a license expressly permitting the user to load the contents of one disk into many computers for use at the same time, it is suggested that you not allow this activity to take place. The fact that you physically can do so is irrelevant. In an effort to make it easier for schools to buy software for each computer station, many software publishers offer lab packs and other quantity buying incentives. Contact individual publishers for details.

Local Area Network Software Use: It is suggested that before placing a program on a local area network or disk-sharing system for use by multiple users at the same time, you obtain a written license agreement from the copyright holder giving you permission to do so. The fact that you are able to physically load the program on the network is, again, irrelevant. You should obtain a license permitting you to do so before you act.

Model District Policy on Software Copyright

It is the intent of [district] to adhere to the provisions of copyright laws in the area of microcomputer software. It is also the intent of the district to comply with the license agreements and/or policy statements contained in the software packages used in the district. In circumstances where the interpretation of the copyright law is ambiguous, the district shall look to the applicable license agreement to determine appropriate use of the software or the district will abide by the approved Software Use Guidelines.

We recognize that computer software piracy is a major problem for the industry and that violations of copyright laws contribute to higher costs and greater efforts to prevent copying and/or lessen incentives for the development of effective educational uses of microcomputers. Therefore, in an effort to discourage violation of copyright laws and to prevent such illegal activities:

1. The ethical and practical implications of software piracy will be taught to educators and school children in all schools in the district (for example, covered in fifth-grade social studies classes).

2. District employees will be informed that they are expected to adhere to section 117 of the 1976 Copyright Act as amended in 1980, governing the use of software (for example, each building principal will devote one faculty meeting to the subject a year).

3. When permission is obtained from the copyright holder to use software on a disk-sharing system, efforts will be made to secure this software from copying.

4. Under no circumstances shall illegal copies of copyrighted software be made or used on school equipment.

5. [Name or job title] of this school district is designated as the only individual who may sign license agreements for software for schools in the district. Each school using licensed software should have a signed copy of the software agreement.

6. The principal at each school site is responsible for establishing practices which will enforce this district copyright at the school level.

The Board of Directors of the International Council for Computers in Education approved this policy statement in January 1987. The members of the 1986 ICCE Software Copyright Committee were:

Sueann Ambron, American Association of Publishers
Gary Becker, Seminole Co. Public Schools, Florida
Daniel T. Brooks, Cadwalader, Wickersham & Taft
LeRoy Finkle, International Council for Computers in Education
Virginia Helm, Western Illinois University
Kent Kehrberg, Minnesota Educational Computing Corporation
Dan Kunz, Commodore Business Machines
Bodie Marx, Mindscape, Inc.
Kenton Pattie, International Communications Industries Association
Carol Risher, American Association of Publishers
Linda Roberts, US Congress—OTA
Donald A. Ross, Microcomputer Workshops Courseware
Larry Smith, Wayne County Int. Schl. Dist., Michigan
Ken Wasch, Software Publishers Association

For more information write to ICCE Software Copyright Committee, ICCE, University of Oregon, 1787 Agate St., Eugene, OR 97403.

OFF-AIR RECORDING OF BROADCAST PROGRAMMING

1. The guidelines were developed to apply only to off-air recordings by non-profit educational institutions.

2. A broadcast program may be recorded off-air simultaneously with broadcast transmission (including simultaneous cable retransmission) and retained by a nonprofit educational institution for a period not to exceed the first 45 consecutive calendar days after date of recording. Upon conclusion of such retention period, all off-air recordings must be erased or destroyed immediately. "Broadcast programs" are television programs transmitted by television stations for reception by the general public without charge.

3. Off-air recordings may be used once by individual teachers in the course of relevant teaching activities and repeated once only when instructional

reinforcement is necessary, in classrooms and similar places devoted to instruction within a single building, cluster or campus, as well as in the homes of students receiving formalized home instruction, during the first 10 consecutive school days in the 45 calendar day retention period.

4. Off-air recordings may be made only at the request of and used by individual teachers, and may not be regularly recorded in anticipation of requests. No broadcast program may be recorded off-air more than once at the request of the same teacher, regardless of the number of times the program may be broadcast.

5. A limited number of copies may be reproduced from each off-air recording to meet the legitimate needs of teachers under these guidelines. Each such additional copy shall be subject to all provisions governing the original recording.

6. After the first 10 consecutive school days, off-air recordings may be used up to the end of the 45 calendar day retention period only for teacher evaluation purposes, that is, to determine whether to include the broadcast program in the teaching curriculum, and may not be used in the recording institution for student exhibition or any other nonevaluation purpose without authorization.

7. Off-air recordings need not be used in their entirety, but the recorded programs may not be altered from their original content. Off-air recordings may not be physically or electronically combined or merged to constitute teaching purpose without authorization.

8. All copies of off-air recordings must include the copyright notice on the broadcast program as recorded.

9. Educational institutions are expected to establish appropriate control procedures to maintain the integrity of these guidelines.

Association for Educational Communications and Technology (AECT)
1025 Vermont Ave., NW, Ste. 820
Washington, D.C. 20005
(202) 347-7834

Software Publishers Association
1730 M St. NW, Suite 700
Washington, D.C. 20036
Phone: (202) 452-1600   Fax: (202) 223-8756
Piracy Hotline: 1 (800) 388-7478

ADDITIONAL RESOURCES FOR COPYRIGHT INFORMATION

Appendix B

MOTION PICTURE PROJECTION SYSTEM

PURPOSES

► To discuss the major components of the motion picture projector system
► To be able to set up and operate an autoload 16mm motion picture projector
► To be able to troubleshoot and perform simple maintenance tasks on a film projector

Motion picture films are still integral to many schools' media collections, so there remains a need for teachers to possess a basic competence in motion picture projector use and a knowledge of film characteristics. Most motion picture projectors and film have three basic elements: optical, mechanical, and sound systems.

Optical System

The optical system makes images appear on the screen. A series of photographic images on film passes through the projector in an inverted position. The projector's bulb and lens project the images on the screen. An illusion of motion is created as the film advance claw on the projector moves the film at 24 frames per second using a rotating shutter in front of the lamp.

Mechanical System

The mechanical system moves the film through the projector. Sprocket holes on the film match sprocket teeth on the mechanical system, which moves the film through the projector, although some types of machines use a friction feed system instead of sprockets.

Sound System

Educational motion picture films have an optical sound track on one edge of the film that consists of a dark line that varies in size and shape to create different sound patterns when the sound track passes over the projector's optically sensitive sound drum. The sound drum focuses a concentrated light beam on it through a condenser lens from a small exciter lamp. The exciter lamp is just a very small projection lamp.

Each of the three systems must function properly for a film to be run successfully. Teachers and other projectionists should become familiar with operations for their schools' equipment by following instructions provided on the machine or its lid; some machines have an accompanying user's guide.

OPERATING THE MOTION PICTURE PROJECTOR

Sprockets must match the film's sprocket holes well to feed film through the projector.

The film should progress through the equipment in a clockwise motion, from the supply reel, with the images upside down and sprockets facing outward. If the film is not in this position to start, it probably wasn't rewound or was rewound incorrectly after the previous showing.

The feed-in sprockets pull film from the supply reel into the projector. The teeth of the sprockets must be engaged properly in the film's sprocket holes. If the sprocket holes in the film are broken or torn, the feed sprockets will not grab the film properly and the film may not play or may break.

The projectionist should form a loop of film immediately after the first feed sprockets and before the film passes behind the lens. If there is no loop, the film may break when it becomes too taut.

Film passes through the film channel in front of the projection lamp and behind the lens. Each image stops for a fraction of a second as the shutter helps to create the illusion of motion. If the film is not positioned properly in the channel, the image on the screen may be incorrect or the sprocket holes may start to tear on the claws.

A second loop is necessary to keep the film and sound track in sync.

The film should form a loop below the lens and before the second sprockets. The size of this loop affects the synchronization of the images and sound track. Normally, autoload projectors automatically thread the proper sized loop here.

The second sprockets feed the film to the sound drum. If the film is not snug as it passes over the sprockets and goes around the sound drum, the sound may be "fuzzy" or of poor quality.

Film passes around the sound drum before it is rewound on the take-up reel. A small light beam from the exciter lamp focuses on the optical sound track of the film to reproduce the sound. This lamp must be turned on and free of dust and lint to transmit good-quality sound. The film then passes by another set of sprockets to move the film out of the machine and onto the take-up reel.

A snub roller is usually the last projector part that the film passes before feeding onto the take-up reel. This snub roller keeps tension on the film to help steer it to the reel. If the projector doesn't automatically thread the film around the snub roller, be sure to thread it manually. This roller also helps provide enough tension on the film to disengage the autothreading mechanism to ready the film for playing.

If the school has no technician or media specialist to service the projection equipment, teachers should be able to perform the following simple maintenance tasks:

► Change a projector's bulb by opening the machine and removing the bulb. Make sure the projector is unplugged and the bulb is cool. Always replace the burned-out bulb with one having the same ANSI three-character code or equivalent. Never touch a bulb with bare hands or any other item that will leave a residue on the bulb.
► Clean the projection lens with special lens cleaning fluid and tissue. Fingerprints, smudges, and dust reduce the projected image brightness.
► Clean excess lint and dust from the projector and film-threading path with a soft brush or compressed air. This will reduce film wear and produce a clearer image. Don't forget to clean around the sound drum, exciter lamp, and condenser lens.
► To replace a burned-out exciter lamp, remove the protective cover panel. This small lamp is part of the optical system that reproduces the film's sound. It is usually located in the lower front section of the projector, but can vary in location with different models.

PROJECTOR MAINTENANCE

Film chatters or image jumps	Adjust top or bottom film loops. Either stop the projector and readjust the loops or push the loop restorer lever on an autothread projector.
Image blurs or film's edge shows	Ensure that the projector lens is completely closed so the film gate forces the film to travel within the film channel.
Out of frame	When parts of two images appear on the screen at the same time, adjust the framing knob.
No sound	Check whether the Amplifier switch is turned to "on." Also check that the exciter bulb has not burned out.
Mushy/garbled sound	Check the film threading, especially the snugness of the film on the sound drum. Also check for dust or lint in front of the tiny lens that focuses light from the exciter lamp onto the film sound track.
Image and sound out of sync	Check the lower film loop in the threading. This loop may be too large or too small. Adjust the lower loop to follow the guideline marked on the projector. This problem normally doesn't occur on autoload projectors.

TROUBLE-SHOOTING TIPS FOR 16MM PROJECTORS

SUGGESTED ACTIVITIES

1. Identify the major operating systems of a motion picture projector and describe what they do.

2. Set up and operate an autoload 16mm motion picture projector using the Performance Checklist. Be able to perform troubleshooting on the equipment.

The projector diagram shown in Figure B.1 may not match your projector, but you should familiarize yourself with the various labeled parts to know their general locations and functions.

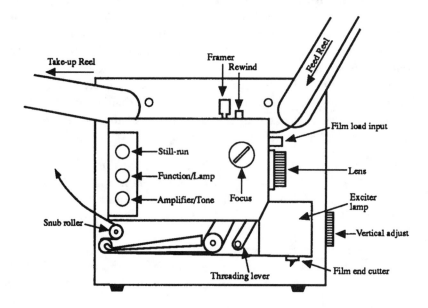

Figure B.1

Components of a Typical 16mm Film Projector

16mm MOTION PICTURE PROJECTOR: AUTOMATIC LOADING
Performance Checklist

Step	Description of Performance	Self Check	Peer Check	Instructor Check
	SET UP PROJECTOR			
1.	Open projector and attach or adjust reel arms.			
2.	Attach feed and take-up reels.			
3.	Plug projector into power outlet.			
4.	Plug in listening headset.			
	TEST AND ADJUST			
5.	Turn on and test the amplifier.			
6.	Turn on and test the fan and lamp.			
7.	Adjust image to screen horizontally.			
8.	Prefocus.			
9.	Turn off and cool lamp.			
10.	Turn fan off.			
	LOAD THE PROJECTOR			
11.	Check and/or cut film end.			
12.	Load film through automatic threading system.			
13.	Attach film to take-up reel.			
14.	Trip release of automatic threader.			
	START AND SHOW FILM			
15.	Turn on motor and lamp.			
16.	Fade sound in and adjust volume.			
17.	Adjust tone.			
18.	Fine focus.			
19.	Adjust frame.			
20.	Reverse film movement (if projector has reverse feature).			
21.	Show still picture (if projector has still frame feature).			
	STOP PROJECTOR AND STORE EQUIPMENT			
22.	Fade sound out.			
23.	Turn lamp off and cool.			
24.	Rewind and store film.			
25.	Store power cord and sound headset.			
26.	Close projector for storage.			

Code for marking:
3 Highly proficient   **2** Proficient   **1** Limited proficiency   **0** Not proficient

INDEX